BLENDER 2025 GUIDE FOR BEGINNERS

OUSIANE WAEKISA

INTRODUCTION

Stepping into the world of 3D design can feel like opening the door to a new dimension. The first glance at the screen of a 3D software like Blender can be overwhelming—a labyrinth of buttons, menus, and hidden features that seem to stretch infinitely. For many beginners, the initial foray into Blender is a dance between excitement and trepidation, as the possibilities appear endless, yet the learning curve daunting. However, with the right guidance and foundational understanding, this intricate tool becomes an empowering platform, transforming visions into reality with the simple click of a mouse and the press of a few keys. The art of mastering Blender is not about knowing every feature at once but building a strong foundation upon which to grow.

At its core, Blender is a gateway to boundless creativity. It allows users to manipulate objects in three-dimensional space, apply stunning materials, and create mesmerizing animations—all within one program. What sets it apart from many other 3D software tools is its versatility and openness. Whether you're aspiring to create visual effects, animations, architectural models, or game assets, Blender accommodates it all. This makes it an essential tool not only for artists but for engineers, architects, filmmakers, and anyone with a passion for visual storytelling. But like any sophisticated software, Blender requires patience, experimentation, and a clear roadmap to unlock its true potential.

Getting comfortable with Blender is about understanding both the broad concepts of 3D modeling and the finer nuances of the interface and tools. Every beginner starts with the same blank canvas—a gray cube floating in the 3D viewport—and it's the journey from this simple form to fully realized, complex designs that makes learning Blender so rewarding. This journey involves mastering the keyboard shortcuts, which are a lifeline for efficiency in 3D work, and familiarizing oneself with the user interface—a space that at first may seem intimidating but, with practice, becomes second nature.

For a novice, the 3D viewport is where most of the action happens. Here, objects are created, modified, and brought to life through movement and texture. Learning to navigate this space is crucial. A beginner needs to understand how to view the scene from different angles, zoom in and out, and pan around with ease. It's much like learning to navigate a virtual world, where the camera—controlled by the user—becomes an extension of their artistic vision. Blender's interface allows for customizability, meaning that, over time, each user can tailor their workspace to fit their specific workflow, enhancing productivity and creativity.

Central to Blender's design philosophy is its focus on objects. In Blender, everything is an object—whether it's a simple cube, a light source, or a camera. Understanding how these objects interact with each other within the 3D space is a key element of learning the software. These interactions aren't just limited to placement; they also encompass relationships formed by constraints, materials, and physics. Once a user grasps the fundamentals of object manipulation, they can begin diving deeper into the more sophisticated features that Blender offers.

Blender's wide array of editing tools opens up new possibilities for shaping and refining objects. Users can push and pull, rotate, scale, and sculpt until the form perfectly matches their vision. With every adjustment, the model becomes closer to a polished, three-dimensional representation of the creator's idea. Along with standard editing, Blender offers a wide range of add-ons—extensions that unlock even more capabilities. These add-ons can introduce tools for specialized tasks, allowing users to focus on specific types of 3D work without needing external software.

As one progresses through Blender, it becomes clear that editing isn't just about manipulating shapes. Modifiers—a core feature of Blender—allow for non-destructive changes to objects. These modifiers can generate new geometry, deform existing shapes, or simulate physics-based effects, transforming basic objects into intricate designs without losing the flexibility to tweak or undo changes. Modifiers can be applied in sequence, layering effects to produce complex results from simple shapes. Understanding how to use and stack these modifiers effectively is one of the most powerful skills a Blender user can develop.

Beyond the world of hard edges and geometric precision, Blender excels in offering organic tools for creating more fluid, natural shapes. Working with curves is one such toolset, giving users the ability to create smooth, flowing designs that feel alive. Curves can be manipulated to follow intricate paths, adding elegance to models that may otherwise feel rigid or mechanical. As with many aspects of Blender, mastering curves is a skill that builds upon earlier lessons in basic modeling, but the results are incredibly rewarding for those looking to add a more artistic flair to their creations.

Materials and textures are where objects in Blender truly come to life. Even the most detailed model will fall flat without the application of materials that give it the illusion of weight, texture, and physical presence. Whether aiming for the sheen of polished metal, the roughness of stone, or the soft folds of fabric, understanding how to apply and manipulate materials is essential for achieving realism in 3D projects. Blender's powerful shading system allows users to fine-tune every aspect of a material, from how it reflects light to the surface patterns created by textures.

Beyond static models, Blender shines as a tool for creating dynamic animations and interactions. Constraints and shape keys allow for controlled movement and deformation, providing the backbone for rigging characters or objects for animation. These features enable the user to define how parts of an object should move or change shape over time, creating smooth, lifelike transitions. When combined with Blender's action editors, which store and manage animation sequences, the possibilities for storytelling and motion design expand exponentially.

One of the most exciting aspects of Blender is its ability to simulate the forces of nature. With particle systems, users can create everything from flowing water to swirling clouds of dust, all controlled by precise parameters that determine how particles behave. When combined with Blender's physics engine, particle systems can interact with objects in realistic ways, colliding, bouncing, or adhering as they would in the real world. This opens up a wide range of creative opportunities, whether it's designing complex environmental effects for a scene or creating abstract, physics-driven art.

As the journey with Blender continues, users are introduced to the intricacies of dynamic painting—a feature that allows for real-time painting of objects as they interact with forces like wind, gravity, or other objects. This technique is particularly useful in animation, where it can be used to simulate effects such as footprints in sand, ripples in water, or paint flowing across a canvas. Dynamic painting combines the power of Blender's physics and material systems, producing results that would be nearly impossible to achieve manually.

For animators, Blender's rigging tools are invaluable. Rigging is the process of adding a skeleton to a model so that it can be posed and animated. Blender's Rigify and AnimBox tools simplify this process, providing pre-built rigs that can be customized to fit a character's unique proportions and movement style. With these tools, even beginners can create animations with professional-level fluidity and realism, breathing life into their characters and scenes.

As one becomes more proficient with Blender, exploring the different render engines becomes essential for achieving specific visual styles and production quality. Blender offers multiple render engines, each optimized for different tasks, from real-time previews with Eevee to high-quality photorealistic rendering with Cycles. Understanding how to leverage these engines allows users to choose the best tool for their project's needs, balancing speed and quality depending on the desired outcome.

Blender's learning curve is undeniably steep, but it is also incredibly rewarding. What begins as a complex, overwhelming interface soon becomes a familiar, intuitive workspace where creativity flows seamlessly. By gradually mastering the software's fundamental tools and concepts, beginners can embark on a journey that unlocks their potential to create stunning 3D art, animations, and designs. Whether it's sculpting an intricate character, simulating realistic physical interactions, or producing a high-quality render, Blender provides all the tools necessary to bring creative visions to life.

Through practice, experimentation, and a clear understanding of Blender's core functionalities, beginners will find themselves equipped to tackle increasingly ambitious projects. With each step forward, new possibilities emerge, and what once seemed out of reach becomes achievable. The world of 3D design is vast, but with a tool as powerful and flexible as Blender, the only limit is one's imagination.

CONTENTS

CHAPTER 1: INTRODUCING TO BLENDER 3D

1.1. WELCOME TO BLENDER 3D

In the ever-evolving world of digital art and animation, a powerful tool has emerged as a beacon for creators ranging from hobbyists to professional studios. This tool is Blender 3D, a comprehensive, open-source software suite that facilitates the entire 3D creation pipeline. From sculpting and modeling to rendering and animation, Blender 3D stands as a testament to what open-source communities can achieve.

1.1.1. What is Blender 3D?

Blender 3D is a free, open-source 3D creation suite that supports the entirety of the 3D pipeline, including modeling, rigging, animation, simulation, rendering, compositing, and motion tracking, even video editing and game creation. Its comprehensive feature set, high-end capabilities, and commitment to fostering creativity and collaboration make it a unique tool in the digital art world.

Originally conceived in the early '90s, Blender started as an in-house tool for a small animation studio. However, it rapidly evolved beyond its initial scope, driven by a growing community of users and developers. In 2002, Blender was released as open-source software, a move that exponentially accelerated its development and adoption worldwide.

Blender's philosophy is rooted in its open-source nature, which ensures that it is not only free to use but also constantly improved upon by contributions from users and developers from all corners of the globe. This community-driven approach has led to Blender being at the forefront of innovation in the 3D world, continually introducing cutting-edge features and capabilities that rival, and often surpass, those of its commercial counterparts.

1.1.2. The Scope of Blender 3D in the World of Digital Art and Animation

Blender 3D's impact on the digital art and animation landscape cannot be overstated. It democratizes access to high-quality 3D creation tools, removing the barrier of cost that often restricts the ability of individual artists and small studios to compete in the industry. By offering a full suite of tools that cater to a wide range of 3D art and animation disciplines, Blender enables users to explore their creativity without limitations.

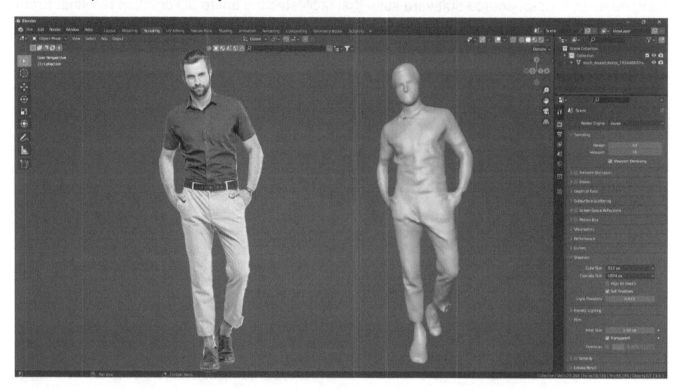

Artists use Blender for creating animated films, visual effects, art, 3D printed models, interactive 3D applications, and video games. Its ability to handle complex simulations, including fluid, smoke, hair, and particle effects, makes it a go-to solution for artists working on ambitious projects that require a high level of detail and realism.

In the realm of animation, Blender provides a robust set of tools for character rigging and animation. The software includes features for inverse kinematics, allowing for natural movement and poses for characters, and a non-linear animation mixer, enabling complex animations that can be edited and refined with ease.

For game developers, Blender offers an integrated game engine, enabling the creation of interactive 3D content. While the focus in recent years has shifted towards better integration with external game engines like Unreal Engine and Unity, Blender remains a valuable asset for game asset creation, including modeling, texturing, and animation.

The software's architecture is designed for extensibility, allowing users to customize and extend its capabilities through scripting with Python. This openness has led to a vibrant ecosystem of plugins and add-ons, further enhancing Blender's functionality to meet specific needs, such as architectural visualization, scientific visualization, and more.

Blender 3D's commitment to providing a comprehensive, open-source 3D creation suite has established it as a beloved tool in the global community of digital artists and animators. Its continual development, driven by feedback and contributions from its user base, ensures that Blender remains at the cutting edge of 3D technology, making it an invaluable resource for anyone looking to explore the vast potential of digital creation.

1.2 A BRIEF HISTORY OF BLENDER 3D

1.2.1 The Origins and Evolution

Blender 3D's journey began in the early 1990s in the Netherlands. It was initially developed by Ton Roosendaal, the co-founder of the animation studio NeoGeo, which was one of the largest animation studios in the Netherlands at the time. The initial goal was to create an in-house tool that would streamline and enhance their 3D content creation process. This need led to the birth of Blender as an integrated application that facilitated modeling, animation, and rendering processes within a single program.

The decision to release Blender as an open-source project in 2002 marked a pivotal moment in its history. This transition was facilitated through a unique crowd-funding campaign, "Free Blender," which raised over 100,000 euros from the community. This effort allowed Blender's source code to be released publicly under the GNU General Public License, ensuring that it would remain free and open to users and developers worldwide.

1.2.2 Milestones in Blender Development

Since becoming open-source, Blender has seen an explosive growth in features, capabilities, and user base. Significant milestones in Blender's development include:

- **The Introduction of Cycles Rendering Engine (2011):** Blender's own rendering engine, Cycles, brought photorealistic rendering capabilities to the software, allowing for more complex and visually stunning outputs.

- **Blender 2.8 and the User Interface Overhaul (2019):** This update introduced a more intuitive and user-friendly interface, making Blender more accessible to new users and streamlining the workflow for all users. It also introduced the Eevee real-time render engine, providing a powerful tool for real-time visualization and game development.

- **Blender 2.83 LTS (2020):** The first long-term support release, offering stability and support for two years, making it a preferred version for studios and individuals working on longer-term projects.

- **Everything Nodes Project:** An ongoing initiative aiming to make all aspects of Blender driven by a node-based system, enhancing the flexibility and power of procedural generation and effects within the software.

1.2.3 Blender's Impact on the Industry

Blender 3D's impact on the digital art and animation industry is multifaceted. Its role in democratizing 3D content creation has been perhaps its most significant contribution, allowing individuals and small studios to access high-quality tools without the burden of expensive licenses. This has led to a surge in creativity and innovation in digital arts, with Blender being used in everything from independent films to major studio productions.

Academically, Blender has become a valuable tool in education, offering students a comprehensive platform to learn 3D modeling, animation, and game design without financial barriers. This has enabled a wider range of individuals to enter the digital arts field, fostering diversity and innovation.

Professionally, Blender's open-source nature has encouraged a culture of collaboration and continuous improvement, with developers and users contributing to its development. This collaborative ecosystem has accelerated Blender's growth and capabilities, making it competitive with, and sometimes superior to, commercial alternatives.

Blender's influence extends into the realms of scientific visualization, architecture, and virtual reality, demonstrating its versatility beyond traditional entertainment industries. Its ability to adapt and integrate with various workflows and industries underlines the power and potential of open-source software in driving innovation and accessibility in digital content creation.

In conclusion, the history of Blender 3D is a testament to the power of community, open-source principles, and the vision of its founders and contributors. From its humble beginnings to becoming a cornerstone in the digital art and animation industry, Blender has continually evolved, reflecting the needs and aspirations of its users. Its impact on the industry, education, and individual creators around the world is a compelling narrative of how technology can empower creativity and change the landscape of digital content creation.

1.3 ACQUIRING BLENDER 3D

1.3.1 Understanding Blender's Subscription Model

Blender 3D, at its core, remains free and open-source, accessible to anyone with a computer and an internet connection. This approach ensures that the software remains inclusive, fostering a diverse community of users and developers. Beyond the software, Blender offers additional resources and services that can enhance the user experience, including advanced tutorials, asset libraries, and professional support. These services operate on a subscription model, designed to provide valuable extras for users who seek to deepen their engagement with Blender's ecosystem.

The subscription model for these services is not a paywall for the software itself but an avenue for users to access enriched content and support. It serves a dual purpose: offering users professional-grade resources and supporting the ongoing development of Blender through financial contributions. This model is a testament to Blender's commitment to remaining free while also offering avenues for growth and sustainability.

1.3.2 Subscription Options and Pricing

Blender offers several subscription options tailored to different user needs. These can range from access to the Blender Cloud, offering assets, courses, and project collaboration tools, to professional support subscriptions for studios and enterprises requiring direct assistance from Blender developers.

1. **Blender Cloud Subscription:** This subscription grants access to an extensive library of training materials, textures, and models. It's designed for individual artists and educators seeking to expand their skills or incorporate Blender into their curriculum. The pricing is structured to be affordable, offering monthly and annual payment options to accommodate different budgets.

The Creators Who Share

Blender Studio is a dedicated team of artists and developers who challenge themselves with creative and technical targets to drive Blender development forward.

Join Blender Studio

Access to all training, assets and films for €11.50/month

2. **Professional Support Subscription:** Aimed at businesses and studios, this subscription provides direct support from Blender developers, prioritizing issue resolution and offering guidance on complex projects. Pricing varies based on the level of support required, with options for small teams to large enterprises.

3. **Blender Development Fund Membership:** While not a subscription for additional services, joining the Blender Development Fund is a way for users to support the software's development financially. Members can contribute monthly, with different tiers offering varying levels of recognition and perks, such as insights into upcoming features and Blender merchandise.

1.3.3 How to Purchase a Subscription

Purchasing a subscription to Blender's additional services is a straightforward process, designed to be as accessible as the software itself. The following steps outline the general process:

1. **Visit the Official Blender Website:** All subscriptions can be initiated from Blender's official site, ensuring security and ease of access.

2. **Choose Your Subscription:** Navigate to the services section and select the subscription that best fits your needs, whether it's Blender Cloud access, professional support, or membership in the Blender Development Fund.

3. **Create an Account:** If you don't already have one, you'll need to create an account on Blender's website. This account will manage your subscriptions and provide access to the services you've subscribed to.

4. **Payment Information:** Enter your payment information. Blender typically accepts various payment methods, including credit cards and PayPal, to accommodate users worldwide.

5. **Confirmation and Access:** Once your payment is processed, you'll receive confirmation, and your subscription will be active immediately. You can then access the resources or support channels as per your subscription plan.

In conclusion, while Blender 3D remains a free and open-source tool, offering unparalleled access to 3D creation software, it also provides additional paid services for those looking to enhance their Blender experience. These subscription options support both the users in their creative pursuits and the ongoing development of Blender, ensuring its sustainability and growth for years to come.

1.4. INSTALLING BLENDER 3D

Before embarking on your journey with Blender 3D, it's essential to ensure your computer system meets the necessary requirements and understand the installation process. This guide will walk you through the system requirements, a step-by-step installation guide, and how to troubleshoot common installation issues.

1.4.1 System Requirements

To ensure Blender 3D runs smoothly on your computer, it's crucial to check if your system meets the software's minimum and recommended requirements. Blender 3D is designed to be compatible with various operating systems, including Windows, macOS, and Linux. However, the software's performance significantly depends on your system's hardware.

⌄ Windows

	Minimum	Recommended
OS	Windows 8.1 (64-bit)	Windows 10 or Windows 11
CPU	4 cores with SSE4.2 support	8 cores
RAM	8 GB	32 GB
GPU	2 GB VRAM with OpenGL 4.3 (see below)	8 GB VRAM

⌄ macOS

	Minimum	Recommended
OS	macOS 11.2 (Big Sur)	macOS 14 (Sonoma)
CPU	Apple Silicon or Intel	Apple Silicon
RAM	8 GB	32 GB
GPU	GPU with Metal 2.2 (see below)	

AMD, **Apple Silicon**, or **Intel** (Skylake and newer).

⌄ Linux

	Minimum	Recommended
OS	Distribution with glibc 2.28 or newer (64-bit)	
CPU	4 cores with SSE4.2 support	8 cores
RAM	8 GB	32 GB
GPU	2 GB VRAM with OpenGL 4.3 (see below)	8 GB VRAM

Minimum System Requirements:

- **Operating System:** Windows 8.1, macOS 10.13, or Linux

- **Processor:** 64-bit dual-core 2Ghz CPU with SSE4.2 support

- **Memory:** 8 GB RAM

- **Graphics:** 2 GB RAM, OpenGL 4.3

- **Storage:** 700 MB available space

Recommended System Requirements:

- **Operating System:** Windows 10, macOS 10.15, or a recent Linux distribution

- **Processor:** 64-bit quad-core CPU

- **Memory:** 32 GB RAM

- **Graphics:** 8 GB RAM, NVIDIA GeForce GTX 1050 Ti or better (with CUDA support for optimal rendering)

- **Storage:** 2 GB available space (SSD preferred)

For users interested in more complex projects, including high-polygon modeling, advanced simulations, or 4K video rendering, investing in hardware that exceeds the recommended specifications is advisable. A powerful GPU will significantly reduce rendering times and improve the overall workflow.

1.4.2 Step-by-Step Installation Guide

Windows:

1. Visit the official Blender website and navigate to the download section.

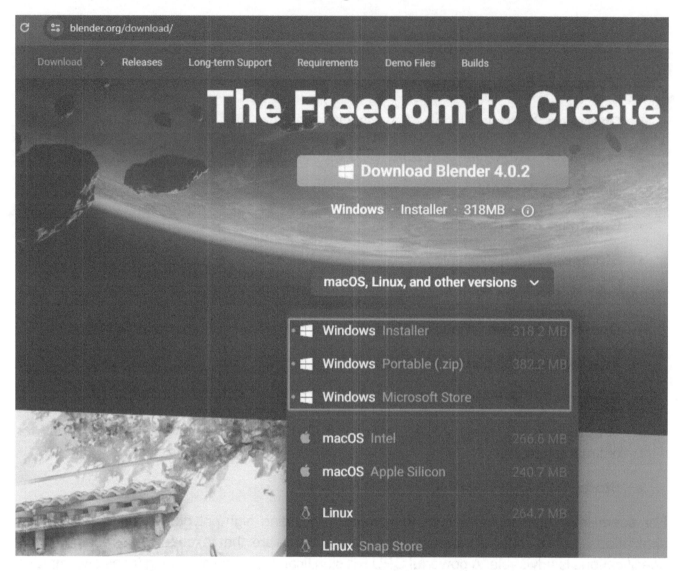

2. Choose the version compatible with your operating system and download the installer.

3. Once the download is complete, run the installer. If you encounter a security prompt from Windows Defender or your antivirus, confirm that you trust the source.

4. Follow the on-screen instructions. You can choose the installation path during this process; the default location is usually sufficient for most users.

5. After completing the installation, you can launch Blender from the Start menu or the desktop shortcut, if created.

macOS:

1. Download the macOS version of Blender from the official website.

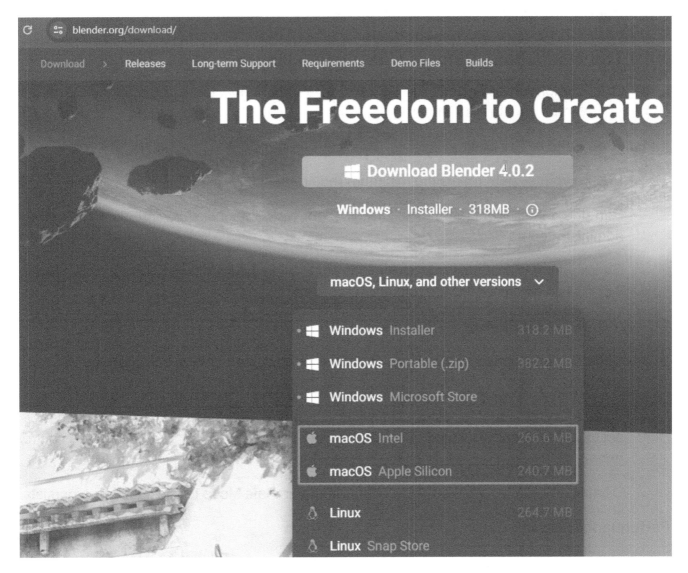

2. Open the downloaded file. Drag and drop the Blender icon into the Applications folder.

3. You might need to authorize the application the first time you open it due to macOS security preferences. Go to System Preferences > Security & Privacy and allow Blender to run.

4. Double-click Blender in your Applications folder to start using it.

Linux:

1. For most Linux distributions, Blender can be installed directly from the official package manager. For example, in Ubuntu, you can use the command **sudo apt-get install blender** in the terminal.

2. Alternatively, download the Linux tarball from the Blender website, extract it, and run the Blender executable from the extracted folder.

3. You might need to install additional dependencies depending on your Linux distribution. Refer to the Blender documentation for detailed instructions.

1.4.3 Troubleshooting Common Installation Issues

Even with a straightforward installation process, users might encounter some issues. Here are common problems and their solutions:

Installation Fails or Freezes:

- Ensure your system meets the minimum requirements.

- Run the installer as an administrator (right-click the installer and select "Run as administrator").

- Check your antivirus software, as it might be blocking the installation. Temporarily disable it or add an exception for Blender.

Blender Crashes on Startup:

- Update your graphics card drivers. Outdated or corrupted drivers are often the cause of crashes.

- If you're using a dual graphics card setup (integrated and dedicated), ensure Blender is set to use the dedicated card. This setting can be adjusted in your graphics card's control panel.

- Disable any incompatible add-ons. Start Blender in Safe Mode to see if the issue persists.

Performance Issues:

- Make sure your graphics drivers are up to date.

- Adjust Blender's performance settings, such as reducing the viewport samples or lowering the subdivision surface modifier's viewport levels.

- Consider upgrading your hardware if you consistently encounter performance issues with complex scenes.

By following these steps and troubleshooting tips, you'll be well on your way to starting your 3D modeling journey with Blender. Remember, the Blender community is vast and supportive. If you encounter any issues not covered here, chances are someone has faced and solved the same problem. Forums, official documentation, and tutorials are great resources to help you overcome any obstacles.

1.5 BLENDER 3D'S DESIGN PHILOSOPHY

1.5.1 The Core Design Concepts Behind Blender

- **Open Source and Free Access:** At the heart of Blender's design philosophy is its status as open-source software. This foundational principle guarantees that Blender remains free to use for anyone, anywhere. This open access is more than just about cost; it's about lowering barriers to entry into the digital creation world, fostering a diverse and vibrant community of users and contributors. It ensures that Blender evolves in response to the needs and feedback of its community, rather than the profit motives of a corporation.
- **Comprehensive Toolset:** Blender is designed to be a 'one-stop-shop' for all things 3D. This means providing a suite of tools that support the entire 3D pipeline—modeling, rigging, animation, simulation, rendering, compositing, and editing. This integration ensures that artists can work within a single software environment without the need for costly plugins or external software, streamlining the creative process and fostering a more intuitive workflow.
- **Customizability and Extensibility:** Recognizing the diverse needs of its user base, Blender is built to be highly customizable. Users can tailor the interface to their workflow, create their own shortcuts, and even develop scripts and add-ons to extend Blender's capabilities. This flexibility ensures that Blender can adapt to the specific needs of individual artists and projects, promoting efficiency and creativity.
- **Community and Collaboration:** Blender's design philosophy places a strong emphasis on community and collaboration. The software is not just developed by its core team but also by contributions from users around the world. This collaborative approach extends to how users interact with Blender, with the community sharing tutorials, resources, and support through forums, social media, and events. Blender's open-source nature fosters a culture of sharing and mutual assistance, which accelerates learning and innovation within the community.

1.5.2 How Blender's Design Philosophy Benefits Users

- **Accessibility and Inclusivity:** By being free and open-source, Blender makes high-quality 3D creation tools accessible to everyone, regardless of financial resources. This inclusivity has opened the doors of digital creation to a global audience, enabling people from diverse backgrounds to express their creativity, learn new skills, and contribute to various fields, including film, animation, video games, and virtual reality.
- **Empowerment Through Education:** Blender's comprehensive toolset, combined with its vast library of community-generated tutorials and documentation, makes it an excellent platform for education. Students and educators have access to a professional-grade software package at no cost, facilitating the teaching and learning of 3D modeling, animation, and more. This accessibility has made Blender a popular choice in schools, universities, and online learning platforms.
- **Innovation and Flexibility:** The customizable and extensible nature of Blender allows users to adapt the software to their specific needs, promoting efficiency and creativity. This flexibility ensures that Blender can be used for a wide range of projects, from small-scale hobbyist creations to large commercial productions. Furthermore, the ability to

extend Blender through scripting and add-ons means that it can keep pace with the latest developments in the 3D field, driving innovation within the community.

- **A Stronger Community:** Blender's emphasis on community and collaboration has cultivated a supportive ecosystem where users share knowledge, resources, and feedback. This collaborative environment accelerates learning and innovation, enabling users to improve their skills and contribute to Blender's development. The community-driven approach also ensures that Blender evolves in a direction that reflects the needs and desires of its users, making it a tool that is continually refined and improved by those who use it the most.

In conclusion, Blender 3D's design philosophy is a reflection of its commitment to openness, inclusivity, and community. By providing a comprehensive, customizable, and free toolset for 3D creation, Blender empowers users around the world to explore their creativity, learn new skills, and contribute to a wide range of projects and industries. The benefits of this philosophy are evident in the vibrant community that has grown around Blender, characterized by a spirit of collaboration, innovation, and shared progress. As Blender continues to evolve, it remains a powerful testament to the impact of open-source principles on the world of digital creation.

1.6 DEVELOPING THE RIGHT MINDSET FOR 3D MODELING

Mastering 3D modeling, especially in a versatile environment like Blender 3D, is as much about cultivating the right mindset as it is about learning the software's ins and outs. This chapter delves into the foundational attitudes and perspectives that can significantly enhance your journey through the 3D modeling landscape.

1.6.1 The Importance of Patience and Persistence

The path to proficiency in 3D modeling is often long and fraught with challenges. Initial excitement can quickly give way to frustration as newcomers confront the complexity of creating their first models or animations. It's here that patience becomes indispensable. Understanding that each obstacle is a stepping stone towards mastery is key. Like learning a musical instrument or a new language, 3D modeling skills are honed over time, through consistent practice and perseverance.

Persistence plays a pivotal role, particularly when progress seems to stagnate or when faced with seemingly insurmountable challenges. The ability to push through, to find solutions to complex problems, and to continue learning and experimenting, even in the face of failure, is what separates those who succeed from those who give up. Remember, every expert in Blender started as a beginner, and their expertise is largely a result of their persistence.

1.6.2 Embracing Creativity and Continuous Learning

Blender 3D offers an expansive set of tools and features, enabling artists to bring even their most ambitious visions to life. However, the true potential of these tools is unlocked only by those who approach their work with creativity and an open mind. Creativity is not just about originality but also about problem-solving. It's about seeing the myriad ways a tool can be used, often in manners not initially intended by its creators.

Continuous learning is equally critical. The field of 3D modeling and Blender's capabilities are continually evolving. New tools, techniques, and best practices emerge regularly. Staying informed about these developments and incorporating them into your work ensures your skills remain relevant and your creations continue to innovate. Fortunately, Blender's vibrant community and wealth of online resources make it easier than ever to keep learning. From official tutorials and forums to user-generated content on social media and video platforms, there's a wealth of knowledge available at your fingertips.

1.6.3 Community and Collaboration in the Blender Ecosystem

One of Blender's greatest strengths is its community. From novices to seasoned professionals, the Blender ecosystem is home to a diverse group of individuals united by their passion for 3D creation. This community is an invaluable resource for learning, inspiration, and support. Engaging with the community can dramatically enhance your learning experience. Sharing your work for feedback, participating in challenges, and contributing to collaborative projects are just a few ways to engage with other Blender users.

Collaboration is another cornerstone of the Blender experience. Whether it's working together on a project, contributing to the open-source code, or sharing assets and resources, collaboration enriches the Blender ecosystem. It fosters a culture of sharing and mutual growth, where more experienced users mentor newcomers, and innovation is driven by collective effort rather than competition.

The community is also a testament to the power of open-source philosophy. Blender's development is significantly shaped by its users, with feedback and contributions directly influencing its evolution. This reciprocal relationship between the developers and the community ensures that Blender continues to meet the needs and exceed the expectations of its user base.

1.7 PREPARING FOR THE FUTURE WITH BLENDER 3D

Blender 3D's evolution is a testament to its adaptability and the forward-thinking approach of its community and developers. As we look to the future, Blender continues to position itself at the forefront of 3D modeling, animation, and rendering technologies, embracing new trends and integrating cutting-edge features. This chapter explores the anticipated directions for Blender in 2024, how users can keep abreast of these developments, and Blender's expanding role in future technologies and industries.

1.7.1 Upcoming Features and Updates in 2024

The roadmap for Blender in 2024 highlights a commitment to innovation, with several key features and updates poised to enhance its functionality, user experience, and application in professional workflows. While specific updates depend on the ongoing development and community feedback, several areas of focus reflect the broader trends in 3D technology and digital content creation:

- **Enhanced Realism in Rendering:** Continuing improvements to both Cycles and Eevee rendering engines aim to achieve greater realism with less computational overhead. This includes better handling of light, shadow, and materials, making photorealistic outputs more accessible to users.

- **AI-Assisted Modeling and Animation:** Leveraging artificial intelligence to streamline the creation process is a significant trend. Blender is expected to incorporate AI-based tools for tasks such as auto-rigging, facial expression generation, and perhaps even AI-driven animation, reducing the time and expertise required to bring characters and scenes to life.

- **Improved Simulation Capabilities:** Simulations for fluids, cloth, and particles are set to become more accurate and less resource-intensive, enabling more complex and dynamic scenes, especially useful in visual effects and scientific visualization.

- **Augmented and Virtual Reality Integration:** With the growing interest in AR and VR, Blender aims to enhance its support for creating content directly usable in these environments, including better real-time previews and integration with popular AR and VR platforms.

- **Interoperability and Industry Standards:** Emphasizing compatibility with other tools and adherence to industry standards remains a priority. This includes improvements in file format support, making Blender more seamless to integrate into mixed-software pipelines.

1.7.2 How to Stay Updated with Blender Developments

Staying informed about the latest Blender developments ensures users can take full advantage of new features and improvements. Several resources and strategies can help:

- **Official Blender Channels:** The Blender website, along with official social media accounts, provides announcements, detailed release notes, and insights into ongoing development projects.

- **Blender Developer Blogs and Forums:** Developers and contributors often share updates, tutorials, and discussions on upcoming features in blogs and forums, offering a deeper understanding of the changes and the rationale behind them.

- **Blender Conferences and Meetups:** Events like the Blender Conference and local Blender meetups are fantastic opportunities to learn from developers and experienced users directly, gaining insights into future directions and networking with the community.

- **Online Tutorials and Courses:** Many educators and content creators regularly update their offerings to include tutorials on new Blender features, providing practical guidance on how to leverage these in your projects.

1.7.3 The Role of Blender in Future Technologies and Industries

Blender's flexibility and comprehensive feature set position it as a key player in the future of various technologies and industries:

- **Film and Animation:** Blender's continued advancements in rendering and animation tools make it increasingly viable for large-scale film and animation projects, challenging the dominance of high-cost proprietary software.

- **Game Development:** With enhancements in real-time rendering and AR/VR support, Blender is set to become an even more integral tool in game development pipelines, facilitating the creation of immersive and complex game worlds.

- **Virtual Production:** The intersection of live-action filming and CGI benefits from Blender's capabilities in real-time rendering and visualization, making virtual production techniques more accessible to filmmakers.

- **Education and Training:** As a free tool, Blender is an invaluable resource for educational institutions, allowing students to develop marketable skills in 3D modeling, animation, and design without financial barriers.

- **Scientific Visualization:** Blender's advancements in simulation and rendering technologies enhance its application in scientific research, enabling more accurate and visually compelling representations of complex data.

In conclusion, preparing for the future with Blender 3D involves not only familiarizing oneself with upcoming features and developments but also understanding Blender's evolving role in broader technological and industrial contexts. As Blender continues to push the boundaries of what is possible in 3D creation, its users stand at the forefront of these changes, equipped to leverage the software's capabilities to explore new horizons in digital art, design, and beyond.

1.8 CHAPTER SUMMARY

1.8.1 Key Takeaways from This Chapter

- **Introduction to Blender 3D:** Blender is a comprehensive, open-source 3D creation suite that supports the entire 3D pipeline. It's accessible to beginners yet powerful enough for professionals, fostering a diverse community of users.

- **The Origins and Evolution of Blender:** Blender's journey from an in-house tool to a global open-source project underscores the power of community and the impact of open-source philosophy on software development.

- **Acquiring Blender 3D:** Despite being free and open-source, Blender offers additional resources through subscription-based services like Blender Cloud and professional support, providing users with enhanced learning tools and support options.

- **Installing Blender 3D:** The installation process is straightforward across different operating systems. System requirements are clearly defined to ensure optimal performance, and the community offers solutions to common installation issues.

- **Blender 3D's Design Philosophy:** Blender's development is guided by principles of openness, innovation, and community collaboration, which manifest in its versatile toolset and adaptive workflow.

- **Developing the Right Mindset for 3D Modeling:** Success in 3D modeling with Blender requires patience, persistence, creativity, and a commitment to continuous learning and community engagement.

- **Preparing for the Future with Blender 3D:** Blender's roadmap is marked by continuous improvement and adaptation, with future updates focusing on realism, AI integration, and support for emerging technologies like AR and VR.

These takeaways underscore Blender's role not just as a software tool but as a platform for learning, creativity, and community. Blender empowers users to explore the vast potential of 3D creation, regardless of their skill level or professional background.

1.8.2 What to Expect in the Next Chapter

As we move forward, the next chapter transitions from Blender's foundational aspects to practical guidance on beginning your 3D modeling journey. It will cover:

- **Navigating Blender's Interface:** An in-depth look at Blender's user interface (UI), including customization options to streamline your workflow and improve efficiency.

- **Basic Modeling Techniques:** Step-by-step tutorials to guide you through the process of creating your first 3D model in Blender, from simple objects to more complex shapes.

- **Material and Texturing Fundamentals:** Understanding how to apply and manipulate materials and textures to bring your models to life with realistic details.

- **Lighting and Rendering:** Techniques for effectively lighting your scene and rendering your creations to produce stunning visuals.

- **Animation Basics:** An introduction to animating objects in Blender, covering keyframes, timelines, and simple animations to bring motion to your models.

- **Project Management and Workflow Tips:** Strategies for managing projects within Blender, including file organization, version control, and efficient use of resources.

- **Community Resources and Further Learning:** A guide to leveraging the Blender community for support, inspiration, and ongoing education.

The upcoming chapter is designed to equip beginners with the necessary skills and confidence to start creating in Blender. Through hands-on tutorials, practical advice, and insights into the software's capabilities, readers will be prepared to embark on their own 3D modeling projects, laying the foundation for more advanced exploration in subsequent chapters.

CHAPTER 2: KEYBOARD SHORTCUTS IN BLENDER

WINDOW HOTKEYS

Certain window managers also use the following hotkeys. So **ALT-CTRL** can be substituted for **CTRL** to perform the functions described below if a conflict arises.

CTRL-LEFTARROW. Go to the previous Screen.

CTRL-RIGHTARROW. Go to the next Screen.

CTRL-UPARROW or **CTRL-DOWNARROW**. Maximize the window or return to the previous window display size.

SHIFT-F4. Change the window to a Data View **SHIFT-F5**. Change the window to a 3D Window **SHIFT-F6**. Change the window to an IPO Window **SHIFT-F7**. Change the window to a Buttons Window

SHIFT-F8. Change the window to a Sequence Window **SHIFT-F9**. Change the window to an Outliner Window **SHIFT-F10**. Change the window to an Image Window **SHIFT-F11**. Change the window to a Text Window **SHIFT-F12**. Change the window to an Action Window

UNIVERSAL HOTKEYS

The following Hotkeys work uniformly in all Blender Windows, if the Context allows:

CTRL-LMB. Lasso select: drag the mouse to form a freehand selection area.

ESC.

- This key always cancels Blender functions without changes.

- or: File Window, Data View and Image Select: back to the previous window type.
- or: the Render Window is pushed to the background (or closed, that depends on the operating system).

SPACE. Open the Toolbox.

TAB. Start or quit Edit Mode.

F1. Loads a Blender file. Changes the window to a File Window.

SHIFT-F1. Appends parts from other files, or loads as Library- data. Changes the window to a File Window, making Blender files accessible as a directory.

F2. Writes a Blender file. Change the window to a File Window.

SHIFT-F2. Exports the scene as a **DXF** file

CTRL-F2. Exports the scene as a **VRML1** file

F3. Writes a picture (if a picture has been rendered). The file format is as indicated in the Display Buttons. The window becomes a File Select Window.

CTRL-F3 (**ALT-CTRL-F3** on Mac OSX). Saves a screen dump of the active window. The file format is as indicated in the Display Buttons. The window becomes a File Window.

SHIFT-CTRL-F3. Saves a screen dump of the whole Blender screen. The file format is as indicated in the Display Buttons. The window becomes a File Window.

F4. Displays the Logic Context (if a Buttons Window is available).

F5. Displays the Shading Context (if a Buttons Window is available), Light, Material or World Sub-contexts depends on active object.

F6. Displays the Shading Context and Texture Sub-context (if a Buttons Window is available).

F7. Displays the Object Context (if a Buttons Window is available).

F8. Displays the Shading Context and World Sub-context (if a Buttons Window is available).

F9. Displays the Editing Context (if a Buttons Window is available).

F10. Displays the Scene Context (if a Buttons Window is available).

F11. Hides or shows the render window.

F12. Starts the rendering from the active camera.

LEFTARROW. Go to the previous frame. **SHIFT-LEFTARROW**. Go to the first frame. **RIGHTARROW**. Go to the next frame.

SHIFT-LEFTARROW. Go to the last frame.

UPARROW. Go forward 10 frames.

DOWNARROW. Go back 10 frames.

ALT-A. Change the current Blender window to Animation Playback mode. The cursor changes to a counter.

ALT-SHIFT-A. The current window, plus all 3DWindows go into Animation Playback mode.

I KEY. Insert Key menu. This menu differs from window to window.

J KEY. Toggle the render buffers. Blender allows you to retain two different rendered pictures in memory.

CTRL-O. Opens the last saved file.

Q KEY. OK? Quit Blender. This key closes Blender.

OBJECT MODE HOTKEYS

These hotkeys are mainly bound to the 3D Viewport Window, but many work on Objects in most other windows, like IPOs and so on, hence they are summarized here.

HOME. All Objects in the visible layer are displayed completely, centered in the window.

PAGEUP. Select the next Object Key. If more than one Object Key is selected, the selection is shifted up cyclically. Only works if the Anim Buttons->Draw Key is ON for the Object.

SHIFT-PAGEUP. Adds to selection the next Object Key.

PAGEDOWN. Select the previous Object Key. If more than one Object Key is selected, the selection is shifted up cyclically. Only works if the Anim Buttons->Draw Key is ON for the Object.

SHIFT-PAGEDOWN. Adds to selection the previous Object Key.

ACCENT. (To the left of the 1KEY in US keyboard) Select all layers.

SHIFT-ACCENT. Revert to the previous layer setting. TAB. Start/stop Edit Mode. Alternative hotkey: **ALT-E. A KEY**. Selects/deselects all.

CTRL-A. Apply size and rotation. The rotation and dimensions of the Object are assigned to the Ob Data (Mesh, Curve, etc.).

At first glance, it appears as if nothing has changed, but this can have considerable consequences for animations or texture mapping. This is best illustrated by also having the axis of a Mesh Object be drawn (**Edit Buttons->Axis**). Rotate the Object and activate Apply. The rotation and dimensions of the Object are 'erased'.

SHIFT-CTRL-A. If the active Object is automatically duplicated (see AnimButtons -> DupliFrames or AnimButtons -> Dupliverts), a menu asks Make dupli's real?. This option actually creates the Objects. If the active Mesh Object is deformed by a Lattice, a menu asks Apply Lattice deform?. Now the deformation of the Lattice is assigned to the vertices of the Mesh.

SHIFT-A. This is the Add Menu. In fact, it is the Toolbox that starts with the 'ADD' option. When Objects are added, Blender starts Edit Mode immediately if possible.

B KEY. Border Select. Draw a rectangle with the Left Mouse; all Objects within this area are selected, but not made active. Draw a rectangle with the Right Mouse to deselect Objects. In orthonormal View Mode, the dimensions of the rectangle are displayed, expressed as global coordinates, as an extra feature in the lower left corner. In Camera View Mode, the dimensions that are to be rendered according to the Display Buttons are displayed in pixel units.

SHIFT-B. Render Border. This only works in Camera View Mode. Draw a rectangle to render a smaller cut-out of the standard window frame. If the option Display Buttons->Border is ON, a box is drawn with red and black lines.

C KEY. Centre View. The position of the 3DCursor becomes the new centre of the 3DWindow.

ALT-C. Convert Menu. Depending on the active Object, a popup Menu is displayed. This enables you to convert certain types of Ob Data. It only converts in one direction, everything ultimately degrades to a Mesh! The options are:

- Font -> Curve
- MetaBall -> Mesh The original MetaBall remains unchanged.
- Curve -> Mesh
- Surface -> Mesh

CTRL-C. Copy Menu. This menu copies information from the active Object to (other) selected Objects.

Fixed components are:

- Copy Loc: the X,Y,Z location of the Object. If a Child is involved, this location is the relative position in relation to the Parent.
- Copy Rot: the X,Y,Z rotation of the Object.
- Copy Size: the X,Y,Z dimension of the Object.
- DrawType: copies Object Drawtype.
- TimeOffs: copies Object time offset.
- Dupli: all Duplicator data (Dupliframes, Dupliverts and so on)
- Mass: Real time stuff.
- Damping: Real time stuff.
- Properties: Real time stuff.
- Logic Bricks: Real time stuff.
- Constraints: copies Object constraints.

OBJECT MODE HOTKEYS

If applicable:

- Copy TexSpace: The texture space.
- Copy Particle Settings: the complete particle system from the AnimButtons.

For Curve Objects:

- a second **X KEY, Y KEY, Z KEY** constrains movement to **X, Y or Z** axis of the local reference.
- a third **X KEY, Y KEY, Z KEY** removes constraints.
- **N KEY** enters numerical input, as well as any numeric key directly. **TAB** will switch between values, **ENTER** finalizes, **ESC** exits.
- **ARROWS**: These keys can be used to move the mouse

- cursor exactly 1 pixel.

Grabber can be terminated with:

- Copy Bevel Settings: all bevelling data from the EditButtons.

Font Objects:

- Copy Font Settings: font type, dimensions, spacing.
- Copy Bevel Settings: all bevelling data from the EditButtons.

Camera Objects:

- Copy Lens: the lens value.

SHIFT-C. Centre Zero View. The 3DCursor is set to zero (0,0,0) and the view is changed so that all Objects, including the 3Dcursor, can be displayed. This is an alternative for HOME.

D KEY. Draw mode menu. Allows to select draw modes exactly as the corresponding menu in the 3D viewport header does.

SHIFT-D. Add Duplicate. The selected Objects are duplicated. Grab mode starts immediately thereafter.

ALT-D. Add Linked Duplicate. Of the selected Objects linked duplicates are created. Grab mode starts immediately thereafter.

CTRL-D. Draw the (texture) Image as wire. This option has a limited function. It can only be used for 2D compositing.

ALT-E. Start/stop EditMode. Alternative hotkey: TAB.

F KEY. If selected Object is a mesh Toggles Face selectMode on and off.

CTRL-F. Sort Faces. The faces of the active Mesh Object are sorted, based on the current view in the 3DWindow. The leftmost face first, the rightmost last. The sequence of faces is important for the Build Effect (AnimButtons).

G KEY. Grab Mode. Or: the translation mode. This works on selected Objects and vertices. Blender calculates the quantity and direction of the translation, so that they correspond exactly with the mouse movements, regardless of the ViewMode or view direction of the 3DWindow. Alternatives for starting this mode:

LMB to draw a straight line.

The following options are available in translation mode:

Limiters:

- **CTRL:** in increments of 1 grid unit.
- **SHIFT:** fine movements.
- **SHIFT-CTRL:** in increments of 0.1 grid unit.

MMB toggles: A short click restricts the current translation to the **X,Y or Z axis**. Blender calculates which axis to use, depending on the already initiated mouse movement. Click Middle Mouse again to return to unlimited translation.

X KEY, Y KEY, Z KEY constrains movement to **X, Y or Z** axis of the global reference.

- **LMB SPACE** or **ENTER**: move to a new position.
- **RMB or ESC**: everything goes back to the old position.

Switching mode:

- **G KEY**: starts Grab mode again.
- **S KEY**: switches to Size (Scale) mode.
- **R KEY**: switches to Rotate mode.

ALT-G. Clears translations, given in Grab mode. The **X, Y, Z** locations of selected Objects are set to zero.

SHIFT-G. Group Selection

- **Children:** Selects all selected Object's Children.
- **Immediate Children:** Selects all selected Object's first level Children.
- **Parent:** Selects selected Object's Parent.
- **Shared Layers:** Selects all Object on the same Layer of active Object

I KEY. Insert Object Key. A key position is inserted in the current frame of all selected Objects. A popup Menu asks what key position(s) must be added to the IpoCurves.

- **Loc:** The XYZ location of the Object.
- **Rot:** The XYZ rotation of the Object.
- **Size:** The XYZ dimensions of the Object
- **LocRot:** The XYZ location and XYZ rotation of the Object.
- **LocRotSize:** The XYZ location, XYZ rotation and XYZ dimensions of the Object.
- **Layer:** The layer of the Object.
- **Avail:** A position is only added to all the current IpoCurves, that is curves which already exists.
- **Mesh, Lattice, Curve or Surface:** depending on the type of Object, a VertexKey can be added

CTRL-J. Join Objects. All selected Objects of the same type are added to the active Object. What actually happens here is that the Ob Data blocks are combined and all the selected Objects (except for the active one) are deleted. This is a rather complex operation, which can lead to confusing results, particularly when working with a lot of linked data, animation curves and hierarchies.

K KEY. Show Keys. The Draw Key option is turned ON for all selected Objects. If all of them were already ON, they are all turned OFF.

SHIFT-K. A popup Menu asks: OK? Show and select all keys. The Draw Key option is turned ON for all selected Objects, and all Object-keys are selected. This function is used to enable transformation of the entire animation system.

LKEY. Makes selected Object local. Makes library linked objects local for the current scene.

OBJECT MODE HOTKEYS

Object will not be deformed. A popup permits to select the bone. This is the option if you are modeling a robot or machinery

CTRL-L. Link selected. Links some of the Active Object data to all selected Objects, the following menu entry appears only if applicable.

- **To Scene:** Creates a link of the Object to a scene.
- **Object IPOs:** Links Active Object IPOs to selected ones.
- **Mesh Data:** Links Active Object Mesh data selected ones.
- **Lamp Data:** Links Active Object Lamp data to selected ones.
- **Curve Data:** Links Active Object Curve data selected ones.
- **Surf Data:** Links Active Object Surf data selected ones.
- **Material:** Links Active Object Material to selected ones.

SHIFT-L. Select Linked. Selects all Objects somehow linked to active Object.

- **Object IPO:** Selects all Object(s) sharing active Object's IPOs.
- **Object Data:** Selects all Object(s) sharing active Object's ObData.
- **Current Material:** Selects all Object(s) sharing active Object's current Material.

Current Texture: Selects all Object(s) sharing active Object's current Texture.

MKEY. Moves selected Object(s) to another layer, a pop-up appers. Use LMB to move, use SHIFT-LMB to make the object belong to multiple layers. If the selected Objects have different layers, this is 'OR'ed in the menu display. Use ESC to exit the menu. Press the "OK" button or ENTER to change the layer seting. The hotkeys (ALT-)(1KEY, 2KEY, ... - 0KEY) work here as well (see 3DHeader).

CTRL-M. Mirror Menu. It is possible to mirror an Object along the X, Y or Z axis.

N KEY. Number Panel. The location, rotation and scaling of the active Object are displayed and can be modified.

ALT-O. Clear Origin. The 'Origin' is erased for all Child Objects, which causes the Child Objects to move to the exact location of the Parent Objects.

SHIFT-O. If the selected Object is a Mesh toggles SubSurf onn/ off. CTRL-1 to CTRL-4 switches to the relative SubSurf level for display purpouses. Rendering SUbSurf level has no Hotkey.

CTRL-P. Make selected Object(s) the child(ren) of the active Object. If the Parent is a Curve then a popup offers two coiches:

- **Normal Parent:** Make a normal parent, the curve can be made a path later on.
- **Follow Path:** Automatically creates a Follow Path constraint with the curve as target.

If the Parent is an Armature, a popup offers three options:

- **Use Bone:** One of the Bones becomes the parent. The
- Use Armature: The whole armature is used as parent for deformations. This is the choiche for organic beings.
- **Use Object:** Standard parenting.

In the second case further options asks if Vertex groups should not be created, should be created empty or created and populated.

ALT-P. Clears Parent relation, user is asked if he wishes to keep or clear parent-induced transforms.

- **Clear Parent:** the selected Child Objects are unlinked from the Parent. since the transformation of the Parent disappears, this can appear as if the former Children themselves are transformed.
- **... and keep transform:** the Child Objects are unlinked from the Parent, and an attempt is made to assign the current transformation, which was determined in part by the Parent, to the (former Child) Objects.
- **Clear Parent inverse:** The inverse matrix of the Parent of the selected Objects is erased. The Child Objects remain linked to the Objects. This gives the user complete control over the hierarchy.

RKEY. Rotate mode. Works on selected Object(s). In Blender, a rotation is by default a rotation perpendicular to the screen, regardless of the view direction or View Mode. The degree of rotation is exactly linked to the mouse movement. Try moving around the rotation midpoint with the mouse. The rotation pivot point is determined by the state of the 3DWiewport Header buttons. Alternatives for starting this mode:

LMB to draw a C-shaped curve.

The following options are available in rotation mode:

Limiters:

- **CTRL:** in increments of 5 degrees.
- **SHIFT:** fine movements.
- **SHIFT-CTRL:** in increments of 1 degree.

MMB toggles: A short click restricts the current rotation to the horizontal or vertical view axis.

XKEY, YKEY, ZKEY constrains rotation to **X, Y or Z** axis of the global reference.

a second **XKEY, YKEY, ZKEY** constrains rotation to **X, Y or Z** axis of the local reference.

a third **XKEY, YKEY, ZKEY** removes constraints.

NKEY enters numerical input, as well as any numeric key directly. **ENTER** finalizes, **ESC** exits.

ARROWS: These keys can be used to move the mouse cursor exactly 1 pixel.

Rotation can be terminated with:

- **LMB SPACE or ENTER**: move to a new position.
- **RMB or ESC**: everything goes back to the old position.

Switching mode:

- **GKEY:** switches to Grab.
- **SKEY:** switches to Size (Scale) mode.
- **RKEY:** starts Rotate mode again.

OBJECT MODE HOTKEYS

ALT-R. Clears Rotation. The X,Y,Z rotations of selected Objects are set to zero.

SKEY. Size mode or scaling mode. Works on selected Object(s). The degree of scaling is exactly linked to the mouse movement. Try to move from the (rotation) midpoint with the mouse. The pivot point is determined by the settings of the 3D Viewport header pivot Menu. Alternatives for starting scaling mode:

LMB to draw a V-shaped line.

The following options are available in scaling mode:

Limiters:

- **CTRL:** in increments of 0.1.
- **SHIFT-CTRL:** in increments of 0.01.

MMB toggles: A short click restricts the scaling to X, Y or Z axis. Blender calculates the appropriate axis based on the already initiated mouse movement. Click MMB again to return to free scaling.

XKEY, YKEY, ZKEY constrains scaling to X, Y or Z axis of the local reference.

a second **XKEY, YKEY, ZKEY** removes constraints.

NKEY enters numerical input, as well as any numeric key directly. **ENTER** finalizes, **ESC** exits.

ARROWS: These keys can be used to move the mouse cursor exactly 1 pixel.

Scaling can be terminated with:

- **LMB SPACE or ENTER:** move to a new position.
- **RMB or ESC:** everything goes back to the old dimension.

Switching mode:

- **GKEY**: switches to Grab.
- **SKEY**: starts Size mode again.
- **RKEY**: switches to Rotation.

ALT-S. Clears Size. The X,Y,Z dimensions of selected Objects are set to 1.0.

SHIFT-S. Snap Menu:

- **Sel->Grid:** Moves Object to nearest grid point.
- **Sel->Curs:** Moves Object to cursor.
- **Curs->Grid:** Moves cursor to nearest grid point.
- **Curs->Sel:** Moves cursor to selected Object(s).
- **Sel->Center:** Moves Objects to their barycentrum.

TKEY. Texture space mode. The position and dimensions of the texture space for the selected Objects can be changed in the same manner as described above for Grab and Size mode. To make this visible, the drawing flag Edit Buttons->Tex Space is set ON. A Popup Menu asks you to select: "Grabber" or "Size".

CTRL-T. Makes selected Object(s) track the Active Object. Old track method was Blender default tracking before version 2.30. The new method is the Constrain Track, this creates a fully editable constraint on the selected object targeting the active Object.

ALT-T. Clears old style Track. Constraint track is removed as all constrains are.

UKEY. Makes Object Single User, the inverse operation of Link (**CTRL-L**) a pop-up appears with choices.

- **Object:** if other Scenes also have a link to this Object, the link is deleted and the Object is copied. The Object now only exists in the current Scene. The links from the Object remain unchanged.
- **Object & ObData:** Similar to the previous command, but now the ObData blocks with multiple links are copied as well. All selected Objects are now present in the current Scene only, and each has a unique ObData (Mesh, Curve, etc.).
- **Object & ObData & Materials+Tex:** Similar to the previous command, but now Materials and Textures with multiple links are also copied. All selected Objects are now unique. They have unique ObData and each has a unique Material and Texture block.
- **Materials+Tex:** Only the Materials and Textures with multiple links are copied.

VKEY. Switches in/out of Vertex Paint Mode.

ALT-V. Object-Image Aspect. This hotkey sets the X and Y dimensions of the selected Objects in relation to the dimensions of the Image Texture they have. Use this hotkey when making 2D Image compositions and multi-plane designs to quickly place the Objects in the appropriate relationship with one another.

WKEY. Opens Object Booleans Menu.

XKEY. Erase Selected? Deletes selected objects.

ZKEY. Toggles Solid Mode on/off. **SHIFT-Z**. Toggles Shaded Mode on/off. **ALT-Z**. Toggles Textured Mode on/off.

EDIT MODE - GENERAL

Again, Most of these hotkeys are useful in the 3D Viewport when in Edit Mode, but many works on other Blender Object, so they are summarized here.

Many Object Mode keys works in Edit mode too, but on the selected vertices or control points; among these Grab, Rotate, Scale and so on. These hotkeys are not repeated here.

TAB or **ALT-E**. This button starts and stops Edit Mode.

CTRL-TAB. Switches between Vertex Select, Edge Select, and Face Select modes. Holding **SHIFT** while clicking on a mode will allow you to combine modes.

AKEY. Select/Unselect all.

BKEY. Circle Select. If you press **BKEY** a second time after starting Border Select, Circle Select is invoked. It works as described above. Use **NUM+** or **NUM-** or **MW** to adjust the circle size. Leave Circle Select with **RMB** or **ESC**.

CTRL-H. With vertices selected, this creates a "**Hook**" object. Once a hook is selected, **CTRL-H** brings up an options menu for it.

NKEY. Number Panel. Simpler than the Object Mode one, in Edit Mode works for Mesh, Curve, Surface: The location of the active vertex is displayed.

OKEY. Switch in/out of Proportional Editing.

SHIFT-O. Toggles between Smooth and Sharp Proportional Editing.

PKEY. Separate. You can choose to make a new object with all selected vertices, edges, faces and curves or create a new object from each separate group of interconnected vertices from a popup. Note that for curves you cannot separate connected control vertices. This operation is the opposite of Join (**CTRL- J**).

CTRL-P. Make Vertex Parent. If one object (or more than one) is/are selected and the active Object is in Edit Mode with 1 or 3 vertices selected then the Object in Edit Mode becomes the Vertex Parent of the selected Object(s). If only 1 vertex is selected, only the location of this vertex determines the Parent transformation; the rotation and dimensions of the Parent do not play a role here. If three vertices are selected, it is a 'normal' Parent relationship in which the 3 vertices determine the rotation and location of the Child together. This method produces interesting effects with Vertex Keys. In Edit Mode, other Objects can be selected with **CTRL-RMB**.

CTRL-S. Shear. In Edit Mode this operation enables you to make selected forms 'slant'. This always works via the horizontal screen axis.

UKEY. Undo. When starting Edit Mode, the original Ob Data block is saved and can be returned to via **UKEY**. Mesh Objects have better Undo, see next section.

WKEY. Specials popup Menu. A number of tools are included in this Popup Menu as an alternative to the Edit Buttons. This makes the buttons accessible as shortcuts, e.g. Edit Buttons->Subdivide is also '**WKEY, 1KEY**'.

SHIFT-W. Warp. Selected vertices can be bent into curves with this option. It can be used to convert a plane into a tube or even a sphere. The centre of the circle is the 3DCursor. The mid-line of the circle is determined by the horizontal dimensions of the selected vertices. When you start, everything is already bent 90 degrees. Moving the mouse up or down increases or decreases the extent to which warping is done. By zooming in/out of the 3Dwindow, you can specify the maximum degree of warping. The CTRL limiter increments warping in steps of 5 degrees.

EDIT MODE - MESH

This section and the following highlight peculiar Edit Mode Hotkeys.

CTRL-NUM+. Adds to selection all vertices connected by an edge to an already selected vertex.

CTRL-NUM-. Removes from selection all vertices of the outer ring of selected vertices.

ALT-CTRL-RMB. Edge select.

CKEY. If using curve deformations, this toggles the curve Cyclic mode on/off.

EKEY. Extrude Selected. "Extrude" in Edit Mode transforms all the selected edges to faces. If possible, the selected faces are also duplicated. Grab mode is started directly after this command is executed.

SHIFT-EKEY. Crease Subsurf edge. With "Draw Creases" enabled, pressing this key will allow you to set the crease weight. Black edges have no weight, edge-select color have full weight.

CTRL-EKEY. Mark **LSCM** Seam. Marks a selected edge as a "seam" for unwrapping using the **LSCM** mode.

FKEY. Make Edge/Face. If 2 vertices are selected, an edge is created. If 3 or 4 vertices are selected, a face is created.

SHIFT-F. Fill selected. All selected vertices that are bound by edges and form a closed polygon are filled with triangular faces. Holes are automatically taken into account. This operation is 2D; various layers of polygons must be filled in succession.

ALT-F. Beauty Fill. The edges of all the selected triangular faces are switched in such a way that equally sized faces are formed. This operation is 2D; various layers of polygons must be filled in succession. The Beauty Fill can be performed immediately after a Fill.

CTRL-F. Flip faces, selected triangular faces are paired and common edge of each pair swapped.

HKEY. Hide Selected. All selected vertices and faces are temporarily hidden.

SHIFT-H. Hide Not Selected: All non-selected vertices and faces are temporarily hidden.

EDIT MODE - MESH

SHIFT-U. Redo. This let you re-apply any undone changes up to the moment in which Edit Mode was entered.

ALT-H. Reveal. All temporarily hidden vertices and faces are drawn again.

ALT-J. Join faces, selected triangular faces are joined in pairs and transformed to quads

KKEY. Knife tool Menu.

- **Face Loop Select: (SHIFT-R)** Face loops are highlighted starting from edge under mouse pointer. **LMB** finalizes, **ESC** exits.
- **Face Loop Cut: (CTRL-R)** Face loops are highlighted starting from edge under mouse pointer. **LMB** finalizes, **ESC** exits.
- **Knife (exact): (SHIFT-K)** Mouse starts draw mode. Selected Edges are cut at intersections with mouse line. **ENTER** or **RMB** finalizes, **ESC** exits.
- **Knife (midpoints): (SHIFT-K)** Mouse starts draw mode. Selected Edges intersecting with mouse line are cut in middle regardless of true intersection point. **ENTER** or **RMB** finalizes, **ESC** exits.

LKEY. Select Linked. If you start with an unselected vertex near the mouse cursor, this vertex is selected, together with all vertices that share an edge with it.

SHIFT-L. Deselect Linked. If you start with a selected vertex, this vertex is deselected, together with all vertices that share an edge with it.

CTRL-L. Select Linked Selected. Starting with all selected vertices, all vertices connected to them are selected too.

MKEY. Mirror. Opens a popup asking for the axis to mirror. 3 possible axis group are available, each of which contains three axes, for a total of nine choices. Axes can be Global (Blender Global Reference); Local (Current Object Local Reference) or View (Current View reference). Remember that mirroring, like scaling, happens with respect to the current pivot point.

ALT-M. Merges selected vertices at barycentrum or at cursor depending on selection made on pop-up.

CTRL-N. Calculate Normals Outside. All normals from selected faces are recalculated and consistently set in the same direction. An attempt is made to direct all normals 'outward'.

SHIFT-CTRL-N. Calculate Normals Inside. All normals from selected faces are recalculated and consistently set in the same direction. An attempt is made to direct all normals 'inward'.

ALT-S. Whereas **SHIFT-S** scales in Edit Mode as it does in Object Mode, for Edit Mode a further option exists, **ALT-S** moves each vertex in the direction of its local normal, hence effectively shrinking/fattening the mesh.

CTRL-T. Make Triangles. All selected faces are converted to triangles.

UKEY. Undo. When starting Edit Mode, the original Ob Data block is saved and all subsequent changes are saved on a stack. This option enables you to restore the previous situation, one after the other.

ALT-U. Undo Menu. This let you choose the exact point to which you want to undo changes.

WKEY. Special Menu. A Popup Menu offers the following options:

- **Subdivide:** all selected edges are split in two.
- **Subdivide Fractal:** all selected edges are split in two and middle vertex displaced randomly.
- **Subdivide Smooth:** all selected edges are split in two and middle vertex displaced along the normal.
- **Merge:** as ALT-M.
- **Remove Doubles:** All selected vertices closer to each other than a given threshold (See Edit Mode Button Window) are merged ALT-M.
- **Hide:** as HKEY.
- **Reveal:** as ALT-H.
- **Select Swap:** Selected vertices become unselected and vice versa.
- **Flip Normals:** Normals of selected faces are flipped.
- **Smooth:** Vertices are moved closer one to each other, getting a smoother object.
- **Bevel:** Faces are reduced in size and the space between edges is filled with a smoothly curving bevel of the desired order.

XKEY. Erase Selected. A popup Menu offers the following options:

- **Vertices:** all vertices are deleted. This includes the edges and faces they form.

- **Edges:** all edges with both vertices selected are deleted. If this 'releases' certain vertices, they are deleted as well. Faces that can no longer exist as a result of this action are also deleted.
- **Faces:** all faces with all their vertices selected are deleted. If any vertices are 'released' as a result of this action, they are deleted.
- **All:** everything is deleted.
- **Edges and Faces:** all selected edges and faces are deleted, but the vertices remain.
- **Only Faces:** all selected faces are deleted, but the edges and vertices remain.

YKEY. Split. This command 'splits' the selected part of a Mesh without deleting faces. The split parts are no longer bound by edges. Use this command to control smoothing. Since the split parts have vertices at the same position, selection with **LKEY** is recommended.

EDIT MODE - CURVE

CKEY. Set the selected curves to cyclic or turn cyclic off. An individual curve is selected if at least one of the vertices is selected.

EKEY. Extrude Curve. A vertex is added to the selected end of the curves. Grab mode is started immediately after this command is executed.

FKEY. Add segment. A segment is added between two selected vertices at the end of two curves. These two curves are combined into one curve.

HKEY. Toggle Handle align/free. Toggles the selected Bezier handles between free or aligned.

SHIFT-H. Set Handle auto. The selected Bezier handles are converted to auto type.

CTRL-H. Calculate Handles. The selected Bezier curves are calculated and all handles are assigned a type.

LKEY. Select Linked. If you start with an non-selected vertex near the mouse cursor, this vertex is selected together with all the vertices of the same curve.

SHIFT-L. Deselect Linked. If you start with a selected vertex, it is deselected together with all the vertices of the same curve.

MKEY. Mirror. Mirror selected control points exactly as for vertices in a Mesh.

TKEY. Tilt mode. Specify an extra axis rotation, i.e. the tilt, for each vertex in a 3D curve.

ALT-T. Clear Tilt. Set all axis rotations of the selected vertices to zero.

VKEY. Vector Handle. The selected Bezier handles are converted to vector type.

WKEY. The special menu for curves appears:

- **Subdivide.** Subdivide the selected vertices.
- **Switch direction.** The direction of the selected curves is reversed. This is mainly for Curves that are used as paths!

XKEY. Erase Selected. A popup Menu offers the following options:

- **Selected:** all selected vertices are deleted.

- **Segment:** a curve segment is deleted. This only works for single segments. Curves can be split in two using this option. Or use this option to specify the cyclic position within a cyclic curve.
- **All:** delete everything.

EDIT MODE - SURFACE

CKEY. Toggle Cyclic menu. A popup Menu asks if selected surfaces in the '**U**' or the '**V**' direction must be cyclic. If they were already cyclic, this mode is turned off.

EKEY. Extrude Selected. This makes surfaces of all the selected curves, if possible. Only the edges of surfaces or loose curves are candidates for this operation. Grab mode is started immediately after this command is completed.

FKEY. Add segment. A segment is added between two selected vertices at the ends of two curves. These two curves are combined into 1 curve.

LKEY. Select Linked. If you start with an non-selected vertex near the mouse cursor, this vertex is selected together with all the vertices of the same curve or surface.

SHIFT-L. Deselect Linked. If you start with a selected vertex, this vertex is deselected together with all vertices of the same curve or surface.

MKEY. Mirror. Mirror selected control points exactly as for vertices in a Mesh.

SHIFT-R. Select Row. Starting with the last selected vertex, a complete row of vertices is selected in the 'U' or 'V' direction. Selecting Select Row a second time with the same vertex switches the 'U' or 'V' selection.

WKEY. The special menu for surfaces appears:

- **Subdivide.** Subdivide the selected vertices
- **Switch direction.** This will switch the normals of the selected parts.
- **Mirror.** Mirrors the selected vertices

XKEY. Erase Selected. A popup Menu offers the following choices:

- **Selected:** all selected vertices are deleted.
- **All:** delete everything.

VERTEX PAINT HOTKEYS

SHIFT-K. All vertex colours are erased; they are changed to the current drawing colour.

UKEY. Undo. This undo is 'real'. Pressing Undo twice redoes the undone.

WKEY. Shared Vertexcol: The colours of all faces that share vertices are blended.

EDIT MODE - METABALL

MKEY. Mirror. Mirror selected control points exactly as for vertices in a Mesh.

EDIT MODE - FONT

In Text Edit Mode most hotkeys are disabled, to allow text entering.

RIGHTARROW. Move text cursor 1 position forward

SHIFT-RIGHTARROW. Move text cursor to the end of the line.

LEFTARROW. Move text cursor 1 position backwards. **SHIFT-LEFTARROW.** Move text cursor to the start of the line **DOWNARROW**. Move text cursor 1 line forward

SHIFT-DOWNARROW. Move text cursor to the end of the text.

UPARROW. Move text cursor 1 line back.

SHIFT-UPARROW. Move text cursor to the beginning of the text

ALT-U. Reload Original Data (undo). When Edit Mode is started, the original text is saved. You can restore this original text with this option.

ALT-V. Paste text. The text file /tmp/.cutbuffer is inserted at the cursor location.

UV EDITOR HOTKEYS

EKEY. LSCM Unwrapping. Launches LSCM unwrapping on the faces visible in the UV editor.

PKEY. Pin selected vertices. Pinned vertices will stay in place on the UV editor when executing an **LSCM** unwrap.

ALT-PKEY. Un-Pin selected vertices. Pinned vertices will stay in place on the UV editor when executing an **LSCM** unwrap.

EDGE SELECT HOTKEYS

ALT-CLICK. Selects an Edge Loop.

FACE SELECT HOTKEYS

ALT-CLICK. Selects a Face Loop.

TAB. Switches to Edit Mode, selections made here will show up when switching back to Face Select Mode with TAB.

FKEY. With multiple, co-planar faces selected, this key will merge them into one "FGon" so long as they remain co-planar (flat to each other).

LKEY. Select Linked UVs. To ease selection of face groups, Select Linked in UV Face Select Mode will now select all linked faces, if no seam divides them.

RKEY. Calls a menu allowing to rotate the UV coordinates or the VertexCol.

UKEY. Calls the UV Calculation menu. The following modes can the applied to the selected faces:

- **Cube:** Cubical mapping, a number button asks for the cubemap size
- **Cylinder:** Cylindrical mapping, calculated from the center of the selected faces

- **Sphere:** Spherical mapping, calculated from the center of the selected faces
- **Bounds to x:** UV coordinates are calculated from the actual view, then scaled to a boundbox of 64 or 128 pixels in square
- **Standard x:** Each face gets default square UV coordinates
- **From Window:** The UV coordinates are calculated using the projection as displayed in the 3DWindow

CHAPTER 3: NAVIGATING THE BLENDER USER INTERFACE

When you launch Blender for the first time, what appears on your computer screen is the User Interface of the program. This layout of panels serves as the means through which you interact with the program by inputting commands (data) via the keyboard and mouse. The panels you see on the user interface are known as Editors or Headers, they facilitate your communication with Blender.

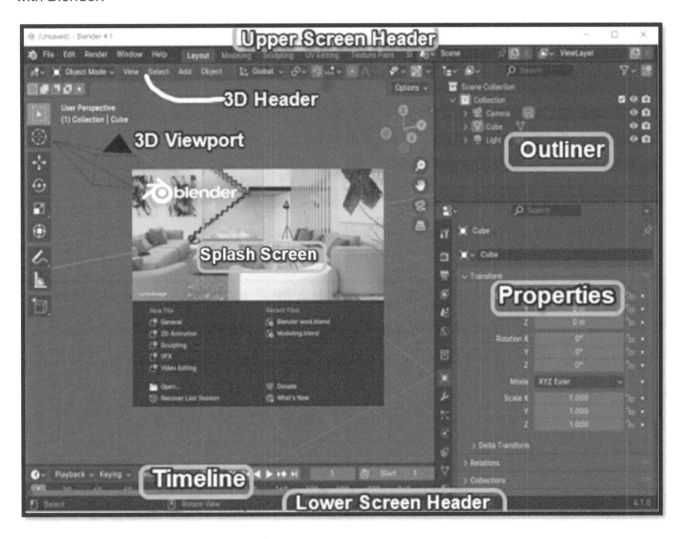

Note: In the diagram above, the various Editors are highlighted to differentiate them from one another. Altering the background colors of Editors essentially modifies the color scheme or theme of the User Interface.

Upon the first launch, Blender's User Interface appears on the computer screen with a default theme or color scheme called **"Blender Dark"**.

If you wish to experiment with different themes and customize Blender to your liking, you can do that in the **Preferences** Editor with the following steps:

1) Click on **"Edit"** and select **"Preferences "** in the Screen Header.

37

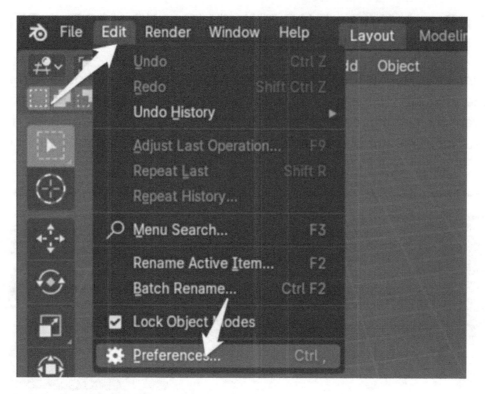

2) Within the **Preferences** Editor, navigate to the **"Themes"** section in the left-hand column. Click on the **"Presets"** menu to reveal a list of available color schemes.

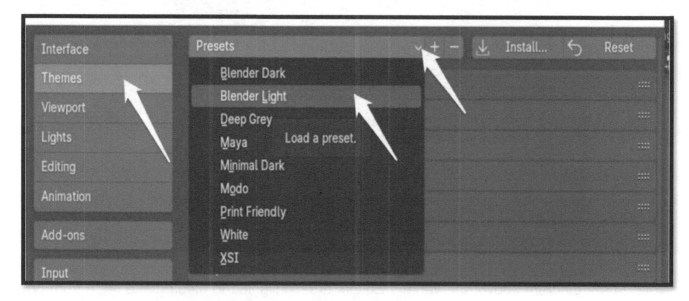

3) The Blender User Interface reflects the change

It's assumed that you're already familiar with the Blender User Interface, including the Preferences Editor and the process of selecting themes. However, these instructions are provided to ensure clarity and to familiarize you with the instructional approach used throughout the book, which includes references to Editors, Headers, Panels, and Tabs.

For further clarification on these terminologies and their usage within the interface, refer to the following diagram.

EDITORS

When you first open Blender, you'll encounter four Editors: the 3D Viewport, Outliner, Properties, and Timeline Editors. T h e Splash Screen, located at the center of the display, greets you with the Blender version and provides access to various functions via buttons. Usually, the Splash Screen image changes with each new Blender release. Screen Headers appear at the top and bottom of the display, while each Editor Panel features its own Editor Header. These headers host Butt on Controls for accessing functions relevant to the screen or editor.

For instance, clicking the Left Mouse Button in the 3D Viewport Editor dismisses the Splash Screen

BLENDER CONTROLS (BUTTONS, SLIDERS AND ICONS)

Controls within the User Interface consist of **Buttons, Icons**, and **Sliders,** each Editor being a distinct panel with its Header containing buttons that either activate functions or reveal submenus with additional function buttons.

A button can take various forms: it might be a text annotation that turns blue when hovered over, an icon representing a function, or a bar with text. Clicking a button triggers an action within the program.

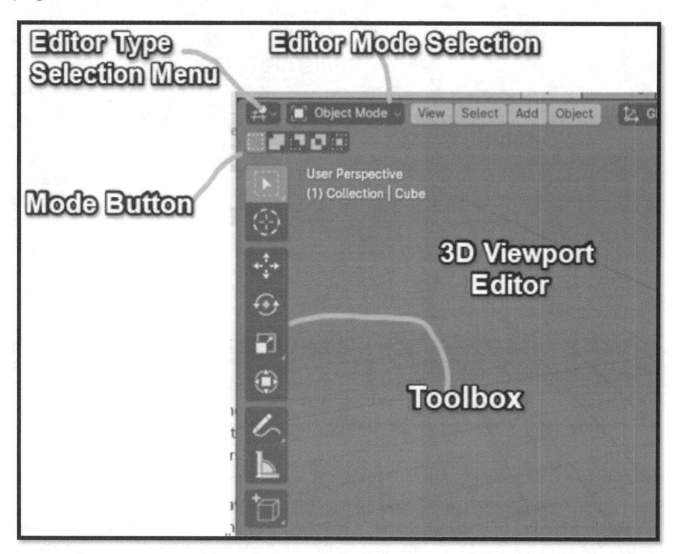

For instance, in the 3D Viewport Editor (the default screen display buttons; these buttons are visible at the top left side of the panel). These instructions refer to the default arrangement of element s on the Blender screen, meaning what appears before any actions are taken.

THE PROPERTIES EDITOR

By default, the Properties Edi to r displays its content having the Object Properties active. In this condition, the default cube object is di-rectly influenced in the 3D Viewport Editor.

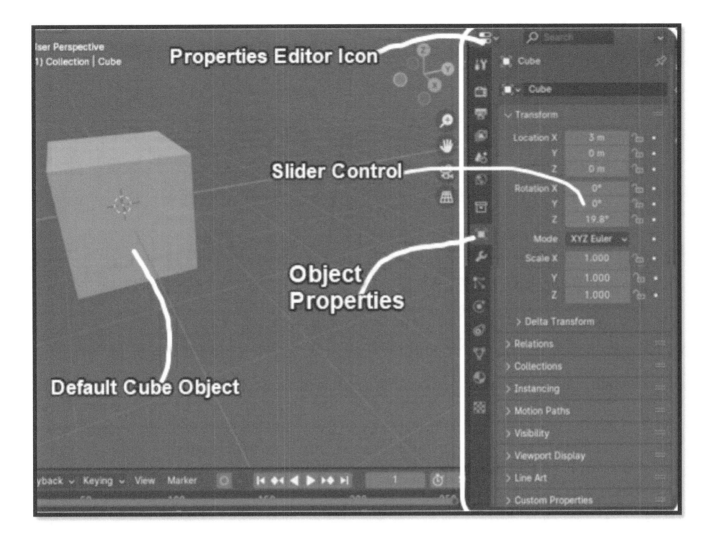

Take Note of the following:

- ✓ In Blender, a **button** can appear as a tiny rectangular area or square on the screen, or if extended, it's referred to as a bar.
- ✓ Some buttons appear with icons, icons are visual representations of functions. For instance, in the diagram, the icon at the upper left corner signifies the Properties Editor's display.
- ✓ A **slider** in Blender is an expanded area typically displaying a numeric value. You can modify this value by clicking, deleting, and retyping the value, or by clicking, holding, and dragging the mouse cursor over it. When hovered over, some sliders reveal small arrows at either end; clicking on these arrows incrementally adjusts the value. Certain sliders directly impact the on-screen display.

SLIDER CONTROL DETAIL

The Slider Controls within the **Transform** tab influence the location of the Cube (selected object) in the 30 Viewport Editor.

When the **Cube** Object is selected in the 30 Viewport Editor, adjusting the **X** Location Slider to **3m** and the X-Axis Rotation Slider to **19.8°** causes the Cube to move forward along the **X-Axis (Red Line)** and rotate about the **vertical Z-Axis.**

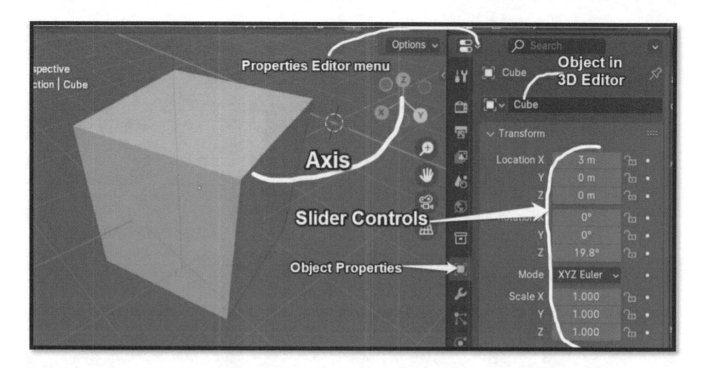

For keyboard input, a command involves pressing specific keys or a group of keys. For instance, pressing "**Shift + Ctrl + T**" means holding down both the **Shift** and **Ctrl** keys simultaneously and then tapping the **T** key. Additionally, Num pad (Number Pad) keys can also be used, where the command "Press Num Pad **0** to **9** or Plus and Minus", means pressing the numeric key son the keyboard's Num Pad along with the **Plus** and **Minus** keys to instruct the application for a command.

Keep in mind: Whenever a control button, icon, or slider is visible on the computer screen, it specifies a specific location. Placing the mouse cursor at this spot and clicking the mouse button or pressing a keyboard button sends a signal to the computer. The computer in-terprets this as follows: signal received at a specific location equal (=) performing a specific computation and producing a result.

For instance, in the **Blender Screen** Header shown below, positioning the mouse cursor over the **Render** Properties button and left-click-ing the mouse button once triggers an action.

In this scenario, the signal received by the computer at the position of the **Render** Properties button prompts it to display the Render Options Sub Menu. Then, by hovering the mouse cursor over **"Render Image"** in the submenu and clicking once, an image of the **Camera View** (what the camera sees) is rendered.

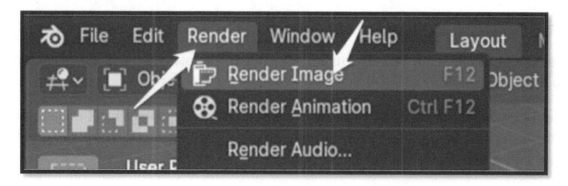

The rendered image appears in a new **Editor** panel called the Image Editor. Although the image can be saved from this location, you can press **Esc** on the keyboard to cancel the rendering process and return to the 3DViewport Editor for now.

Note: when you press Num Pad 0, the 3D Viewport Editor shows the preview of what will be rendered in the Image **"What the Camera sees".**

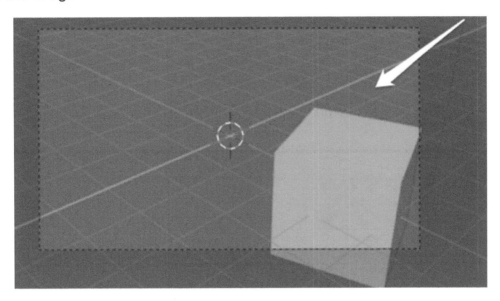

The annotation **F12** shown beside the Render image is the shortcut to render the image

BLENDER VIEWPOINT AND SHORTCUTS

Viewpoint allows you to align the viewing direction of the 3D Viewport Editor to a specific axis. You can use **XYZ** Navigation Gizmo or **Shortcut** keys as shown below. Viewpoint: **View > Viewpoint.**

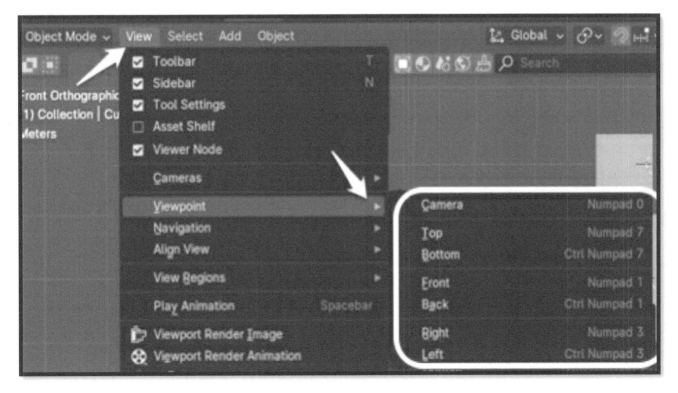

SHORTCUTS KEY	AXIS
Num Pad 0	Camera View
Num Pad 3	Right Orthographic View
Ctrl + Num pad 3	Left Orthographic View
Num pad 1	Front Orthographic View
Ctrl + Num pad 1	Back Orthographic View
Num Pad 7	Top Orthographic View
Ctrl + Num Pad 7	Bottom Orthographic View
Num Pad 5	Toggle User Orthographic/User Perspective

The above shortcuts align the view to a global (world) axis. You can align to a local axis of the selected object by additionally holding down

the **Shift** key with the above shortcuts. In this manner, you can view any mesh face head-on, regardless of its orientation. (To opt out of the Local view point, simply align to a global axis again).

CHAPTER 4: UNDERSTANDING OBJECTS IN THE 3D VIEWPORT

In the 3D Viewport Editor, objects include the models and characters you craft as basic parts of a scene. This category extends to lights that illuminate the scene and cameras designed to capture specific portions you want to render. Essentially, anything introduced into a scene within Blender is classified as an object.

When embarking on modeling, a common starting point is the use of basic object primitives, which are initially introduced into a scene. These primitives serve as foundational shapes that can be subsequently modified or edited to generate new shapes, which is the founda-tion of modeling.

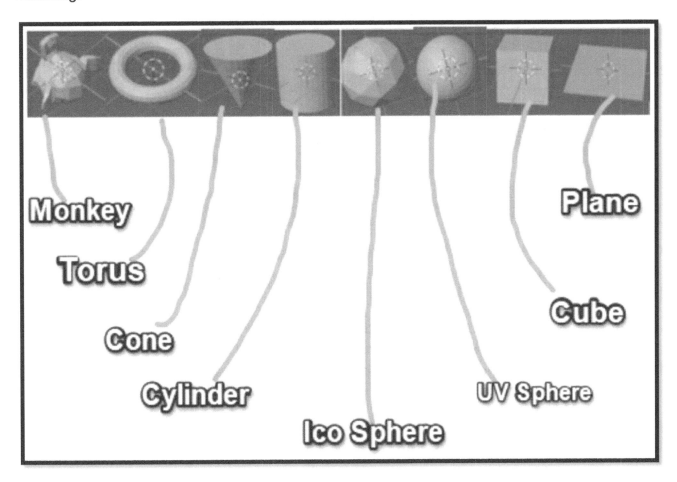

OBJECT PRIMITIVES

To add object primitives, you can do that from **Add> Mesh** in the 3DViewport Editor Header.

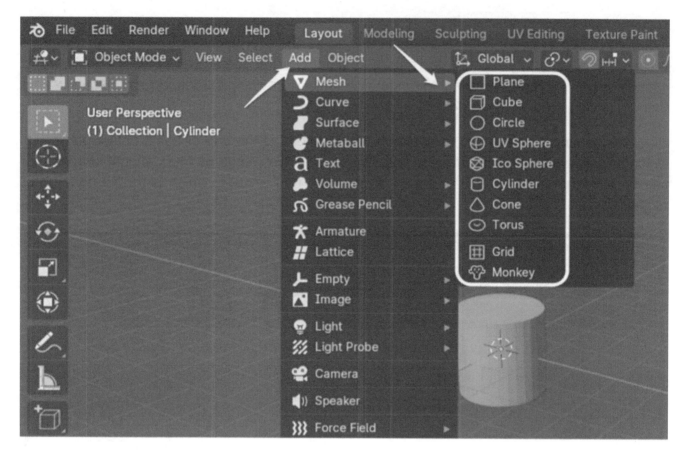

Note: Mesh primitives represent one category of objects; others can be found in the **Add** Menu. These objects are classified as such because once they are introduced into a scene, they can be manipulated to generate effects.

Additionally, aside from the **Mesh Primitive** object, a range of other object types can be accessed from the **Add** Menu located in the **3D Viewport** Editor Header. **Curve** object types, for example, are used in modeling and supplement model processing or for producing scene effects.

Note: The Bezier Curve is among the five curve types available, which include **Bezier, Circle, Nurbs Curve, Nurbs Circle, and Path**.

In **Edit** Mode, the Nurbs Torus contains a surrounding cage that facilitates shaping adjustments. (Nurb torus can be found in surface grouping in the Add menu).

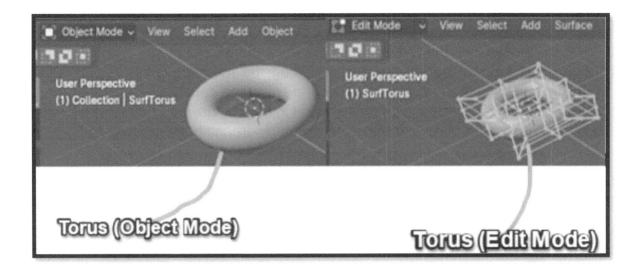

Select the **Cage vertices** and Drag.

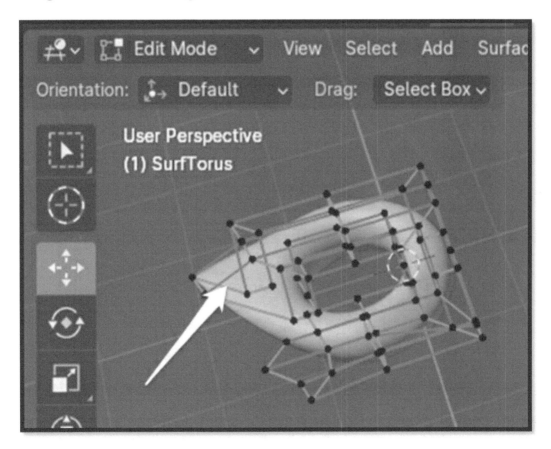

Once the desired shaping is achieved, switch to Object Mode, right-click with the mouse, and choose Convert To> Mesh from the menu options.

Note: Some object types selected from the Add menu do not render in the final output. For instance, the Bezier Curve does not render, whereas the Surface- Nurbs Torus does render.

THE ADD CUBE TOOL

Within the 3D Viewport Editor's Object Mode, the Tool Panel includes **the Add Cube** Tool, this tool offers a convenient method for intro-ducing objects into a scene.

To access the tool options, use the following steps:

1) hover the mouse over the **tool** and left-click the mouse button.
2) While holding down the left mouse click, drag the mouse over an option, which will highlight blue, and then release the mouse to select the option.
3) Once an option is selected, the mouse cursor in the 3D Viewport Editor transforms into a grid, allowing you to position it within the scene by dragging the mouse.

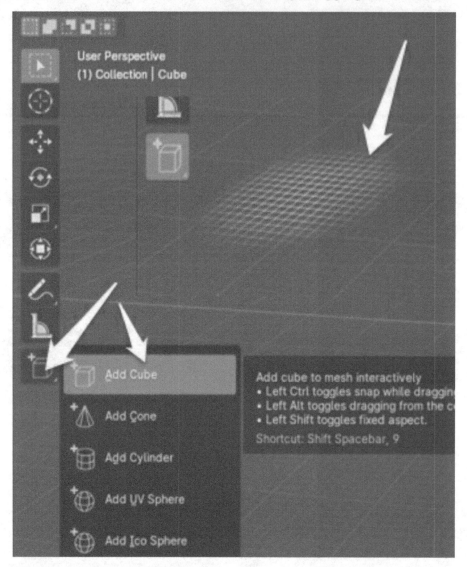

4) Move the grid to the desired location within the scene. Left-click the mouse and then drag the mouse to create a **rectangle** (which may not necessarily be a perfect square).

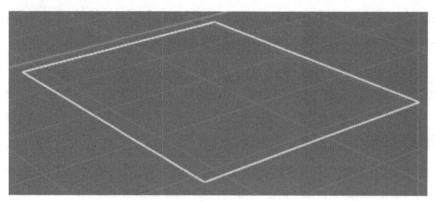

5) Release the left mouse click and then drag the mouse upward to form a cuboid shape.
6) Finally, left-click the mouse again to confirm and set the shape.

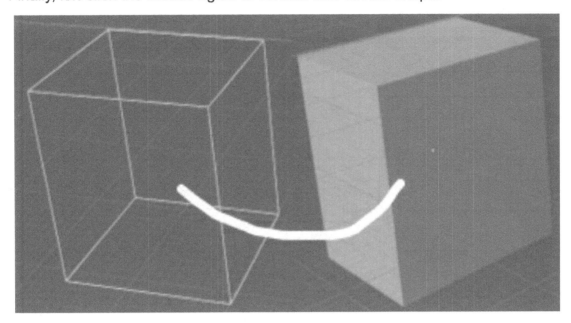

Clicking the left mouse button switches the cursor back to its default state with the grid still attached. You can repeat this process to create an additional cuboid or any other object of your choice.

To cancel the construction process, select the **Select Box** Tool locate d at the top of the Tool Panel.

Note: The Add Cube Tool can be used in both Object Mode and Edit Mode. To switch to Edit Mode, you must have an existing mesh object in the scene. If you create a new object using the Add Cube (shape) Tool in Edit Mode, the new shape will be joined to the original mesh object.

OBJECTS FROM ADD-ONS

The default choice in the Add Menu within the 3D Viewport Editor encompasses mesh objects and various other types of objects. It's important to note, however, that Blender offers additional mesh objects that aren't readily accessible. To access these, you'll need to acti-vate specific add-ons within the Preferences Editor.

To open the Preferences Editor:

1) click on **"Edit"** in the Blender Screen Header and then select **"Preferences."**
2) Within the **Preferences** Editor, navigate to the left-hand side and select **"Add-ons."** In the right-hand side, scroll down until you locate the section labeled **"Add Mesh Add-ons"**.
3) Tick the checkbox beside the add-ons name to activate the desired add-ons.

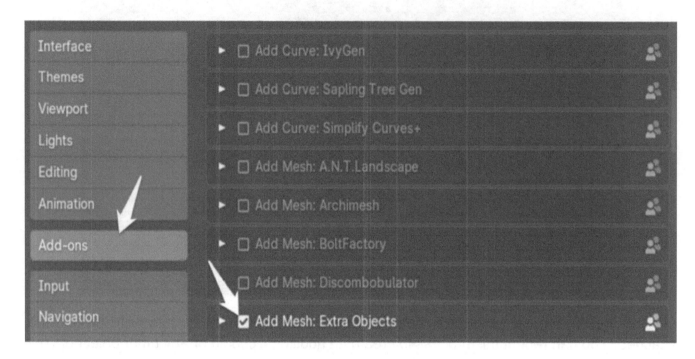

4) Click the disclosure triangle to show Add-on details.

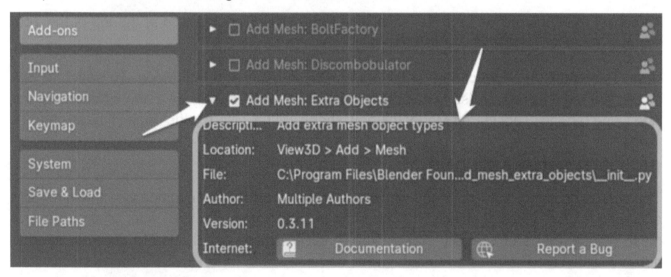

Play around various add-ons to figure out new objects and features. Each ad d-on you add will be reflected on the **3D ViewPoint > Add** menu. For instance, other objects have been added to the Mesh menu in this case.

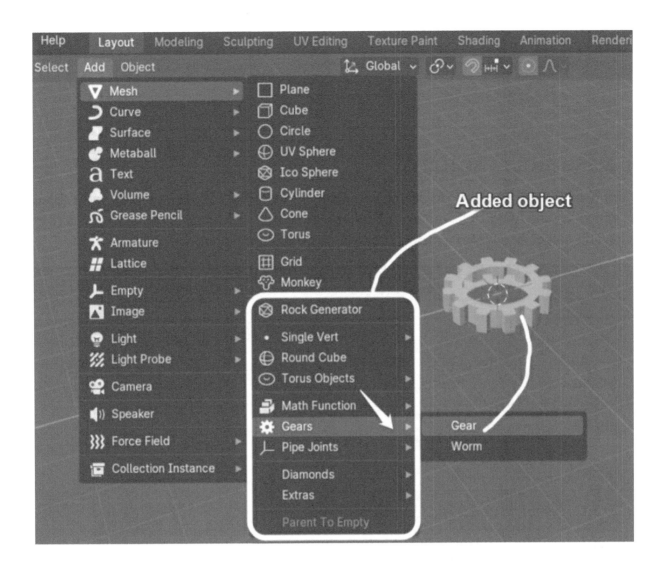

ADD MESH (ARCHIMESH)

The **"Archimesh"** add-on offers a range of architectural components.

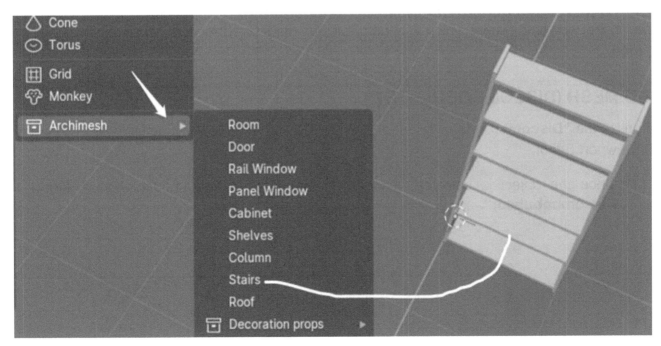

ADD MESH (BOLT FACTORY)

Use the "Bolt Fact or y" add-on to create various configurations of bolts and nuts within Blender. After activating the "Add Bolt " add-o n Pref-erence Editor, navigate to the 3D Viewport Editor Header and select Add > Mesh > Bolt to display a default bolt in the viewport.

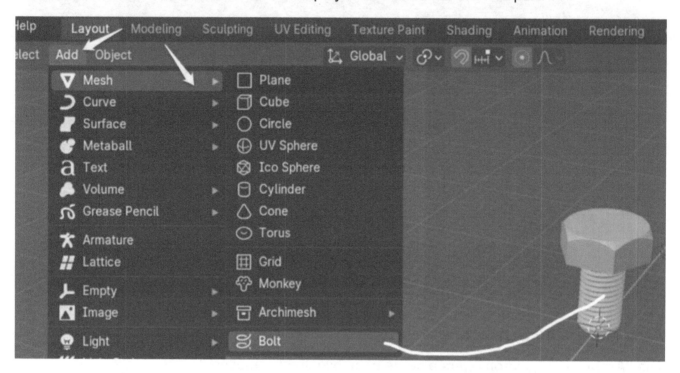

To further customize the bolt or nut, expand the Last Operator Panel located on the lower left side of the viewport, where you'll find con-trols for adjusting the type and specifications as needed.

ADD MESH (DISCOMBOBULATOR)

To utilize the **"Discombobulator"** add -on, ensure you have a mesh object selected within the 3D Viewport Editor.

1) Once the object is selected, navigate to the Header and choose **Add > Mesh > Discombobulator"**.

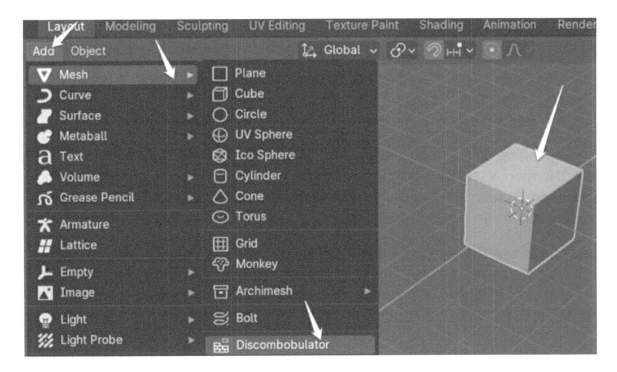

2) This action triggers the discombobulation process, which generates a duplicated version of the selected object. This duplicate is then subdivided and reconfigured into a puzzling shape based on the settings specified in the Discombobulator panel. You can alter the Discombobulator settings.

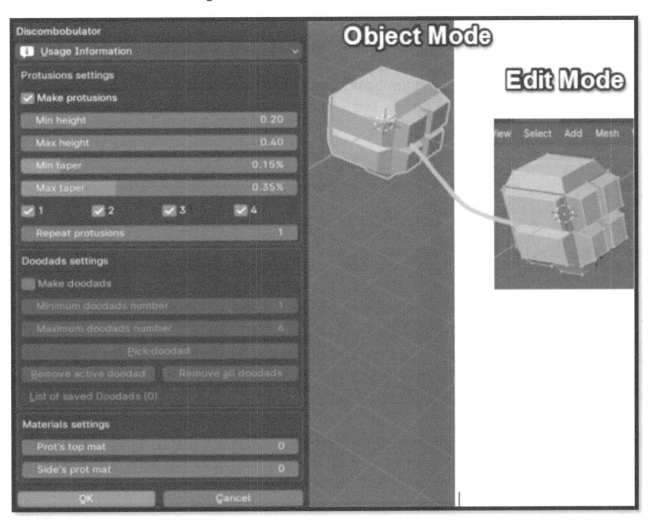

BLENDER ASSETS

In Blender, an asset refers to a pre-constructed model, a material (color), a material texture, or any other useful element. Objects them- selves serve as assets by offering a foundation for modeling and scene creation components.

Computer graphics artists frequently rely on assets to enhance their work or simplify their workflow. Numerous online sources provide downloadable assets, prompting Blender to incorporate an Assets Browser within the program, which connects to an Assets Library. Addi-tionally, users can install add-ons in Blender to access additional asset resources.

The **Assets Library** is essentially a folder created on the hard drive, which is usually empty at first, where users can add assets. These assets can then be viewed and selected in the Assets Browser and subsequently inserted into the scene within the current Blender file. The Assets Browser can thus be called a specialized Editor.

The type of add-on is **BlenderKit**, which offers a variety of models, scenes, materials, brushes, and HOR images. To access **BlenderKit**, users need to download and install it in Blender, register as a user, and choose between free and paid selections. Many online asset sources provide both free and paid assets.

VIEWING THE ASSETS BROWSER

The Assets Browser, as previously mentioned, connects to the Assets Libra ry. As of the time of writing, this feature is still under devel-opment, so the operation procedure may vary depending on the version of the Blender program being used. Initially, access to the Assets Browser can be obtained by clicking on the **Editor Type** Icon and selecting **"Assets Browser"** from the selection menu as shown below.

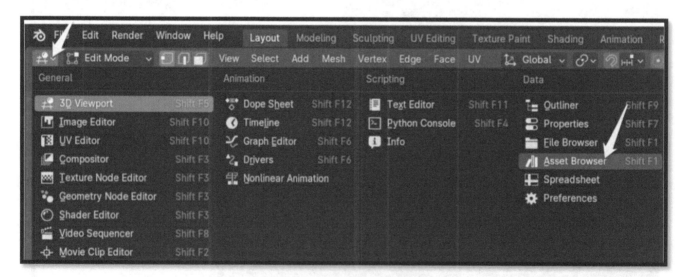

For practical purposes, you can split the 3D **Viewport Editor** vertically, dedicating one half to the **Assets Browser**. To do that open the Asset Browser from different Editor Types aside from the **Editor Type** at the Top Left corner as shown below.

When you select either the **Assets Library** or **User Library**, you will receive the following message:

No asset icons are displayed when **"Current File"** is selected because no assets have been created or marked.

Additionally, the message **"Path to Asset Library"** appears when the file path to the library hasn't been set or the library hasn't been cre-ated yet.

Asset libraries are essentially folders created on your hard drive, where you can save Blender files containing content marked as assets. These asset libraries are straightforward folders that you create on your hard drive. You can organize them by creating sub folders to clas-sify your assets effectively.

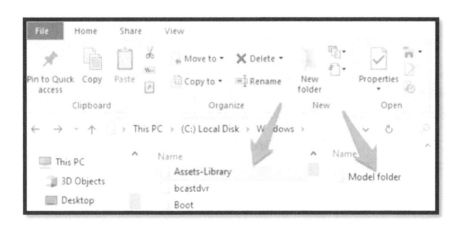

To enable the Assets Browser to locate the Assets Library folder, you need to set the **File Path** in the **Preferences Editor**.

Before creating a library, assets can still be generated when **"Current File"** is selected. For instance, a modified default cube object can serve as an asset. To mark the modified cube as an asset, follow these steps:

1) With the modified cube selected in the 3D Viewport Editor, go to the **Outliner Editor.**
2) Select the modified cube object, right-click, and choose **"Mark as Asset"** from the menu that appears.

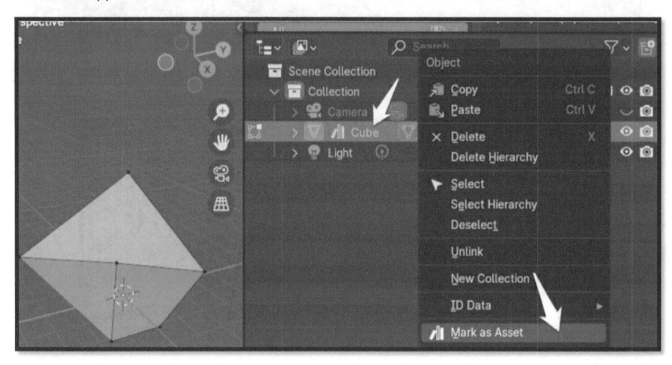

3) An icon representing the modified cube will then appear in the **Assets Browser** when "Current File" is selected.

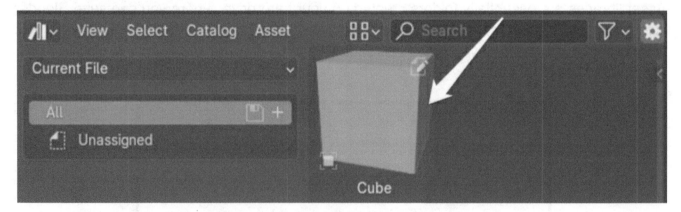

4) click the **Cube** icon in the **Assets Browser**, then hold and drag it into the **3D Viewport** Editor to create duplications.

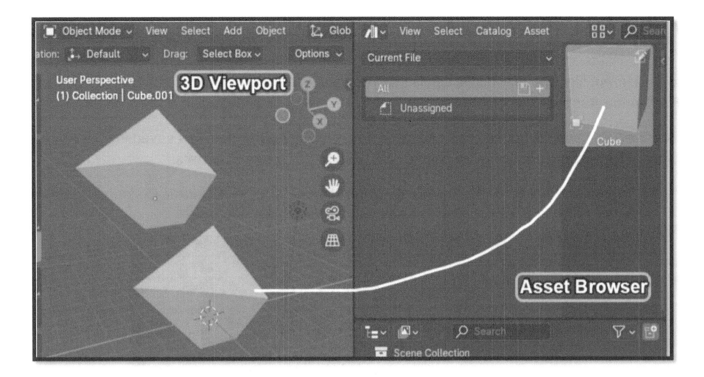

By following these steps, assets have been both created and applied using the Assets Browser in **"Current File"** mode. Saving the Blender file will preserve these assets, making them available when the file is reopened.

However, note that when a new Blender file is opened, the assets created in previous files are not accessible. To ensure assets are available across all Blender files, it's necessary to create an Assets Library.

WHAT IS THE ASSETS LIBRARY?

The Assets Library Folder is created with subfolders organized into categories in the previous section. For ease of access, the **Assets Li-brary** Folder has been established on the **C: Drive** of the computer. You have the flexibility to create a folder and assign it any desired name to serve as an Assets Library. Simply ensure to assign the **file name** and **file path** to the folder in the **Preferences** Editor as shown below.

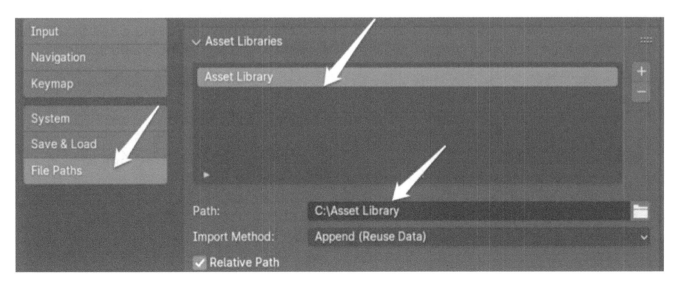

ADDING ASSETS TO THE ASSETS LIBRARY

To add assets to the library, follow the same process as previously discussed for adding assets to the current file. The only distinction is that you select **"Assets_Library"** rather **than "Current File"** in the **Asset Browser.**

However, it's essential to Hint: to add assets, you must have **Blender files** saved in your **Assets Library Directory** containing the content you wish to designate as assets.

1. To add any asset to the **Assets Browser**, navigate to the **Outliner** Editor, click on the asset which **is "Suzanne"** in this case, and select **"Mark as Asset".**

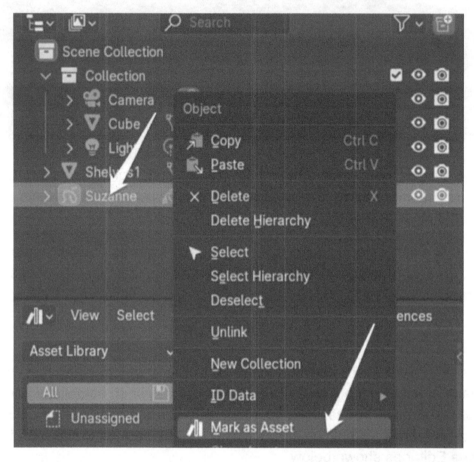

2. This will place an icon in the Assets Browser as shown above. To insert the model into the 3DViewport Editor, click, hold, and drag the icon from the Assets Browser into the 3DViewport. You may need to adjust the rotation and scale to fit the scene accordingly.

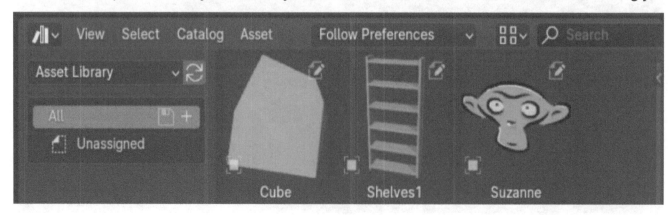

ASSETS PACKS

Asset Packs are collections of Blender files comprising pre-constructed models. Since models can be complex and time-consuming to create, Asset Packs offer a convenient solution to save time when building scenes. Many websites provide Asset Packs, some free of charge, while others require payment.

An example of a free Asset Pack is the Ground Foliage Pack, which can be downloaded from: **[https://www.motionblendstudio.com/ blender-vfx-assets).**

✓ When you download this specific Assets Pack, you'll receive a **ZIP** file named "blender Ground Foliage. zip".When you extract the contents, you'll find two folders: **"MACOSX"** and **"blender GroundFoliage"**.

✓ Inside the **"blenderGroundFoliage"** fold e r, you 'll discover several Blender files. The Ground Foliage Pack is stored within the file named **"groundFoliage,"**which is one of the Blender files contained in this folder.

✓ When you open **"groundFoliage.blend** "in Blender, you'll see a variety of models that can be added to other Blender files.

✓ Additionally, you have the option to select each model individually in the **Outliner** Editor and "**Mark it As Asset** "thus ad ding it to your Assets Library.

You can populate your Assets Library with as many assets as you desire, provided that you have Blender files saved on your PC containing these assets. These saved assets will remain accessible when you open a new Blender file.

Over time, your Assets Library may become quite extensive, accumulating numerous Blender files. Alternatively, you can use online re- sources such as the **BlenderKit Online Assets Library** to access a wide range of assets.

BLENDERKIT

BlenderKit is an add-on designed for Blender. You can download it from [this link) **(https://www.blender kit.com/get-blenderkit/).**

The downloaded file," **blenderkit v3.11.024,**"comes in the form of a compressed ZIP file. It's important not to unzip this file.

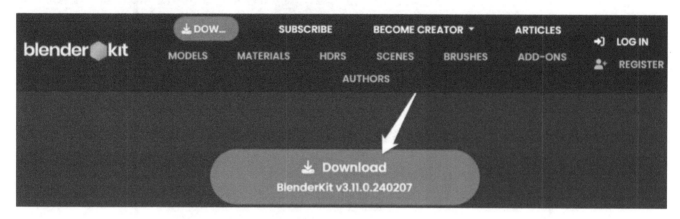

To install the add-on, follow these steps:

1) Open the **Preferences** Editor in Blender, navigate to the **"Add-ons"** section, and click on the **"Install"** button.

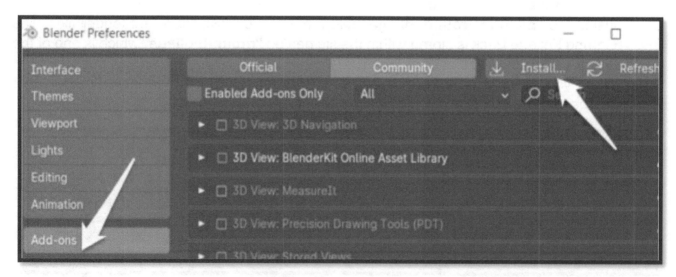

2) Locate the **"blenderkit v3.11.024"** file in your Downloads folder using the **Blender File View**.

3) Select the **"blendrekit v3.11.024"** file and click on **"Install Add-on"** at the bottom of the panel.

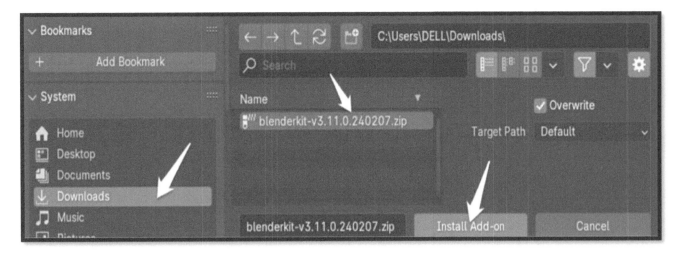

4) Once the add-on is installed, remember to activate it in the Add-ons section to start using its features.

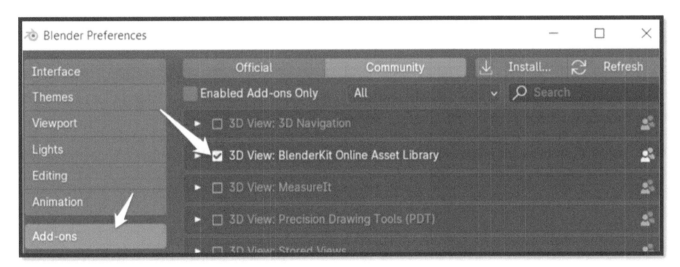

5) Once BlenderKit is installed and activated, you'll notice a new tab labeled **"BlenderKit"** icon in the **Properties** Panel within the 3D Viewport Editor.

BlenderKit serves as a link between **Blender** and an **online assets** library, meaning assets are not stored locally on your PC.

It's worth noting that assets are categorized into two types: **Locked** and **Unlocked**. Unlocked assets are available for free, while locked as- sets require payment to access.

Hover over an asset, click, hold, and drag it into the 3D Viewport Editor. Then, zoom in and rotate the view as needed.

To apply material assets, first select a model in the 3DViewport Editor. Then, click, hold, and drag the material asset over the selected model.

Hint: some materials may take a while to load and will only display in the 3D Viewport Editor when in Material Preview or rendered View- port Shading Mode.

CHAPTER 5: BASICS OF EDITING AND ADD-ONS

Editing objects lays the groundwork for modeling. Essentially, you shape basic primitives, known as mesh objects to craft characters and elements within a scene. This shaping occurs in both Object Mode and Edit Mode, where you can manipulate objects as a whole or refine individual vertices on the object's mesh surface. The 3D Viewport offers editing tools, including widgets and procedures to aid in the modeling process. While these tools are visible in the Tool Panels within the Editor Panel in both modes (Edit and Object), navigating the available options might not always be straightforward. Additionally, there are various add-ons accessible in the Preferences Editor to fur-ther help the editing process. This chapter aims to guide users on accessing editing tools and add-ons effectively.

In subsequent sections, we will look into **Object** Mode and **Edit** Mode, explore the tool panels associated with each, and discuss the use of add-ons for editing. Finally, we'll illustrate the basic modeling process by transforming a sphere into a humanoid character suitable for animation.

THE OBJECT AND EDIT MODE

In both **Object** Mode and **Edit** Mode, the 3D Viewport Editor presents default **Tool** Panels. These panels offer essential tools for editing objects within the scene. If needed, you can hide these Tool **Panels** by simply pressing the **T** key on your keyboard; pressing it again toggles between hiding and showing them.

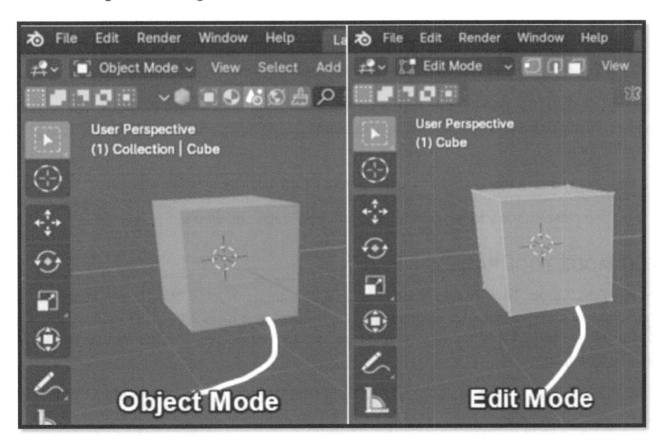

OBJECT MODE TOOL PANEL

Within the **Object Mode Tool** Panel, you'll find tools dedicated to fundamental operations like **translation, scaling, and rotation**. When you activate the Scale Tool, it adds scale manipulation handles, often referred to as widgets, onto the selected object, allowing you to adjust its size.

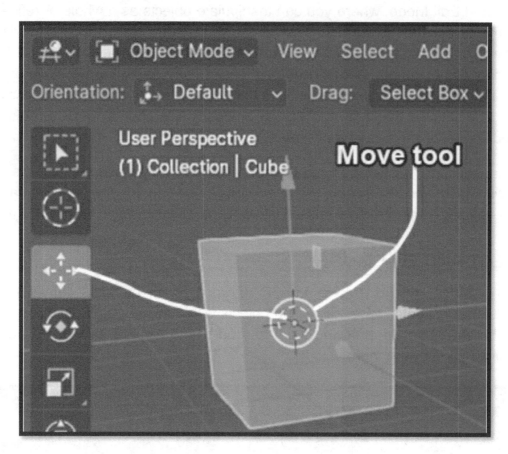

Note: By default, the **Select Box** Tool is active. To choose a different tool, hover your mouse over the desired tool and left-click the mouse button. Hovering over a tool displays a description of its function.

To cancel any active tool and return to the Select Box Tool, simply select it again.

Try out the different tools to get comfortable with how each one works.

EDIT MODE TOOL PANELS

In the **Edit Mode Tool** Panel, you'll find a wide range of tools specifically designed for manipulating mesh objects. It's worth noting that the first nine tools are similar to those found in Object Mode. Note: hovering your mouse over a tool and holding the left mouse button will display tool options.

Hint: the initial nine editing tools are applicable in both **Objec**t Mode and **Edit** Mode. Whenever you encounter a triangle icon in the comer of a **Tool** Panel, simply hover your mouse over it, then **click** and **hold the left mouse** to reveal **additional tool options.**

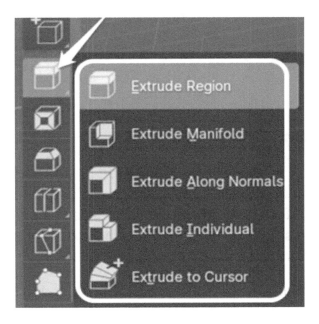

In the **Edit Mode Tool** Panel, you'll notice it displays in three stages. To customize the view, simply hover your mouse over the panel and drag the double-headed arrow to compress the display, revealing the tool names.

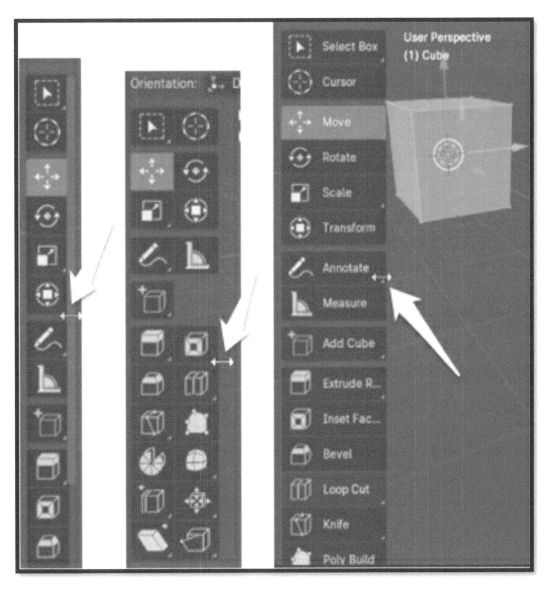

ADD-ONS FOR EDITING

In addition to the editing tools available in the 3DViewport Edi to r Tool Panel, Blender also offers several useful add-ons for adding basic objects to a scene and for editing objects. These add-ons can be found in the **Preferences** Edit or, you can access them from the **Blender Screen Header** by clicking **Edit** and selecting **Preferences** at the bottom of the menu. To view add-ons, navigate to the **"Add-ons"** group on the left-hand side.

Add-ons are arranged alphabetically and are somewhat categorized for ease of navigation. As an example of implementing add-ons for editing, consider the following:

ADD MESH EXTRA OBJECT:

One of the add-on s is **"Add Mesh Extra Object, "**which can be found around the top of the listing (scroll down in the **Preferences** Editor). By default, the **add-on** is inactive. To activate it, simply check **(tick)** the checkbox located before the add-on name.

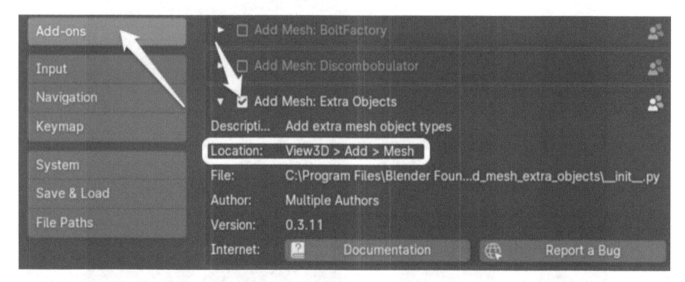

Once activated, you'll find the add-on details displayed, including the location of the controls, typically under Location: **"View 3D > Add > Mesh"**

With the **"Add Mesh: Extra Object"** add-on enabled, you 'll have access to additional objects in the **"Add"** menu under **"Mesh."** Before activating the add-on, the available mesh objects are limited to the default options provided by Blender.

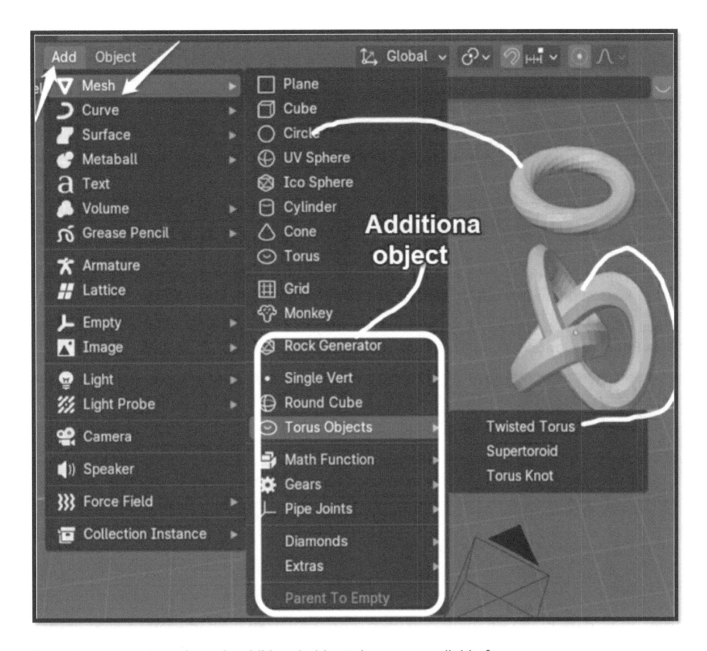

Once the add-on is activated, additional objects become available for use.

Hint: the controls for some add-ons are accessible in the 3DViewport Editor Header, while others are found in the Object Properties Panel within the 3D Viewport.

EDIT MESH TOOLS (ADD ON MESH):

Next, we shall consider the **"Mesh: Edit Mesh Tools"** add-on. To access its controls, first enable it in the Preference Editor, then:

1) First, consider the location of the **"Mesh: Edit Mesh Tools"-(View 3D >Sidebar > Edit Tab/ Edit Mode Context Menu).**

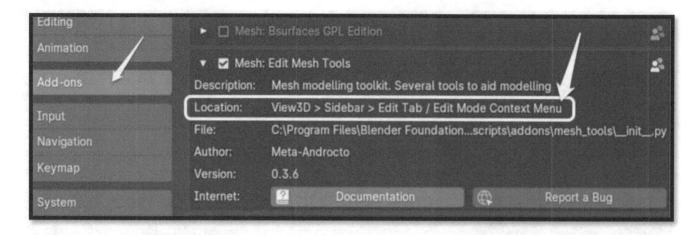

2) With an **object** selected in the 3D Viewport, switch to **Edit** Mode by pressing **Tab** on the keyboard. This will display the controls for the **"Mesh: Edit Mesh Tools"** add-on.

Press the **N** key on your keyboard to reveal the **Object Properties** Panel (also known **as the Side Panel or Context Menu)** in the upper right- hand side of the 3D Viewport Editor.

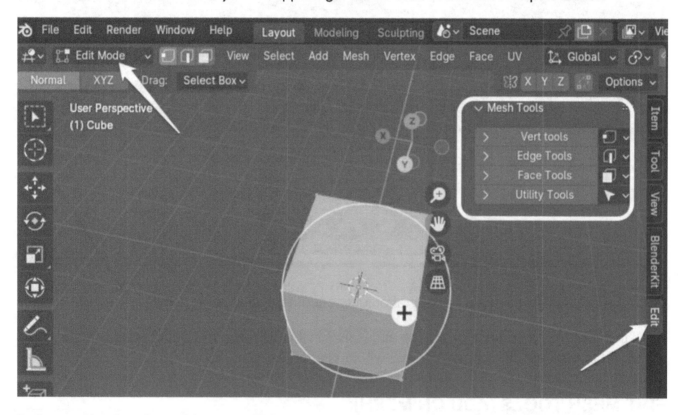

Before activating the add-on, you'll interact with mesh objects using the default tools. After activation, you'll have access to a wider range of objects and tools provided by the add-on.

with the object selected in the **3DViewport** (for example, **a cube**) in Object Mode, using the **Subdivide** tool will subdivide the cube's mesh when switched to **Edit** Mode.

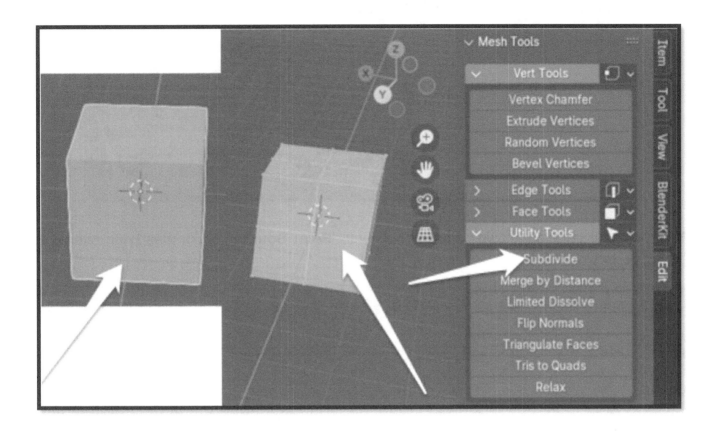

CELL FRACTURE (ADD ON OBJECT):

Another add-on, called **"Cell Fracture"** exhibits different locations within the 3D Viewport.

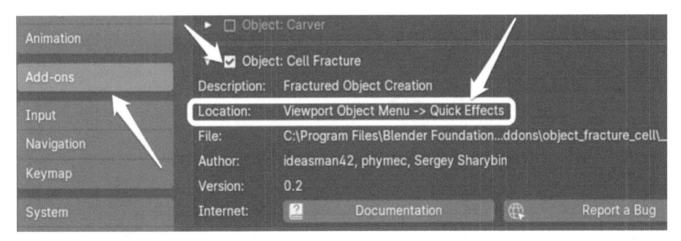

Now, what exactly is Cell Fracture?

When you click on **"Cell Fracture"** in the **Quick Effects** menu, it opens up the **Cell Fracture** control panel within the 3D Viewport Editor. These controls are specifically designed for the currently selected object. Cell Fracture essentially breaks down (fractures) a mesh into mul-tiple parts, based on the settings chosen in the control panel.

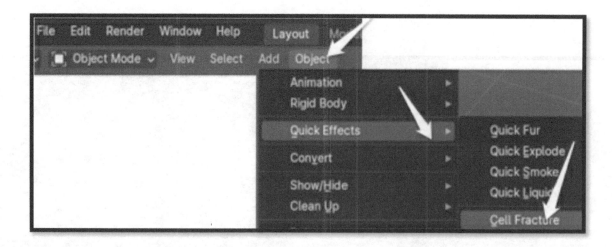

Hint: in the illustration shown below, the default **"Point Source"** option has been altered to **"Own Verts".**

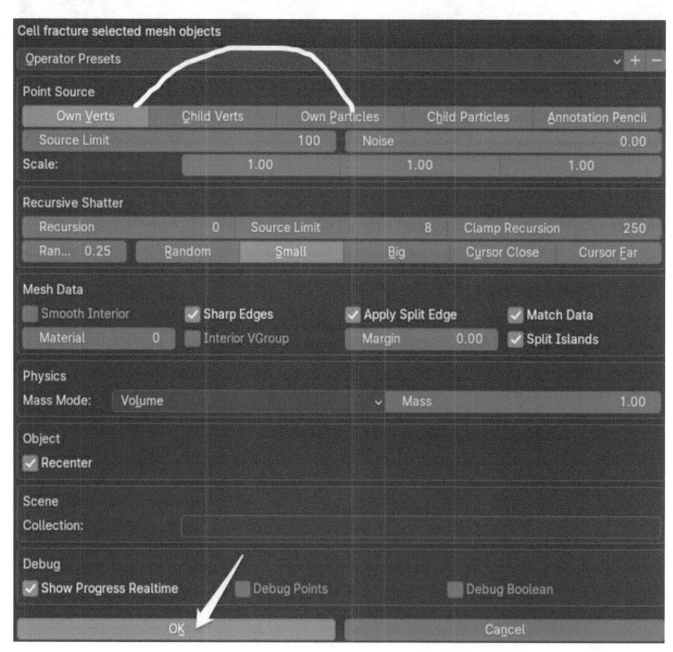

By default, when an **Icosphere** is selected in the 3D Viewport Editor, it will be divided (fractured) into parts based on the arrangement of its vertices. However, it's worth mentioning that other settings can also influence the number of cells produced.

Here's an Icosphere with the Cell Fracture effect applied, revealing two cells that have been removed.

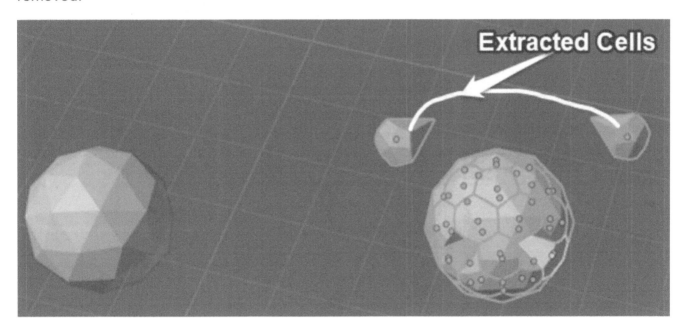

CHAPTER 6: EDITING WITH GENERATE MODIFIERS

Modifiers are automated operations that impact an object in a non-destructive manner, enabling the creation of effects that would otherwise be cumbersome to achieve manually. They function by altering how an object appears and is rendered within the viewport. Importantly, the original geometry of the mesh remains intact until the modifier is applied. This allows for editing of the mesh's underly-ing geometry as needed before commit ting to the modifier's changes permanently.

To access modifiers, navigate to the **Properties** Editor and select the **Modifiers** tab under Properties.

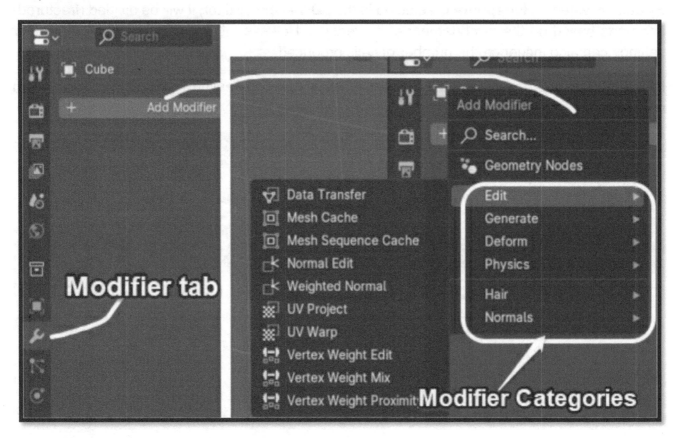

THE MODIFIER SELECTION MENU

The Modifier Selection Menu is categorized into six sections, as illustrated above.

Modifiers listed under **"Edit"** apply procedural or operational effects to the selected object in the 3DViewport Editor. Note that this cate- gory doesn't physically alter the shape of the object.

"Generate" and **"Deform"** Modifiers, on the other hand, physically modify the shape of the selected object. Additionally, **"Physics** "Modifiers apply real-world physical attributes to an object. We will only discuss the first four modifiers in this book.

You can apply multiple modifiers to a single object, combining their effects to create a Modifier Stack.

THE GENERATE MODIFIER

In the **"Generate"** category, you'll find modifiers that serve as building tools, altering the overall appearance or automatically adding new geometry to an object.

An example of a modifier in this category is the **Bevel** Modifier, which is listed second alphabetically.

The Bevel Modifier is relatively straightforward to grasp, making it an ideal choice for demonstrating how modifiers work. To apply a modifier:

1) begin by selecting the **object** you wish to modify within the 3D Viewport Editor. The modifier will add specifically to the chosen object.

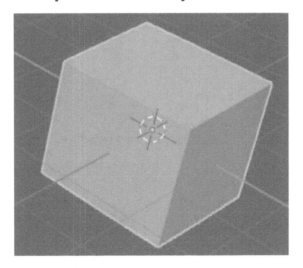

2) Next, go to the **Properties** Editor and access the **Modifier** Properties section. Click on the "**Add Modifier** " button to reveal a Modifier selection.
3) Within the **"Generate"** category, lo ca t e and select "**Bevel**" as shown below. This action prompts the Bevel **Modifier** panel to appear within the Modifier **Properties** sect ion of the Properties Editor

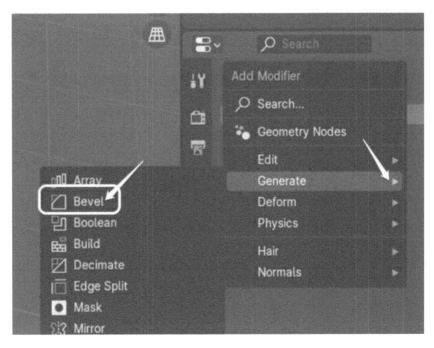

Hint: The settings within the Bevel Modifier Panel are tailored to the object selected within the 3D View port.

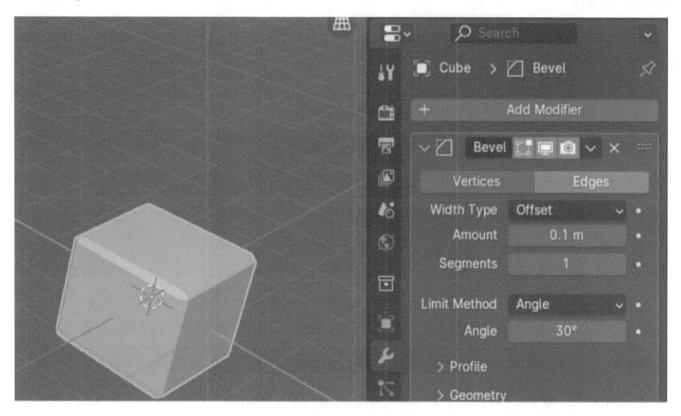

Once the Bevel Modifier is applied, the selected object will show its edges with a beveled effect in **Object** Mode. However, in Edit Mode, you'll notice the bevel, but with only eight vertices visible.

The modifier has been added to the object, but its effects have not yet been permanently applied. To apply the modifier, click on "Apply" in the menu.

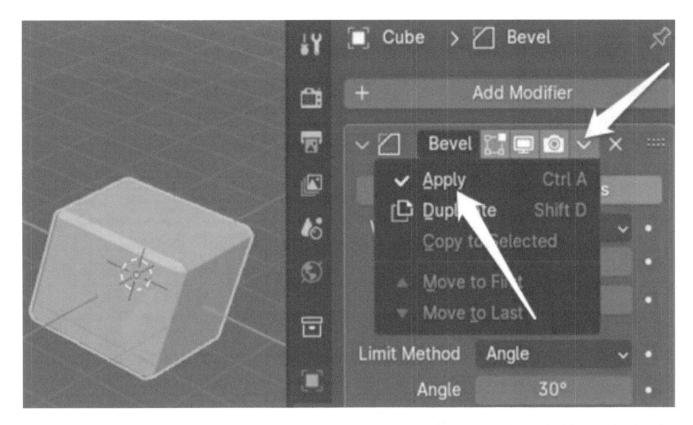

Once the modifier is applied, vertices are permanently added to the selected object, altering its shape permanently.

USING ARRAY MODIFIER

The Array Modifier is a tool that duplicates an object and arranges the copies in an array, with each copy positioned at a specified offset from the original. For example, this illustrates a Monkey Object duplicated using an Array Modifier in Front Orthographic view.

To apply the Array Modifier, see the steps below:

1) Select the **object** you want to duplicate (e.g., the **Monkey {Suzanne}**) in the 3D Viewport Editor.

2) Navigate to the **Properties** Editor, then to the **Modifier** Properties section.
3) Click on **"Add Modifier "**and choose **"Array"** from the Generate menu.

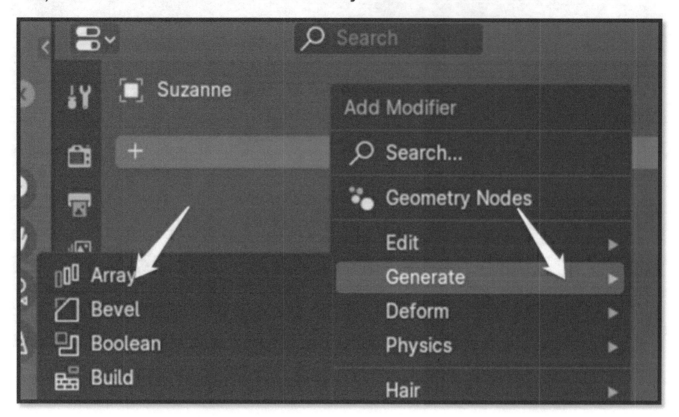

4) input the **Relative Offset** values as shown below. Additionally, setting the Count to **4** instructs Blender to generate four monkeys in the array, including the original object and three duplicates.

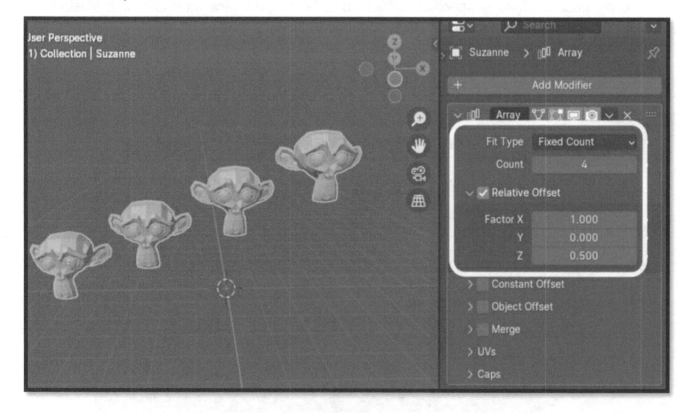

The **offset** is determined based on the object's bounds. Each object has a bounding volume that surrounds its shape. You can visualize this bounding volume by enabling the "**Bounds**" checkbox in the **Properties** Editor, within the **Object** Properties under the **Viewport Display** tab.

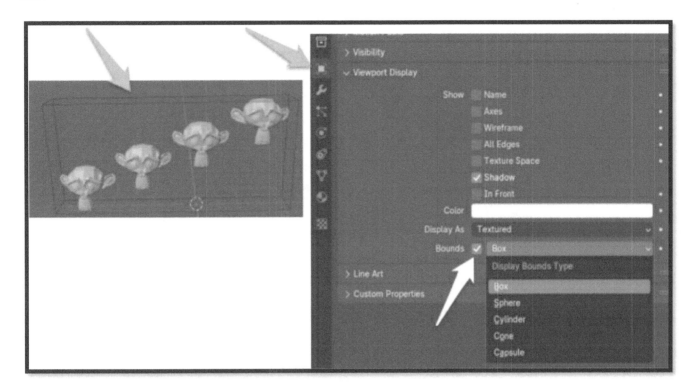

Next, we shall discuss the distinction between **relative** and **constant** offset. **Constant offset** of **(1)** one **Blender unit** means shifting the center of the object by one unit regardless of its size. This results in the Monkey's center being offset by **one Blender unit**, causing overlap in the display. On the other hand, relative offset considers the overall size of the object.

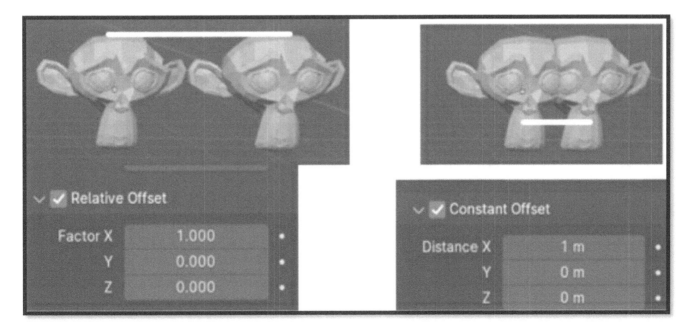

OBJECT OFFSET:

1) When using **Object** Offset, the displacement of one object influences another. To use **Object Offset**, position the **Control** Object (a **UV Sphere**) in the 30 Viewport Editor.

After adding the modifier, you can translate, rotate, and scale it as desired. By default, **Relative Offset** is enabled in the **Properties** Editor under Modifier **Properties.**

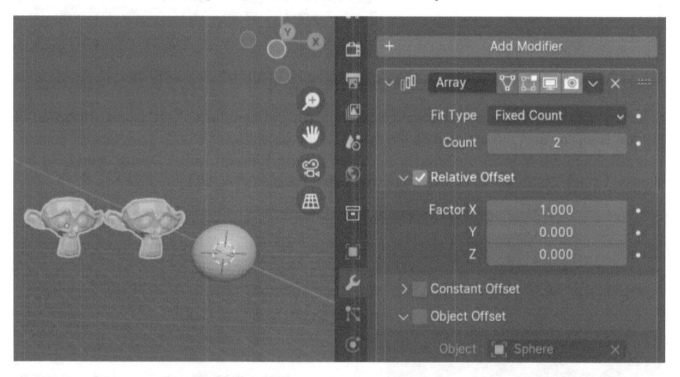

2) To switch to **Constant** Offset, tick the corresponding option and check **Object** Offset.

Then, click on the bar below **Object** Offset and select your **Offset Object** (the Sphere) from the displayed menu, as shown below.

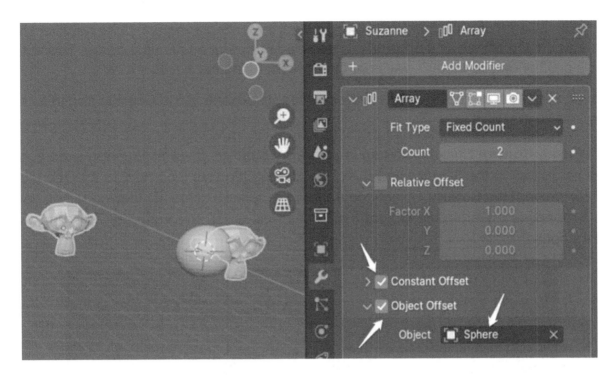

3) As shown below **Suzanne** (the **Monkey)** is shown with an **Array** Modifier applied, where both **Constant** Offset and **Object** Offset are enabled. The Viewport displays the Front Orthographic View. Additionally, a **UV Sphere** is introduced into the scene, strate-gically placed **(2)** meters along the **X**-axis and two meters along the **Z**-axis, as shown below. This Sphere is then scaled down to 0.500 of its original size.

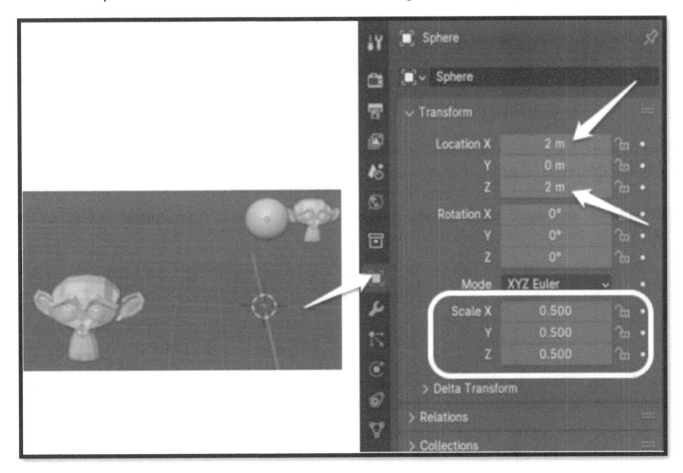

4) With a Count of **2** specified in the **Array** Modifier for **Suzanne** and **Object** Offset chosen, with the Object set as the **Sphere**, a duplicate is produced at half the size. This duplicate is positioned one meter away from the Sphere, along the positive X-axis.

The position of the control **Object** for **Objec**t Offset is defined in the **Object** Properties for the Sphere, as illustrated above.

Note: When a **Control** Object is utilized in the **Array** Modifier, it will still render, even if you opt to hide its display in the 3D Viewport Editor by clicking the **Eye** Icon next to it in the **Outliner** Editor. To prevent the **Control** Object from rendering, select it in the 3D Viewport, then navigate to the **Properties** Editor, in the **Object** Properties, and within the **Visibility** Tab, uncheck the **Renders** option.

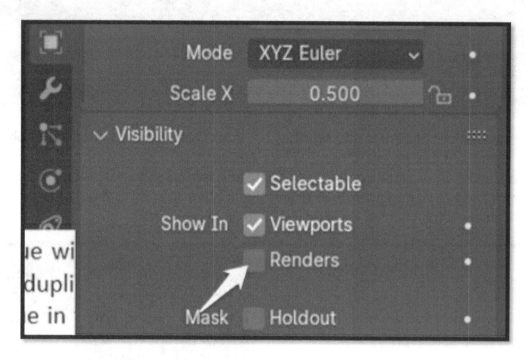

Increasing the **Count** Value within the **Array** Modifier panel results in duplicating objects. When **Object Offset** is used, the duplicated object adjusts its position and scale accordingly. Furthermore, **increasing** the **Count Value** in the **Modifier** replicates the original object, altering its position and scale exponentially. Any adjustments made to the **Control** Object will be reflected in these duplications, as shown here.

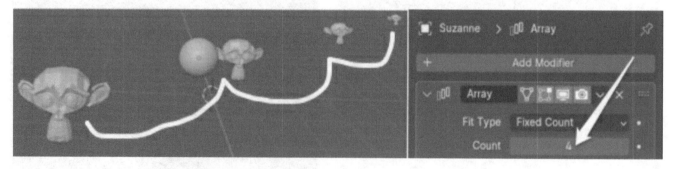

The **Array** displays the **Count Value** increased to 4, accompanied by the **UV Sphere Control** Object being both scaled and rotated.

USING THE BOOLEAN MODIFIER

The Boolean Modifier is utilized to generate shapes by either adding or subtracting one object from another. Within the Modifier panel, you'll find three options: **Difference, Intersection, and Union.**

To illustrate various operations,

1) start by placing a **UV Sphere** Object alongside the default **Cube**, as shown below. Adjust the size of the sphere to fit within the top face of the cube.

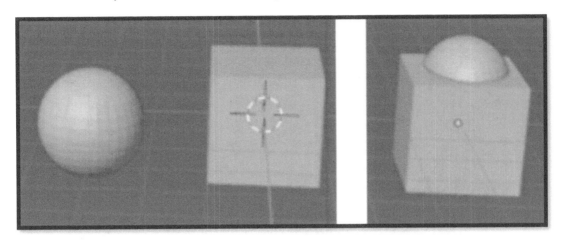

This setup of the cube and sphere will serve as the basis for demonstrating all three Boolean operations.

2) select the **Cube** and add the **Modifier** to the Cube. Choose the desired **Operation Type**, in this case, Boolean **Difference**. Specify the **Boolean Object**, which in this example is the **Sphere**. Finally, click on **Apply** to execute the operation

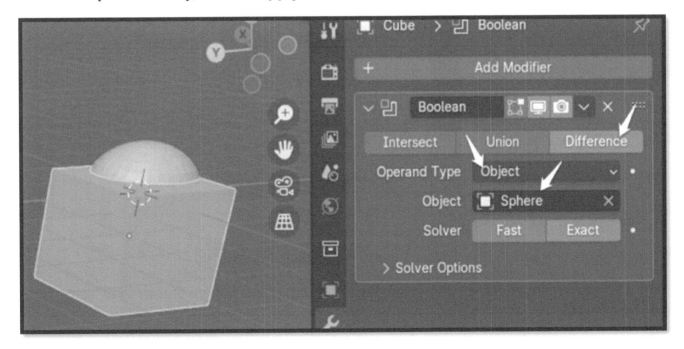

✓ For the **Boolean Difference** operation:

When you select the **Difference** operation, the part of the Boolean Object (the Sphere) that overlaps with the Cube will create a depression or dish-like feature on the surface of the Cube.

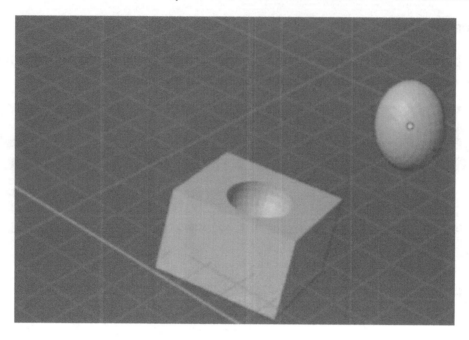

For **the Boolean Intersect** operation:

When you select the **Intersect** operation, the part of the Cube that intersects with the Boolean Object (the Sphere) is isolated and becomes a new object on its own.

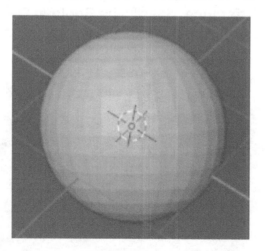

For the **Boolean Union** operation:

When you choose **Union**, the surfaces of the two objects are merged.

Hint: after performing the Union operation, the lower part of the Sphere that was inside the Cube no longer exists.

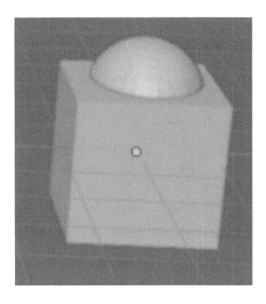

USING THE BUILD MODIFIER

The Build Modifier is used to simulate the gradual construction of an object over time. While this modifier can be applied to any object, achieving a smooth and impressive effect typically requires a high vertex count.

To prepare for applying the Build Modifier:

1) In the 3D View Editor, adjust the scale of the default **Cube** along the Y axis.

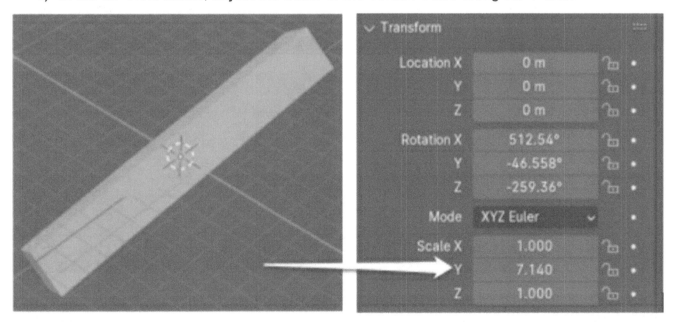

2) Switch to **Edit** mode by pressing **Tab**, right-click, and choose **subdivide** on the context menu to subdivide the surface by specifying the number of cuts (e.g., set Number of Cuts to **8**).

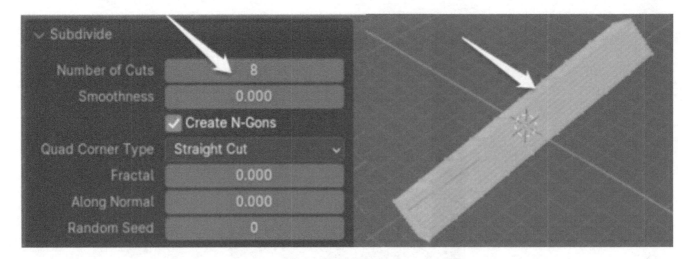

Switch back to **Object** mode, and then add a **Build Modifier** to the object as shown below. You'll notice that the object disappears from view. By adding a Build Modifier, you essentially create an animation indicating the gradual construction of the object over time.

To control this animation, navigate to the **Timeline** Editor located at the bottom of the screen. Here, you can click, hold, and drag the Timeline Cursor to the right. As you do so, sections of the object will be reconstructed in the 3D Viewport Editor.

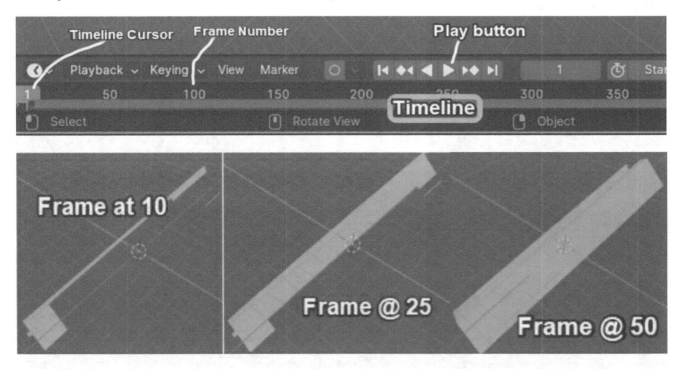

To start the animation playback, simply click the Play Button located in the Timeline Editor. This action will display the reconstruction process. Hint: the object is completely reconstructed by Frame 100, as a result of **Length** the setting adjustment in the **Properties** Editor, in the **Build** Modifier. For a more dynamic and dramatic reconstruction effect, consider enabling the Randomize option within the Modifier settings.

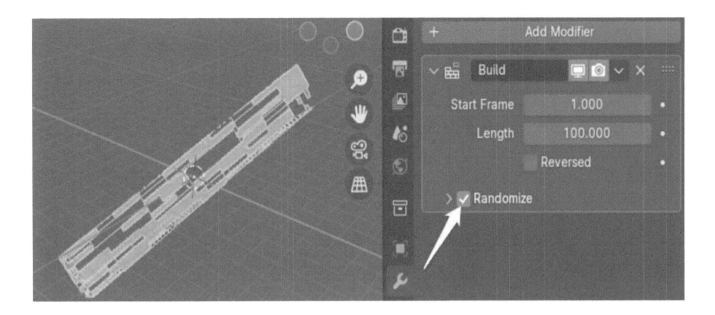

USING THE DECIMATE MODIFIER

The Decimate Modifier comes in handy when dealing with mesh objects that have been intricately modeled. Such objects often contain a multitude of vertices, resulting in a high vertex-face count. Blender relies on Vertex/ Face count to compute various shading effects, dis-tinct from the actual vertices and mesh faces used in constructing the model. Essentially, it's about triangulation within mesh faces. utilizing the Decimate Modifier offers an instant and straightforward method to decrease the vertex/face count. To illustrate how to use it,

1) begin with the default Blender scene. Delete the **cube** object and replace it with a **monkey.**
2) The **monkey,** with its complex shape composed of numerous faces and vertices, serves as an ideal example for demonstrating deci-mation. In **Object** mode, the **monkey's shape** signifies the **vertices** that you see in **Edit** mode.

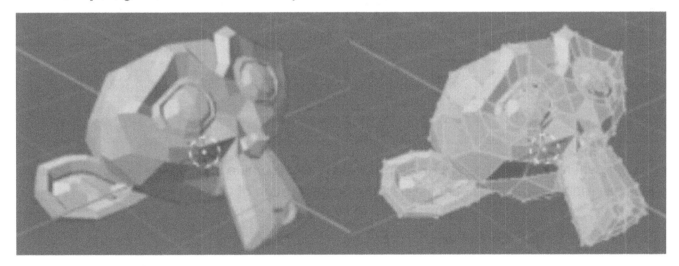

3) When you apply **a Decimate Modifier** and decrease the **Ratio** value to around **0.3** as shown below, you'll notice a significant change in the shape displayed in the 3D View Editor.

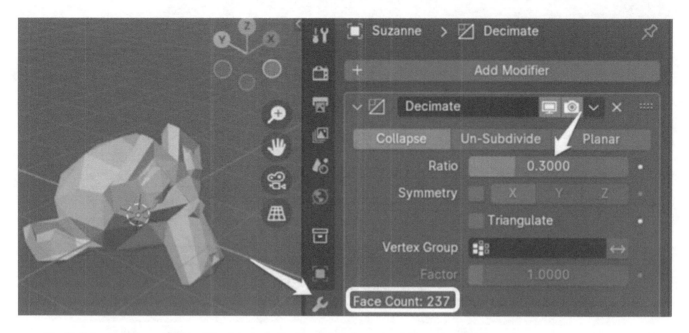

4) If you begin again with the **original monkey** object and subdivide it with a count of **10** in **Edit** mode, you'll generate numerous vertices as shown here.

5) With this increased vertex count, applying a **Decimate** Modifier and lowering the Ratio value to 0.3 doesn't noticeably alter the display in the 3D Viewport Editor or a rendered view.

However, when there are many vertices, reducing the Ratio value to 0.3 in the Decimate Modifier effectively reduces the face count, im-pacting the generation of shading effects.

USING THE EDGE SPLIT MODIFIER

Although it's called the Edge Split Modifier, it's not limited to splitting edges only; it allows you to divide an object by selecting vertices, edges, or faces.

Here's a demonstration:

1) In the default 3D Viewport Editor, select the **cube** object in **Object** Mode. Then, add and apply an **Edge Split** Modifier as shown below. Once applied, the Modifier panel in the Properties Editor will disappear.

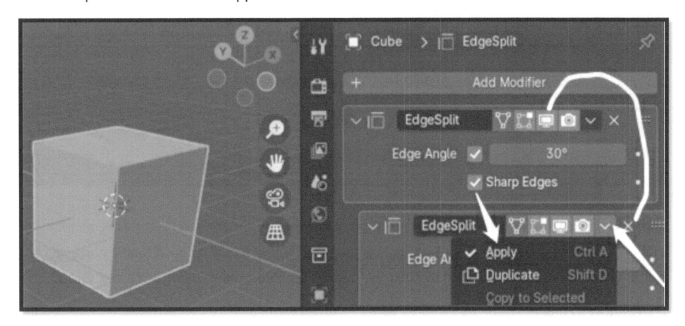

2) Switch to **Edit** Mode by pressing **Tab** after applying the modifier.

Take note of the selection options available in the Viewport Header. The **selection option** you choose determines how the **Edge Split** Mod-ifier will function. Once applied in **Object** Mode, the modifier remains operational in **Edit** Mode.

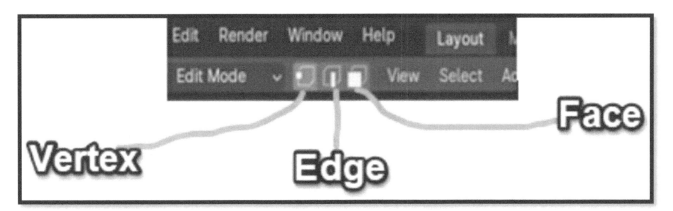

✓ **Edge Split (Vertex):**

When you select a vertex, you can lift or move a corner of the object.

✓ **Edge Split (Edge):**
✓ Choosing an edge will open a face, similar to how you'd open a lid on a box (you can also check:
✓ **Edge Split (Face):**

With the **Edge Split** Modifier, when a face is separated, it remains part of the object. To separate a face, select it and then use the Move Tool Widget to pull it away from the cube.

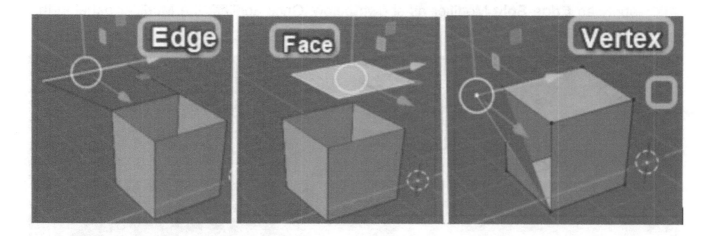

USING THE MASK MODIFIER

The Mask Modifier is a handy tool for controlling which parts of a mesh are visible in the 3DView Editor or during rendering. You can spec-ify the portion of the mesh using a **Vertex** Group.

Here's how to use it:

1) Add a **UV Sphere t**o the scene. Then, in **Edit** Mode, select the vertices you want to include in the mask as shown below.
   Once selected, create a **Vertex** Group. By default, the vertex group is named **"Group."**

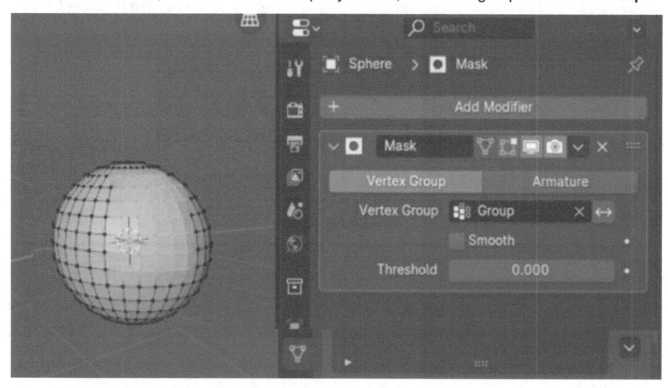

2) Switch to **Object** Mode to view only the portion of the sphere that is defined by the Vertex Group, as shown below.

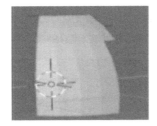

You don't have to apply the modifier unless you want this change to be permanent.

3) To reverse the display and show the entire sphere except for the section defined by the Vertex Group, simply click the double-headed arrow in the Modifier panel, as shown below.

With this modifier, you can control visibility without needing to remove any vertices from the UV sphere.

USING MIRROR MODIFIER

The Mirror Modifier is a powerful tool that enables you to create or modify a mesh on one side of a center point and have it automatically mirrored on the opposite side.

Here's how to use it:

1) Start by adding a **UV Sph**ere to the scene while in **Top Orthographic** View (Num Pad **5**). Switch to **Edit** Mode and ensure that **no vertices** are selected.

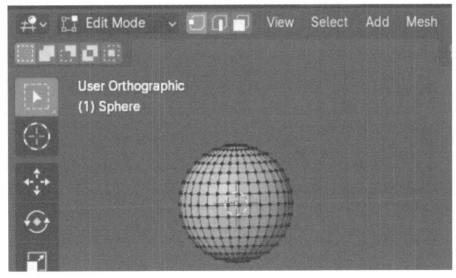

2) With **X-Ray** mode toggled on as shown below, use the **Box Select** tool (activated with the **B** key) to drag a rectangle and select one- half of the sphere's vertices.

Remember to enable **X-Ray** mode in the 3D Viewport Editor Header before dragging the rectangle. Then, press the **X** key and select **ver-tices** on the menu to delete the selected **vertices**, as illustrated below.

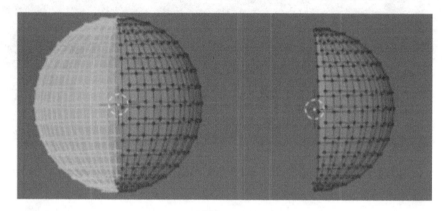

3) Next, in **Object** Mode (with the half sphere selected), navigate to the **Properties** Editor and click on the **Modifier** buttons to add a **Mirror** Modifier as shown here.

The half of the UV Sphere that was deleted will reappear in the 3DView Editor as illustrated below.

It's worth noting that by default, the Mirror Modifier panel has the **X** axis selected, meaning the mirroring occurs along the X axis.

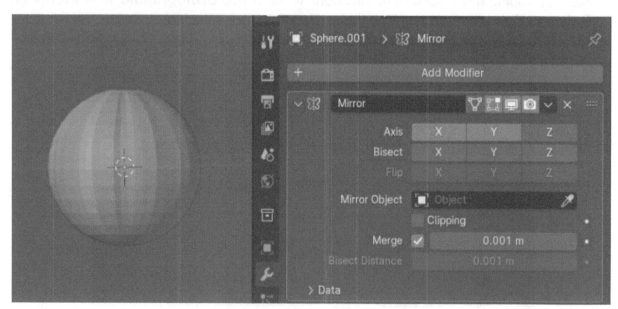

4) Addition ally, in **Edit** Mode, you'll notice that vertices are present only on one side of the sphere. If you select and translate a single vertex, you'll observe that the mesh on the opposite side is mirrored, effectively duplicating

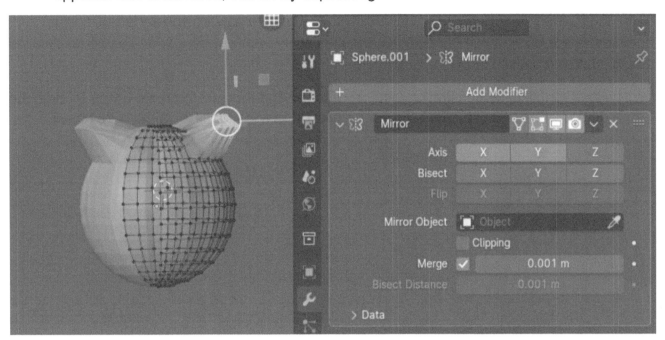

5) Once you apply the modifier (by clicking" **Apply**" in the Modifier Panel), vertices are generated on the mirrored side.

At the center of the Mirror Modifier panel, you'll find the **Mirror Object** option. By adding an object to the scene and typing its name into the **Mirror Object** field, the mirror operation will occur around the centerline of the new object rather than the original object's centerline as shown here.

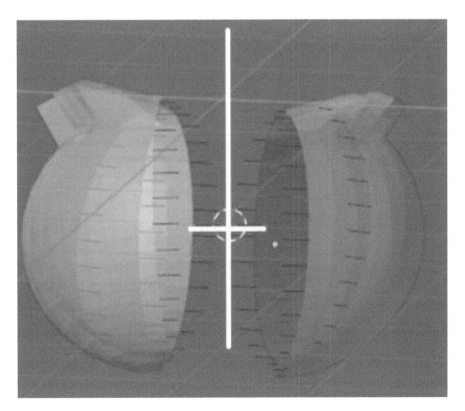

USING THE MULTIRESOLUTIONAND MESH MODIFIER

The Multiresolution Modifier is specifically intended for use with the Sculpt Tool.

As for the Remesh Modifier, it offers the ability to reconfigure how a mesh surface is constructed. In cases where basic mesh shapes lack the necessary vertices, edges, and faces for detailed modeling, this modifier comes in handy.

1) For a practical demonstration, you can use a cylinder object to create a hole through the default **cube** object by applying a **Boolean Difference** Modifier to the cube object.

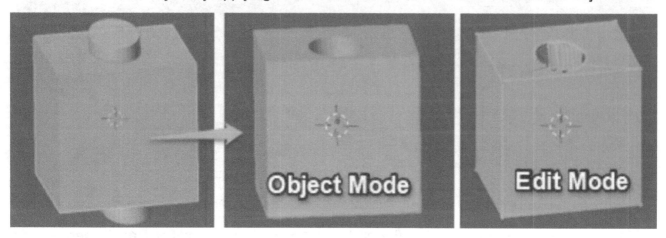

After applying the **Boolean Modifier**, you'll notice that the mesh construction becomes minimal, restricting detailed modeling. To en-hance the vertex count and allow for more intricate modeling, you can apply a Remesh Modifier.

2) Remember to switch the mode to **Object** Mode before applying a modifier. With the **cube** selected in **Object** Mode, add a **Remesh** Modifier. In Object Mode, you'll observe a deformation at the rim of the hole.

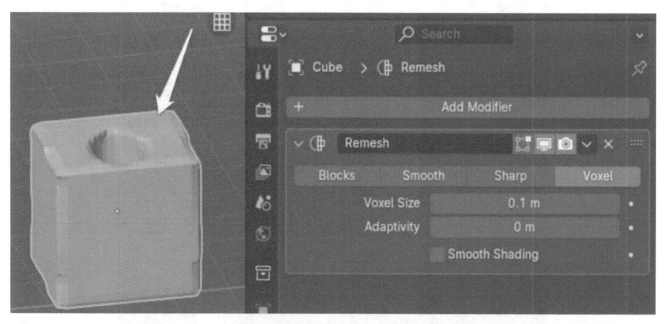

Hint: the default Remesh Mode is **Voxel**. Change this by selecting **"Sharp"** mode. Addition ally, in the **Modifier** Panel, the default Octree Depth value is **4**, and the Scale is set to **0.900**.

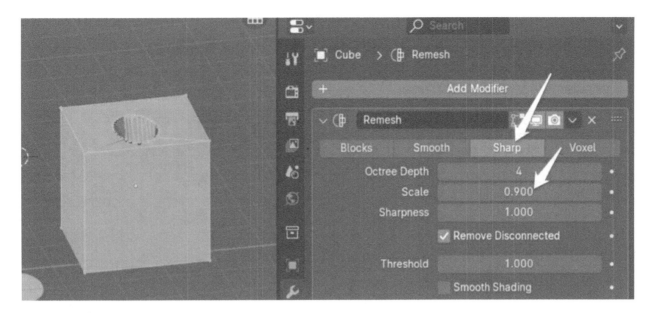

With the default settings, after applying the modifier (by clicking the **Apply** button), you'll notice a substantial increase in the number of vertices, edges, and faces on the mesh surface of the cube in Edit Mode as shown here.

3) After applying the **Remesh** Modifier, the Modifier Panel disappears. To tweak the Octree and Scale values, you can press the **Ctrl + Z** keys to undo and step back through the operations until the panel reappears.
4) Increasing the Octree Depth not ably increases the number of vertices on the mesh. Even a small increase, like going from 4 to 5, has a significant impact.

However, it's crucial to exercise caution: rising to values like **6, 7, or 8** will exponentially inflate the vertex count and can severely impact computer performance.

USING THE SCREW MODIFIER

The Screw Modifier creates a spiral shape by revolving either a profile or an object around an axis, which is defined by another object known as the Axis Object. To illustrate this, let's create a spiral using a Plane Object revolving around an Axis defined by a Cylinder.

1) By default, the **Plane** is added to the scene in the horizontal plane. Rotate it (press **R**, then **X**, then **90**) to stand it on edge, and then move it back along the **X**-axis of the scene.
2) Next, add a **Cylinder** Object to the scene, scale it down, and then scale it up along the vertical **Z**-Axis as shown below.

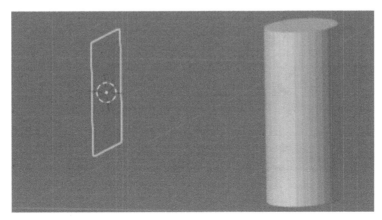

3) With the **Plane** selected, add a **Screw** Modifier in the **Properties** Edi to r under the **Modifier** buttons. Once the **Screw** Modifier is added, the Plane will appear as a flat circular shape in the **XZ** Plane

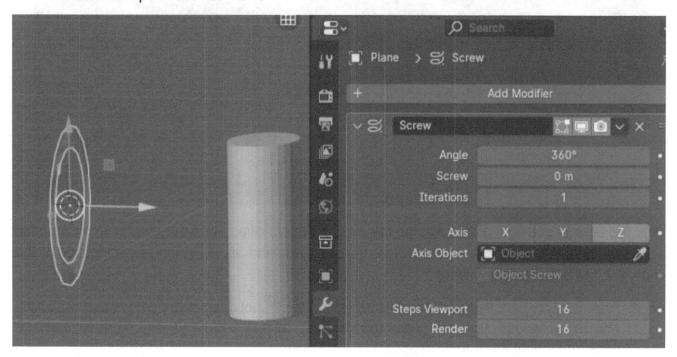

If no Axis Object is specified in the **Modifier** panel, the Plane is duplicated and rotated **360°** around its own Y-Axis. The angle of rotation is determined by the Angle value in the Modifier panel, while the number of duplications is controlled by the Steps Viewport value within the Modifier panel (note: there are separate **Steps** values for the Viewport and Render, with default values set to 16).

4) While this effect may have its uses, it's not the intended behavior of the Screw Modifier. To achieve the intended effect, you need to specify an **Axis** Object in the Modifier panel, such as a **Cylinder.**

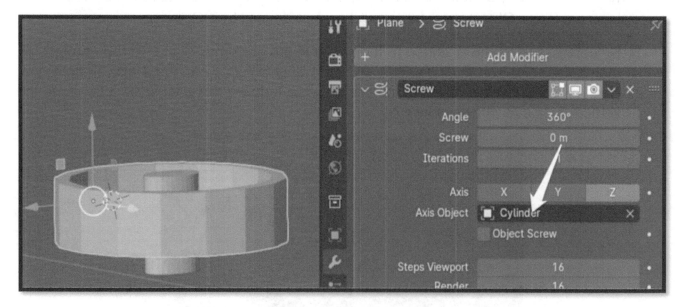

5) Switch to **Edit** Mode in the 3D Viewport Editor. In Edit Mode, you'll observe that the vertices of the **Plane** are duplicated in a circular arrangement around the vertical axis of the **Cylinder Object** as shown below.

The radius of this circle is determined by the Angle value set to 360 ° in the Modifier panel.

By increasing the **Screw** value, the final duplication is displaced vertically, resulting in a screw-like effect as shown here.

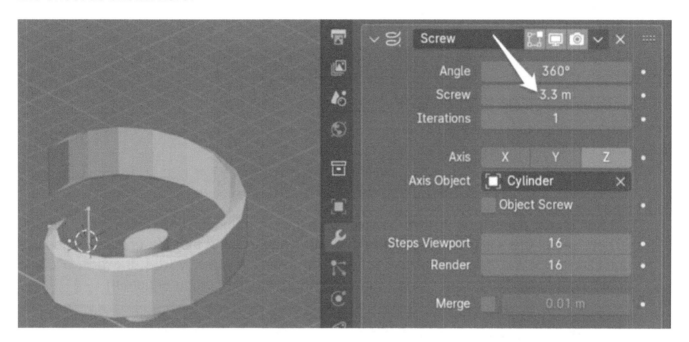

To add more coils to the spiral, increase the **Iterations** value in the **Modifier** panel.

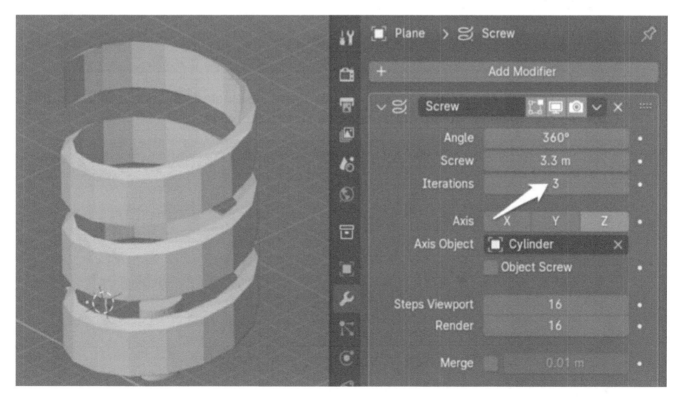

THE SKIN MODIFIER

The Skin Modifier empowers you to craft a three-dimensional form from a simple stick arrangement, requiring only a minimal number of vertices.

To illustrate this process,

1) let's start with a **Plane** Object in the 3D Viewport Editor. The Plane, a straightforward object, consists of **four vertices, four edges, and one face.** Rotate the **Plane** around the Z-Axis. This action merely shifts the edges of the Plane away from the background grid lines, enhancing visibility while in Edit Mode.

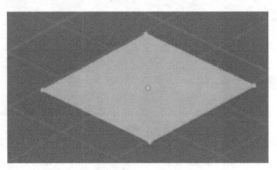

2) In Edit **Mode**, delete **one vertex** to leave two edges, forming the basic stick arrangement. Then, select one **vertex** and **extrude** it t**wice**. Keep in mind that the original edges are positioned on the X-Y axis of the scene. The two new eges will be drawn in a plane passing through the center of the scene and normal to the computer screen.

3) Switch to **Object** Mode, ensure that the **stick figure** is selected, and add a **Skin Modifier.** Click **"Apply"** to generate the solid shape as illustrated below.

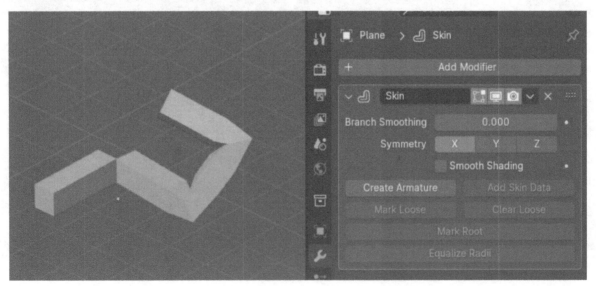

The **Skin** Modifier process involves extruding vertices from a basic object to shape a simple stick figure in Edit Mode. Once the stick figure is formed, the Skin Modifier is applied to it in **Object** Mode. This modifier envelops the stick with a cage-like structure, which transforms into a mesh object when the modifier is applied.

It's important to distinguish between adding and applying the modifier. You add the **modifier** in the Properties Editor's **Modifier Prop-erties** by clicking the **"Add Modifier"** button and selecting it from the menu. The Modifier panel appears, allowing you to adjust values affecting the selected object in the 3D Viewport Editor. Once adjustments are complete, you apply the modifier by clicking the **"Apply"** but - ton in the Modifier panel menu.

THE SOLIDIFY MODIFIER

The Solidify Modifier offers a valuable tool for transforming thin-walled objects into solid objects. To display this:

1) start by selecting a simple **Plane** Object in the 3D Viewport Editor. Then, add a **Solidify Modifier** via the **Properties** Editor.

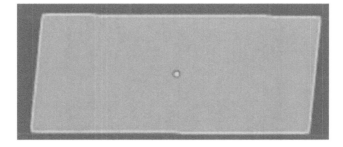

2) When you look closer to the plan e as shown in the screenshot below, you'll notice that it now possesses a thickness. In the Modifier panel, you'll find the **Thickness** setting set to **0.15m** and the **Offset** set to **-1.0000.**

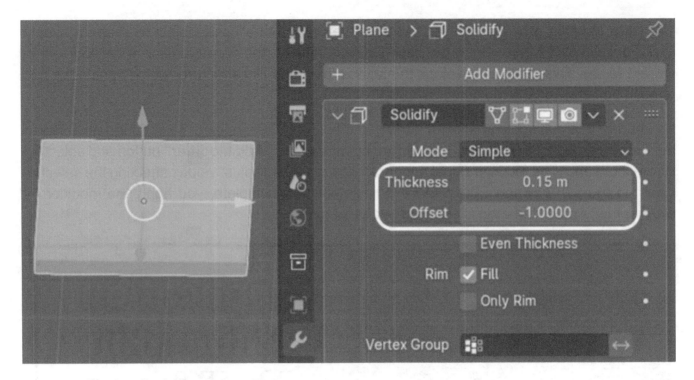

The **Thickness** setting determines the surface thickness. Increasing this value, for example, to 10 cm provides a clearer view.

3) The **Offset** setting ranges from **-1.0000** to+ **1.000**, this enables you to position the thickness below or above the mid-plane. An Off- set value of 0.0000 places the thickness precisely at the mid-plane.

Switching to **Edit** mode, you'll observe that the original vertices of the plane object remain positioned on the mid-plane of the scene if you enter **0.0000** as the **Offset** value.

4) To demonstrate the application of the **Solidify** Modifier, start by creating a new scene with a **Cylinder** object instead of the default **Cube**. Next, delete the **upper face** of the **Cylinder**. This action leaves you with a thin-walled container.

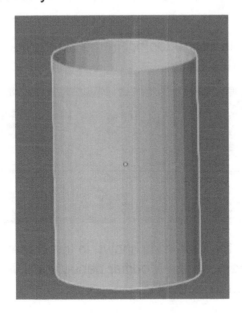

5) Switch to **Object** mode and add a **Solidify** Modifier to the **Cylinder** object. Adjust the **thickness** value to 0.1m. This modification results in the container having a wall thickness.

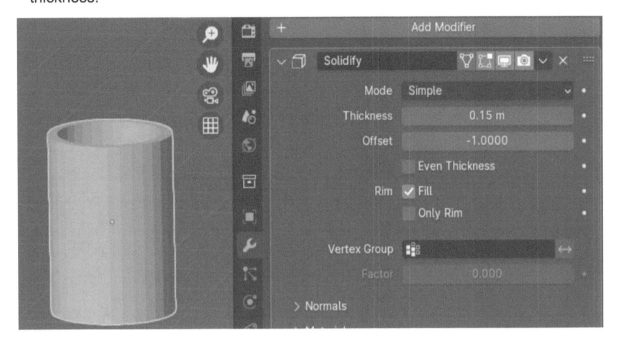

Hint: in **Blender,** dimensions are proportional. For instance, when considering a default **Cylinder** with dimensions of **2m** in diameter by **2m** high, a wall thickness of 0**,01 m** (equivalent to 1.0cm) results in a thin wall thickness. You can view these dimensions by pressing the N key.

When using an **Offset** value of **-1.0000,** the wall thickness is created inside the original surface of the Cylinder. Conversely, an Offset value of **+1.0000** generates the thickness outside the original surface.

1) In **Edit** Mode, the original **vertices, edges**, and **faces** remain unchanged until you click **"Apply"** in the **Modifier** Panel with the **Cylinder** selected in the 3D View Editor in **Object** Mode.

THE SUBDIVISION SURFACE MODIFIER

The Subdivision Surface Modifier enhances the surface of an object by subdividing it, which results in the addition of vertices, edges, and faces. This process gives the object's surface a smoother and more rounded appearance, while also allowing for more detailed modeling. To experiment with this effect, you can use the container created in the previous exercise without the modifier.

1) first, add a **Subdivision Surface** Modifier to the object without applying it, then add the **Solidify** Modifier

Once added, the **Subdivision Surface** Modifier is placed in the Modifier Stack within the **Properties** Editor, positioned above the Solidify Modifier. Do not forget that the Modifier at the top of the stack takes precedence over those below it. So, in this case, the Subdivision Modi-fier has precedence over the Solidify Modifier.

In the **Subdivision Surface Modifier** panel, you can adjust the Subdivisions-Levels values. These values determine the level of subdivision applied to the object.

Hint: the rendered figures are views produced by rendering (Press **F12**).

At this stage, neither the **Solidify** Modifier nor the **Subdivision Surface** Modifier have been applied. The **Apply** button for both modifiers has not been activated. While the modifiers display their effects in the 3D Viewport Editor, switching the **Cylinder** Object to **Edit** Mode re-veals that the original vertices, edges, and faces remain.

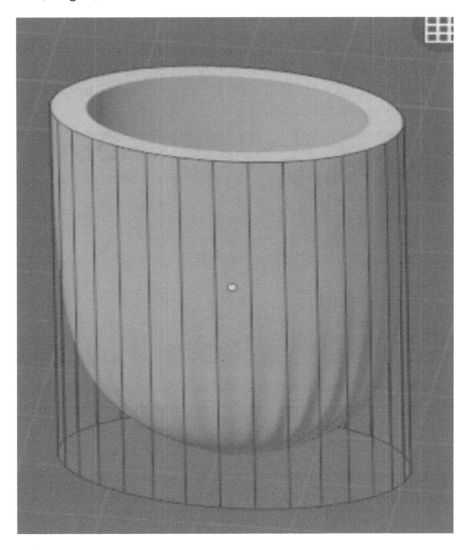

USING THE TRIANGULATION AND WELD MODIFIER

The Triangulation Modifier comes into play when a mesh model has been split and vertices have been added to enhance fine details. This modifier confirms that the triangulation remains consistent, especially during export or rendering processes. If the model is animated using armatures, it's recommended to place the Triangulation Modifier above the armature modifier in the modifier stack.

Additionally, the Triangulation Modifier is used during baking before exporting and importing. Baking involves pre-calculating and stor-ing data to speed up the conversion process from viewport data to image or video files, which is known as rendering.

On the other hand, the Weld Modifier serves to merge vertices in a non-destructive manner. In complex modeling scenarios, vertices may sporadically be duplicated, resulting in two vertices occupying the same 3D space. It's crucial to keep the number of vertices to a mini- mum, particularly in animations, to ensure the correct visual appearance.

Let's create a shape from a Plane Primitive using Modifiers:

1) In the default 3D Viewport Editor, delete the **Cube** Object and add a **Plane.**
2) Scale the **Plane thrice** along the **X**-axis and add a **Bevel** Modifier.
3) It's crucial to press **Ctrl + A** while in **Object** Mode and select **Apply> Scale** to ensure that the object's scale is applied correctly.

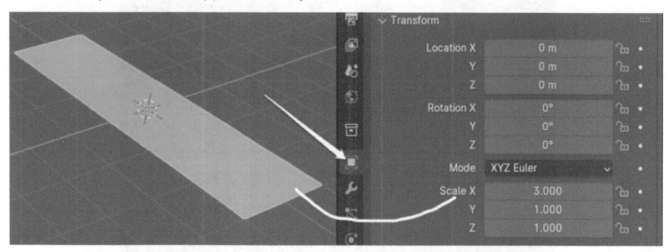

4) In the **Properties** Editor, navigate to the **Bevel** Modifier settings. Enable the **"Vertices"** option and adjust the **"Segments "** to 5. Then, modify the **"Amount"** value to 1 m to achieve a fully rounded end on the Plane. Hint: in **Edit** Mode, the original geometry re- mains intact.

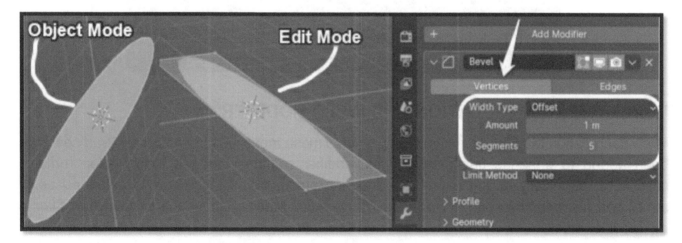

5) Next, add a **Solidify Modifier**. In the **Properties** Editor, under the **Solidify** Modifier, increase the **"Thickness"** value to 1.8

In **Edit** Mode, you can observe the results of the **"Offset"** value and "Segments "set in the Bevel Modifier.

6) In **Object** Mode, right- click and choose **"Shade Smooth."** Go to the **Object Data** in the **Properties** Editor and enable **Auto Smooth** in the Normal tab.

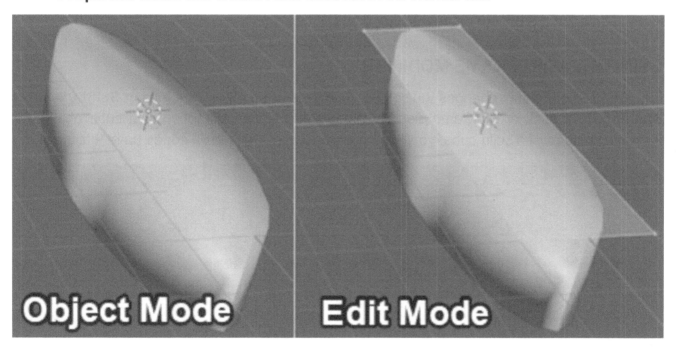

7) This option smooths out the appearance of the selected object. When in Object Mode or Edit Mode, you'll notice that the shape ap-pears with rounded, smooth ends. In **Edit** Mode, you can st ill see the original geometry with four vertices intact.

Despite the smooth ends, there may be a visible shadow line due to a seam. Keep in mind that the shape is created using the **Bevel** Modifier. Currently, the modifier hasn't been applied, as evident in **Edit** Mode. However, if the modifier were to be applied, there would be a duplica-tion of vertices where the seam is shown.

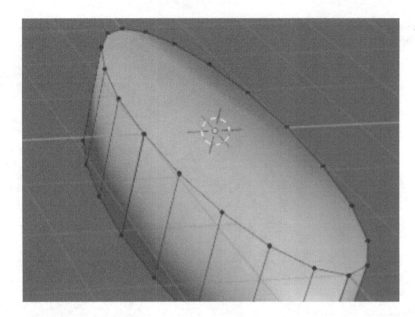

8) Select **one** vertex and move it aside. Because the modifier hasn't been applied, you can't merge vertices manually to remove duplicates.

Hint: in complex models, it's recommended to avoid applying modifiers to reduce the number of vertices.

9) To tidy up the seam, add the **Weld** Modifier. Remember, each modifier added will be placed at the bottom of the modifier stack.

USINGTHE WIREFRAME MODIFIER

The Wireframe Modifier changes the solid appearance of an object, such as in **Solid Viewport Shading,** to a stick or wireframe display. When the modifier is applied to a cube object, for instance, instead of a solid cube, you'll see a frame where the cube's edges have thickness.

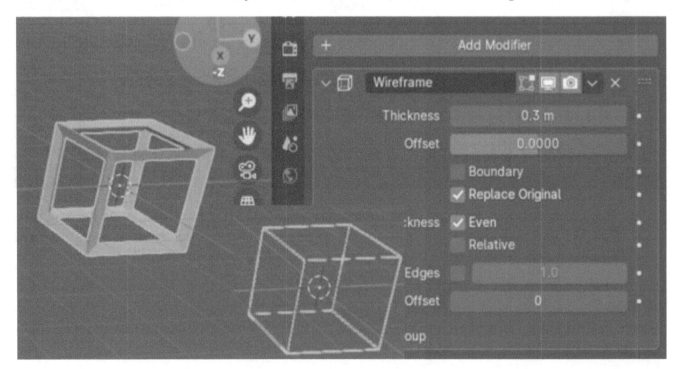

CHAPTER 7: UTILIZING DEFORM MODIFIERS

The Deform group of Modifiers lets you alter the shape of an object without introducing new geometry. These modifiers apply to meshes,

curves, texts, surfaces, or lattices. Specifically, the Mesh Deform modifier enables you to use any closed-shaped mesh to serve as a deforma-tion cage around another mesh object.

The Deform group of Modifiers offers tools for modifying or shaping a mesh Object in its entirety. Some of these modifiers require an un-derstanding of other Blender features, so they will be explained as we come across those features

ARMATURE MODIFIER

In Blender, armatures are objects utilized to manipulate and pose other objects, such as character models. Posing involves animating fig-ures. The Armature Modifier will be covered in detail alongside armatures and character rigging in Chapter **11**

CAST MODIFIER

The Cast Modifier is used to deform a basic object, like the default Cube Object in the scene. To use it,

1) Select the **Cube** Object, enter **Edit** Mode, and subdivide it (with the number of cuts set to 4).
2) Then return to **Object** Mode. In the **Properties** Editor, navigate to **Modifier** Properties and add a Cast Modifier.

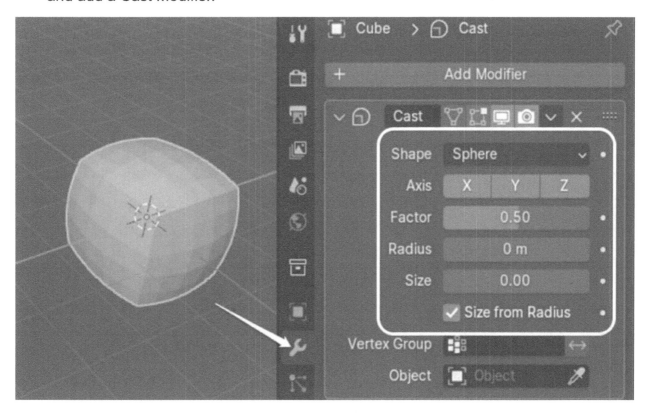

3) By adjusting parameters such as **Cast Type, Factor, Radius, and Size**, and limiting effects to specific axes, you can control the de- formation of the cube.

CORRECTIVE SMOOTH MODIFIER

The Corrective Smooth Modifier is primarily intended to smooth out any incorrect mesh deformations that may occur when Armatures are used to manipulate a mesh.

CURVE MODIFIER

The Curve Modifier utilizes the form of a curve to alter the shape of a mesh.

1) The illustration shown below is the default Blender cube that has been scaled down. Then scaled along the Y axis and subdivided in **Edit** Mode with the number of cuts set to 10.

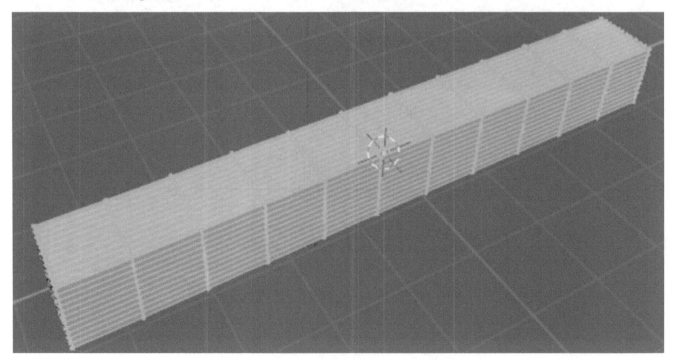

2) Next, in **Object** Mode, the extended Cube is deselected, and a **Bezier Curve** is added. The Curve is then rotated and scaled up to align with the length of the Cube.

3) After deselecting the **Curve** and selecting the **Cube**, remain in **Object** Mode and add a **Curve** Modifier. Specify **"BezierCurve"** as the name in the Object panel.
4) In Edit Mode, manipulate the Curve by altering its shape and position to influence the shape of the Cube.

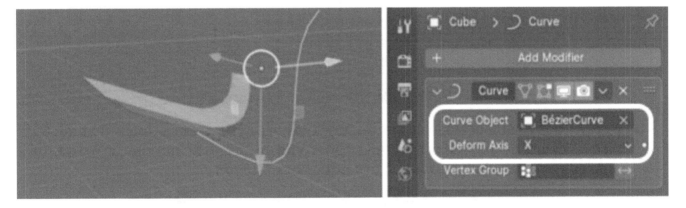

Note: In the **Curve** Modifier panel, the Deformation **Axis** is set to the **X-Axis**.

DISPLACE MODIFIER

The Displace Modifier is used to manipulate the vertices of a Mesh Object. When vertices are assigned to a **Vertex** Group and that group is specified in the Modifier, only the vertices belonging to the group will be affected. Additionally, adding a texture allows displacement based on the dark and light values within the texture.

1) To get started, begin with the default Blender Scene and replace the **Cube** with a **Plane**. With the Plane selected, enter **Edit** Mode and subdivide it sixteen (**16**) times.

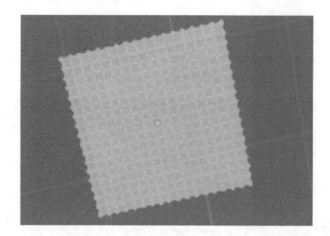

2) Next, select a group of **vertices** and create a **Vertex Group** in the **Properties** Editor under the **Object Data** buttons.

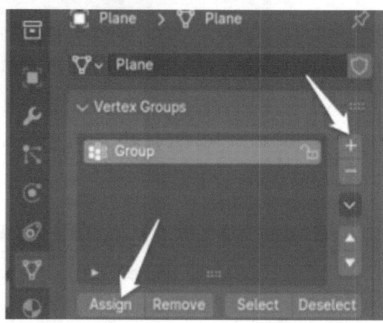

3) Switch back to **Object** Mode. In the **Texture Type** section, include a **Noise Texture.** Click on the Texture button, select **New,** and in the **Type** dropdown menu, choose **Noise**. Take note of the Texture Name, which in this example is **"Texture"**

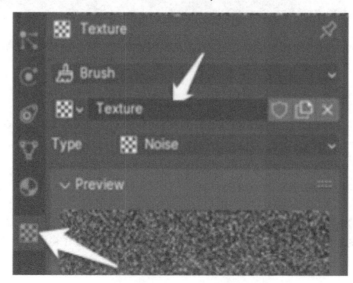

4) In the **Properties** Editor, with the **Plane** selected, navigate to the **Modifier** buttons and add a **Displace** Modifier. Within the **Displace** Modifier panel, specify the **Texture** and the **Vertex Group** to dis place the vertices.

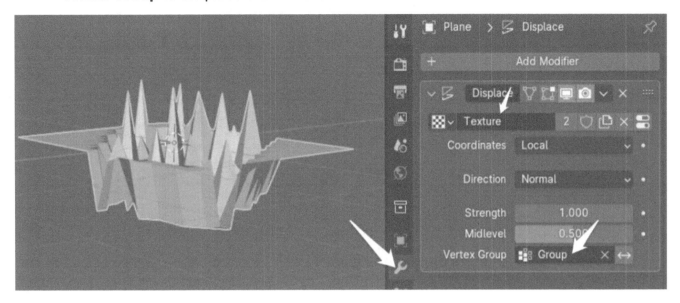

HOOK MODIFIER

The Hook Modifier enables you to manipulate or animate specific vertices of a mesh while in Object mode. These vertices are linked (hooked) to an Empty Object, which, when moved in Object Mode, pulls the selected vertices along with it. This technique can be applied for static mesh deformation or animated movement.

1) To get started, begin with the default scene with the **Cube** Object selected. Switch to **Edit** mode and choose a **single vertex(corner)**.
Press **Ctrl +H** and select **"Hook to New Object"**. This adds an **Empty** Object to the scene.

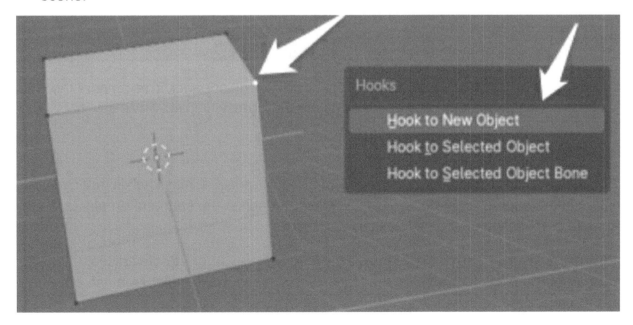

2) In the **Properties** Editor under **Modifiers** Properties, you'll notice a **Hook Modifier** named **"Hook-Empty"** has already been added.

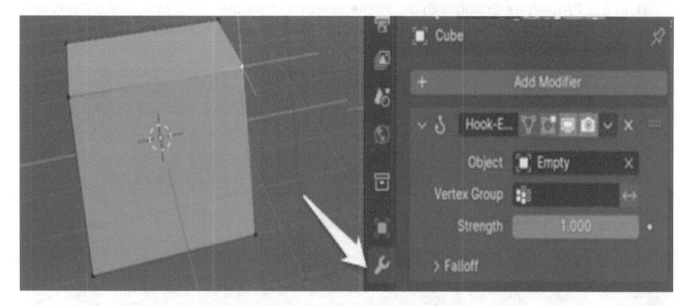

3) Choose and relocate the **Empty** in **Object** Mode to shift the vertex. While in Edit Mode, you'll observe the Empty in its new position, but the selected **vertex** will stay in its original placement.

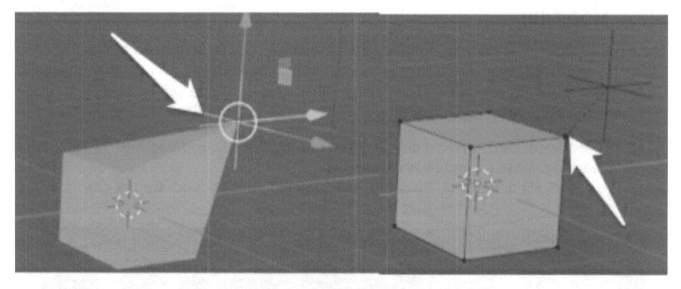

4) Return to **Object** Mode and click **"Apply"** in the Modifier panel. This renders the Cube 's deformation permanent. You can now delete the **Empty** Object.

LAPLACIAN DEFORM MODIFIER

The Laplacian Deform Modifier provides a method to pose a mesh while maintaining the geometric information of its surface. This allows you to adjust the shape of an object in **Object** Mode while preserving the original mesh in **Edit** Mode.

This technique involves assigning a **Hook-Empty** to a vertex or group of vertices, to effectively anchor part of the mesh in place. As the Hook-Empty is moved, it pulls the mesh out of shape against the anchored vertices.

follow these steps carefully to demonstrate the Laplacian Deform feature:

1) Begin with a **Plane** Object, enter **Edit** Mode, and subdivide the mesh of the **Plane** ten times to achieve the desired level of detail.

2) While in **Edit** Mode, select the **single comer vertex**. Press **Ctrl + H** and choose "**Hook to New Object**" from the menu that appears. This attaches a **Hook** in the form of an Empty Object to the selected vertex.

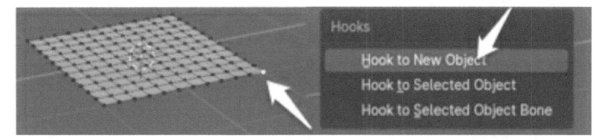

3) Switch to **Object** Mode, you will observe that a **Hook-Empty** Modifier has been automatically added in the **Properties** Editor under **Modifier** Properties.

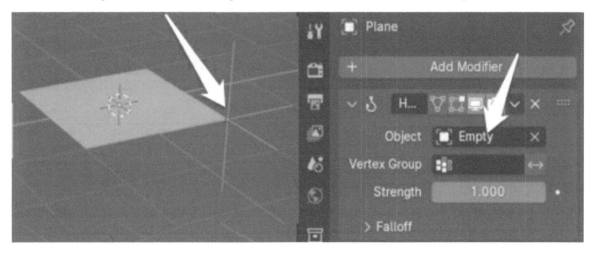

4) In the 3D Viewport Editor, with the **Plane** still in Edit Mode and the single vertex and Hook-Empty also selected, select the **vertices** forming the **two edges** of the **Plane** opposite the single vertex with the Hook-Empty.

5) With the **edge vertices** selected, remain in **Edit** Mode and navigate to the **Properties** Editor. Go to **Object Data** Properties and create a Vertex Group. Assign the selected vertices to this newly created group.

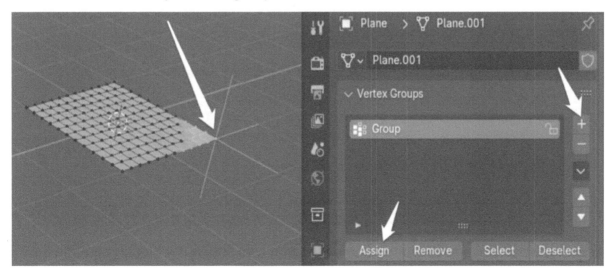

Note: Ensure that the single vertex with the Hook-Empty attached and the edge vertices are all selected when assigning vertices to the **Vertex** Group. By default, the Vertex Group is named **"Group."**

6) Switch back to **Object** Mode, and choose the **Plane** to complete the procedure. In the **Properties** Editor, navigate to **Modifier** Proper- ties and add a **Laplacian Deform** Modifier. Within the **Anchor Weights** p an el, specify **"Group"**(the Vertex Group created earlier), and click **"Bind"**(which will change to "Unbind").

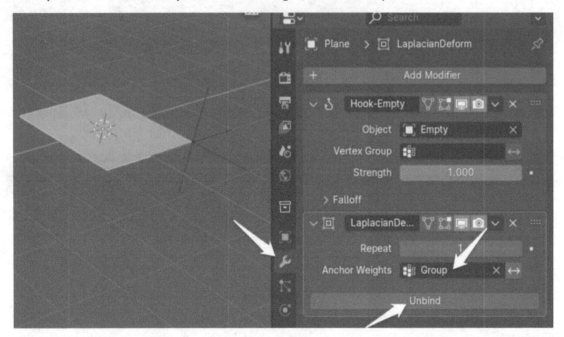

7) Next, by selecting the **Hook-Empty** and pressing the **G** key while dragging the mouse, you can move the corner of the Plane, while the two opposite edges remain in place.

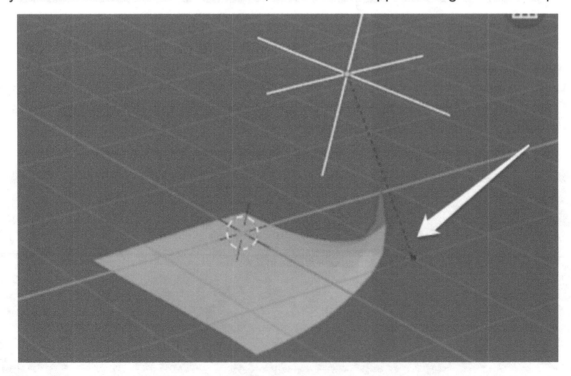

This technique could be used to unveil something that was previously hidden beneath the Plane. Additionally, you can animate the Hook- Empty to achieve dynamic effects.

LATTICE MODIFIER

The Lattice Modifier serves two main purposes: deforming a mesh object and controlling the movement of particles (as discussed in Chap-ter 13). This modifier simplifies the process of shaping a mesh object, particularly when dealing with objects with numerous vertices.

When deforming a mesh object using the **Lattice** Modifier, two components are involved in the scene: the object to be deformed and a lattice. The lattice is a special non-render able object, essentially a non-render able grid of vertices. You can use the same lattice to deform multiple mesh objects by assigning each object a modifier that points to the lattice.

The basic practice involves surrounding the mesh object or objects with a lattice, followed by adding a Lattice Modifier to each object and directing it to the lattice. Please Note that the lattice doesn't necessarily have to fully enclose an object.

To illustrate this, let's deform a UV Sphere object using a Lattice Modifier.

 The object to be deformed should have a reasonable number of vertices for the modifier to work effectively.

1) In the default scene, start by deleting the **Cube** object and adding a **UV Sphere**. Remember that when objects are added to a scene, they appear at the position of the 3D Cursor, which is typically located at the center of the scene. Move the **UV Sphere** to one side, although this movement is purely for demonstration purposes.
2) Add a **lattice** to the scene, as shown below. Upon adding the lattice, it will be positioned at the center of the scene, matching the location of the 3D Cursor.

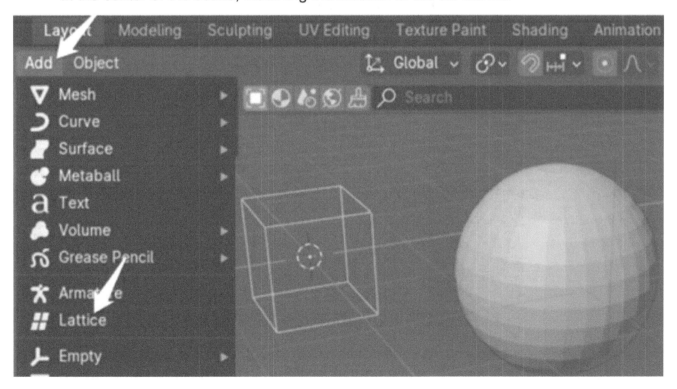

3) In the **Properties** Editor, you'll find a button labeled **"Lattice Object Properties"**. It's worth noting that both the UV Sphere and the lattice are initially entered with a default scale of 1.000, though the lattice appears at half the size of the sphere.

4) For this example, the **lattice** will encapsulate the object being deformed. Therefore, scale up the **lattice** and position it around the **UV Sphere**.

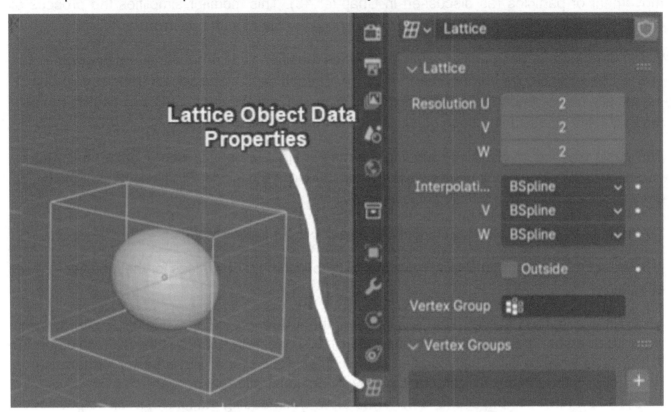

5) Switch to **Edit** Mode. If desired, you can subdivide the lattice by adjusting the Resolution **U, V**, and **W** values in the **Lattice Object Data** Properties panel. The number of subdivisions depends on the level of detailed control needed for the deformation. For example, change the Resolution values to **U, V,** and **W = 3.**

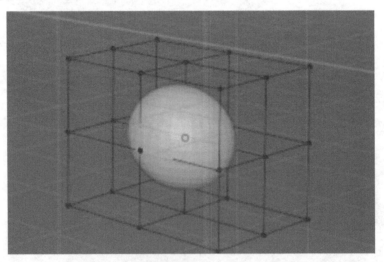

6) when you're satisfied with the subdivision, return to **Object** Mode. S elect the **UV Sphere**, and in the Properties Editor, add a **Lattice Modifier**. In the **Object** panel of the **Modifier**, specify **"Lattice"** to point to the lattice. This sets up the connection between the UV Sphere and the lattice for deformation purposes.

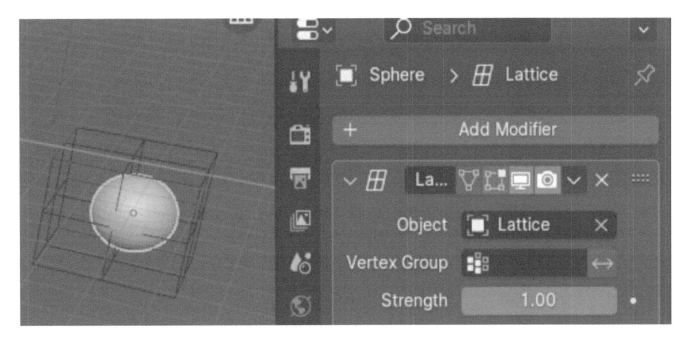

7) Deselect the **UV Sphere**, then select the **Lattice** and switch to **Edit** Mode. Choose a single vertex and press the **G** key(Grab) to trans-late the vertex. Observe how the UV Sphere deforms in response to this vertex movement.

Note: You can select several **lattice vertices** to attain the desired deformation. Experiment with various configurations to gain proficiency in using the Lattice Modifier.

MESH DEFORM MODIFIER

The Mesh Deform Modifier is designed to deform a mesh using a Cage Mesh. Similar to a Lattice Modifier, the cage mesh provides a way to sculpt the deformation around the object being modified. However, unlike a lattice, the cage mesh isn't constrained to a regular grid layout and can be customized to precisely fit the shape of the mesh object being deformed.

To use the **"Mesh Deform"** Modifier, the cage mesh must full yen close the portion of the mesh that is to be deformed, with only the vertices inside the cage being affected. Usually, the cage mesh will have significantly fewer vertices than the mesh being deformed.

To demonstrate this:

1) start by creating a **UV Sphere** object. Scale it along the **Y** axis, (press **Z** and then Num **4** to view the object in Wireframe mode).\

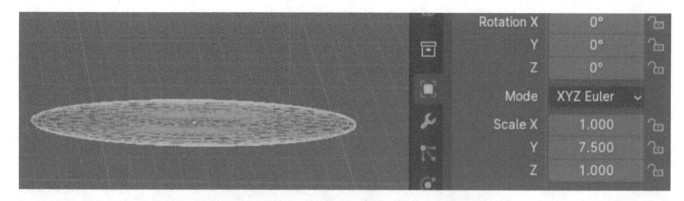

Rotation X	0°	
Y	0°	
Z	0°	
Mode	XYZ Euler	v
Scale X	1.000	
Y	7.500	
Z	1.000	

2) Next, craft a simple cage mesh around the extended sphere by scaling a cube to encompass it. Then subdivide the cage mesh into **5** cuts.

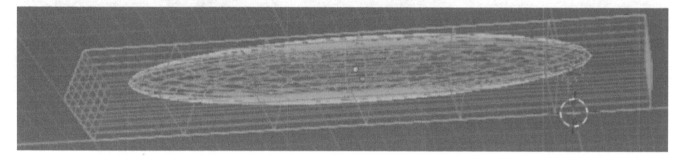

3) Then, in **Edit** Mode, select **vertices** and extrude them as necessary to refine the cage mesh's shape.

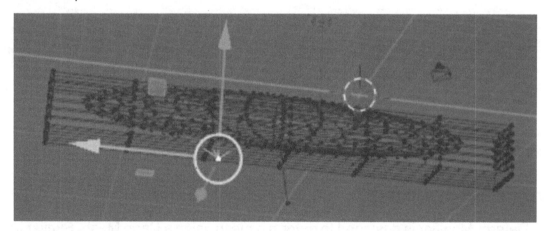

4) Add a **Mesh Deform** Modifier to the scaled **UV Sphere**. In the Modifier panel, specify the name of the cage mesh (in this case, **"Cube"**) in the Object panel. Then, click on **"Bind "** to establish the link between the **two meshes**. Depending on the complexity of your model, the **Bind** operation may take a few seconds to calculate. Wait until **"Bind"** changes to **"Unbind"** before proceeding to select vertices on the cage.

5) Once the meshes are bound, you can deform the **UV Sphere** by **moving, scaling**, and **rotating** the selected **vertices** on the cage. Hint: the closeness of the cage to the original object influences how the **deformation** behaves. Adjusting the position of the cage relative to the UV Sphere can yield different deformation effects.

Note: The **Cage** Mesh will be visible in the scene. With the **UV Sphere** selected in **Object** Mode, apply the **Modifier** and then delete the **Cage**.

THE SHRINKWRAP MODIFIER

The Shrinkwrap Modifier is used to shrink a mesh, enveloping it around another object. This enables the deformed mesh to be offset to generate shapes between the original and deformed states.

1) To demonstrate, begin by deleting the **Cube** in the default Blender Scene and adding a **UV Sphere** al on g with a **Cone** mesh object. Ensure that the **Cone** is positioned inside the **UV Sphere**, which can be easily observed when both objects are viewed in **Wireframe** Mode.

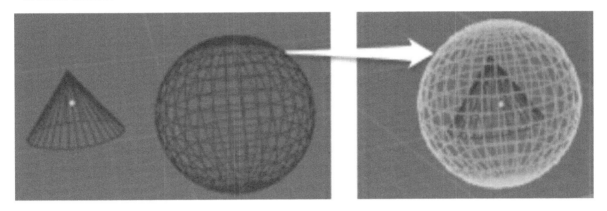

2) Add a **Shrinkwrap** Modifier to the **UV sphere** and type **"Cone "**in the **Target** panel. Adjusting the **Offset** value in the **Modifier** panel affects the size of the modified **UV Sphere.**

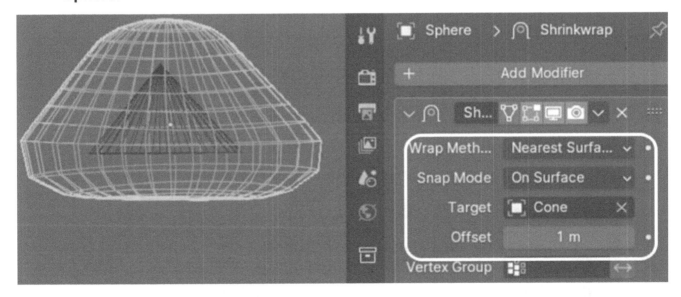

3) Take some time to experiment with different **Wrap** Method and **Snap Mode** values to observe their effects. This allows you to fine- tune the **shrinkwrap** effect according to your desired outcome.

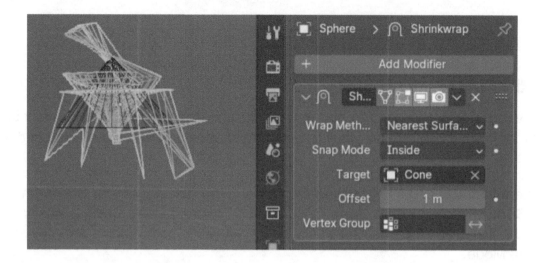

SIMPLE DEFORM MODIFIER

The **Simple Deform** Modifier is used to deform a mesh by adjusting values within the **Modifier** and introducing a second object to influ-ence the deformation.

To witness the effect of this modifier:

1) begin by adding a **UV Sphere** to the default scene. Inside the sphere, position a **scaled-down cube** at its center as shown below. Activate **Wireframe Display** Mode (**Z** key + Num **4**).

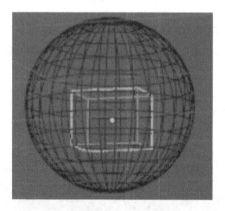

2) Add the **Simple Deform** Modifier to the **UV Sphere**, and specify **"Cube"** as the Origin.

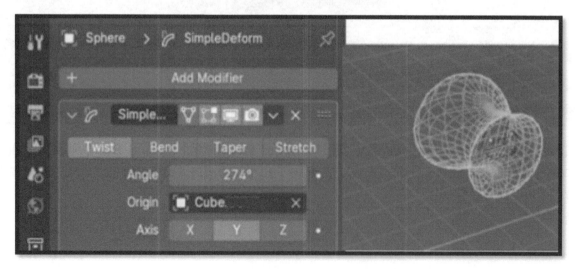

Upon adding the modifier, you'll immediately notice the **mesh of the sphere** skewing. Hint: by default, the **Twist** option is selected in the modifier, indicated by its blue highlighting.

3) Explore the options available within the **Simple Deform** Modifier: **Twist, Bend, Taper, and Stretch**. Use the **Angle** slider to adjust the degree of **skewing**. Experiment with different settings within the **Modifier** to achieve various deformation effects.

Hint: when you combine settings such as **translation, rotation**, or **scaling** either the **Cube** or the **UV Sphere** will influence deformation. Deleting the **Origin** object will also affect the outcome.

4) Additionally, try out the **Stretch** option with **Factor** set to **0.785** and **Origin** set to Cube along the **X**-axis.

For more advanced settings, explore the options available in the Modifier's Restrictions Tab.

THE SMOOTH MODIFIER

The Smooth Modifier is designed to smooth the mesh object by softening the angles between adjacent faces. This process also reduces the size of the original object. Hint: the smoothing effect only impacts how the object's surfaces are visually represented in the 3D viewport. No additional vertices, edges, or faces are added to the object during smoothing.

1. To add the **Smooth** Modifier, select an **object** in the 3D viewport and then add the modifier in the **Properties** Editor under **Modifier** Properties.

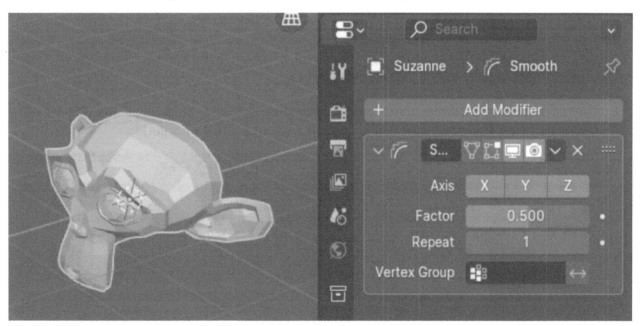

2. Adjust the **Factor** slider to increase or decrease the level of smoothing. The **Repeat** value multiplies the **Factor** value, and you can restrict the smoothing to specific axes using the **X, Y**, and **Z** axis options.

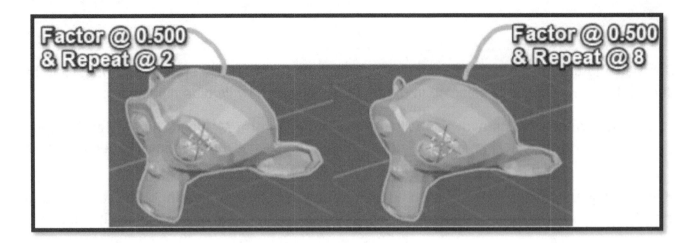

When setting the **Factor** and **Repeat** values, the operation logic involves first establishing a smoothing value (**Factor**) and then applying the calculation (**Repeat**) multiple times to attain the desired level of smoothing. Once you're satisfied with the smoothing effect, apply the modifier.

Ensure that the object has a reasonable number of faces before applying the modifier for it to be effective. For instance, the Monkey object with its default faces will shrink in size as repeats are applied. However, when subdivided three or four times, it will exhibit a fully differ-ent effect.

THE SMOOTH CORRECTIVE MODIFIER

The Smooth Corrective Modifier is utilized to smooth out and correct deficiencies in a model that arise during surface deformation.

THE SMOOTH LAPLACIAN

The Smooth Laplacian Modifier serves to refine the shape of a mesh that has become irregular due to vertex manipulation during detailed modeling.

1. Consider adding a plane object and subdividing it into 7 cuts, with one vertex moved upwards using **Proportional** Editing with **Random Falloff** enabled.

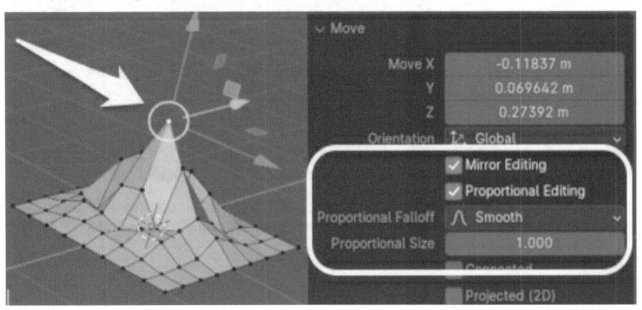

2. By adding the **Smooth Laplacian Modifier** in **Object** Mode, with a **Repeat Value** of **1** and a **Lambda Factor** of **1.100**, the mesh undergoes smoothing. However, in **Edit** Mode with the **Modifier** added but not applied, **vertices** retain their original positions. To make the smoothness permanent, the Modifier needs to be applied.

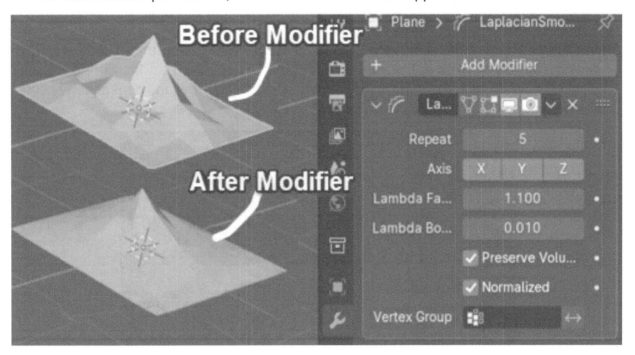

THE SURFACE DEFORM MODIFIER

The Surface Deform Modifier functions similarly to the Mesh Deform Modifier, shaping one mesh based on another. However, unlike the **Mesh Deform** Modifier, the controlling mesh doesn't need to fully enclose the object being shaped.

1) The Illustration below shows that a **Cube Object** is scaled along the **Y**-Axis in **Object** Mode, then subdivided in **Edit** Mode with **10 cuts**.

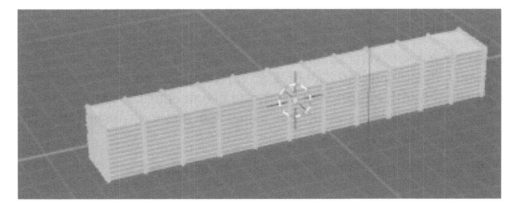

2) Additionally, a **Plane** Object is introduced, rotated on the **Y**-Axis, and scaled to intersect the elongated **Cube**. The Plane is also subdi-vided into10 cuts in Edit Mode.

3) In **Object** Mode, ensure that the elongated **Cube** is selected, and a **Surface Deform** Modifier is added. In the **Target** Panel, **"Plane"** is specified as the controlling object. Clicking **"Bind"** sets the Plane as the control. Deforming the Plane consequently deforms the elongated Cube.

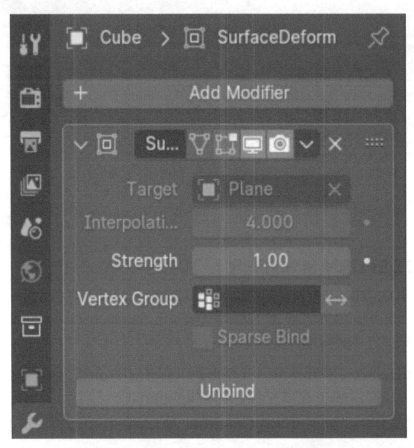

4) When the center row of vertices on the Plane is selected in **Edit** Mode and moved forward, consequently deforming the Cube. Dur-ing this operation, **Proportional** Editing is activated with **Smooth Falloff**, and the **Circle** of Influence is expanded to encompass the entire Plane. After shaping the Cube using this method, ensure that the Modifier is applied, and the Plane is deleted.

We shall discuss more on Proportional Editing in Chapter **Six (6).**

THE WARP MODIFIER

The Warp Modifier enables you to distort a mesh surface in Object mode by manipulating Target Objects. If you prefer not to see the Tar- gets in the Scene, you can use Empty Objects. The mesh deformation occurs in a gradient between the two Targets.

To better understand this concept, let's try a simple exercise in Blender:

1) Create a new Blender Scene, add a **Plane Object**, then zoom in on it and Subdivide the Plane in **Edit** Mode with **10** cuts.

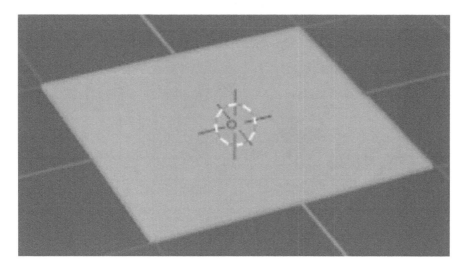

2) In **Object** Mode, add two Empty objects and position them as shown below. observe the names of the **Empty objects** in the **Outliner** Editor; they will be named **Empty** and **Empty.001**, but you can rename them if you prefer.

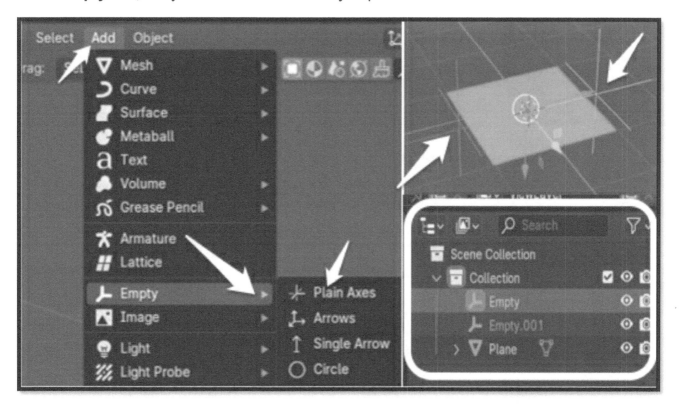

3) Select the **Plane**, then navigate to the **Properties** Editor and click on the **Modifier** buttons to add a **Warp Modifier.**

4) Within the Modifier panel, input the names of the **Empty Target Objects** in the **"From"** and **"To"** panels (From: **Empty** and To: **Empty.001**). Immediately, you'll observe the Plane deforming in the 3D View Editor.

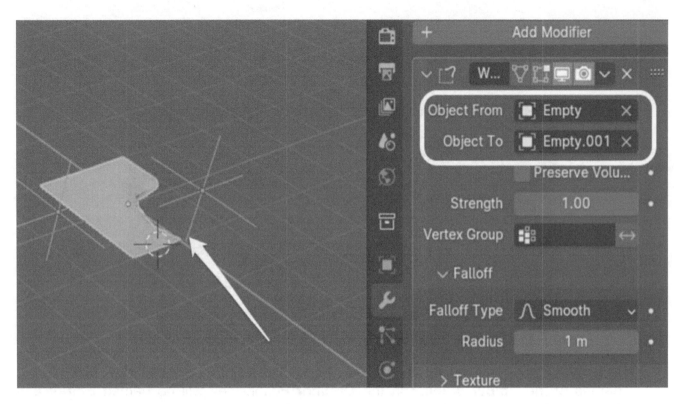

Think of the Modifier as instructing the mesh to deform from **Empty** to **Empty.0 01.**

5) You can further manipulate the deformation of the Plane by selecting either **Empty** in the 3DView Editor and translating it as shown below.

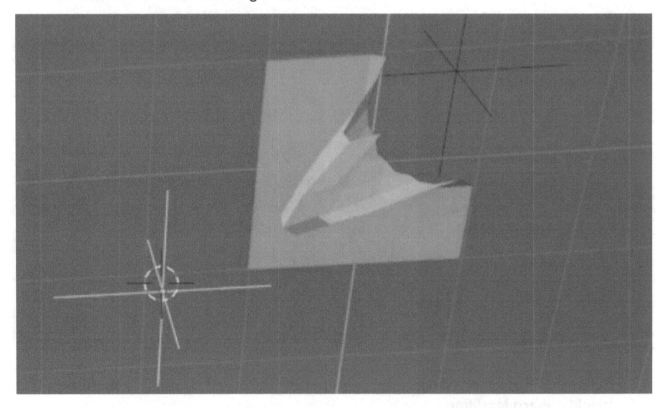

6) Within the **Modifier** pan el, you have the option to select a different **Falloff Type** by accessing the **Falloff** Tab. You can then fine-tune the deformation by adjusting the **Strength** and **Radius** sliders.

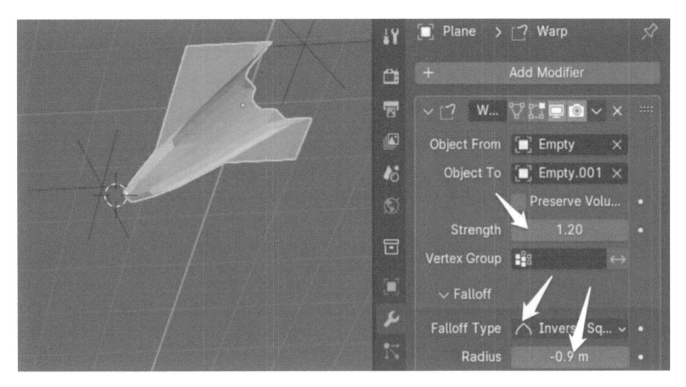

Note: Once the Modifier is applied, the shape of the Plane becomes permanently set.

THEWAVE MODIFIER

The Wave Modifier is used to apply a deformation that generates an animation resembling a wave. To illustrate its function:

1) start with the default Blender Scene by deleting the **Cube** and adding a Plane. Scale the Plane up six times, then switch to **Edit** mode by pressing Tab.
2) Subdivide the **Plane** by right -clicking and select in g **"Subdivide"** in the **Mesh Context** menu. In the Subdivide panel, set the Number of Cuts to **15**.

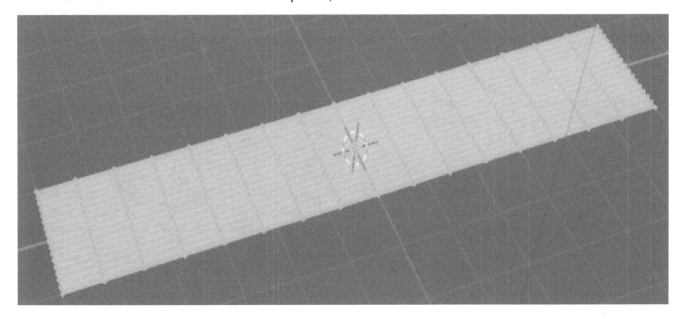

3) Return to **Object** Mode by pressing **Tab** again. Next, with the **Plane** selected, navigate to the **Properties** Editor and click on the **Mod-ifiers** Properties to add a **Wave** Modifier.

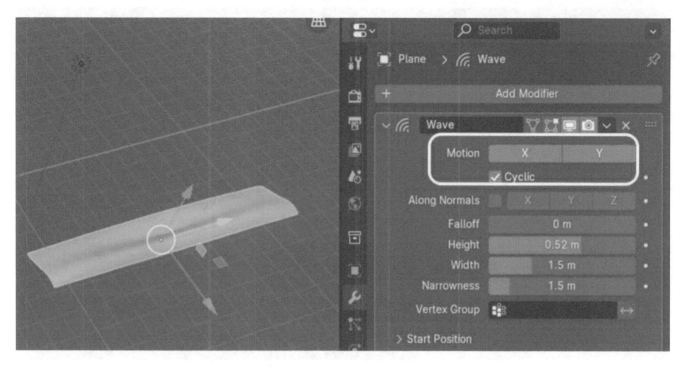

4) After adding the **Wave** Modifier to the Plane, you'll promptly observe the deformation in the 3D Viewport Editor. Pull the Plane up- wards from the center and indent at the top of the bulge.

   The Wave Modifier has been applied to both the **X** and **Y** axes. In the Modifier panel, you'll notice that **X, Y,** and **Cyclic** are selected. **"X"** and **"Y"** refer to the axes, while the "Cyclic" option indicates that the wave animation will repeat continuously.

5) To preview the animation, simply press the **Play** button in the **Timeline** Editor Header.

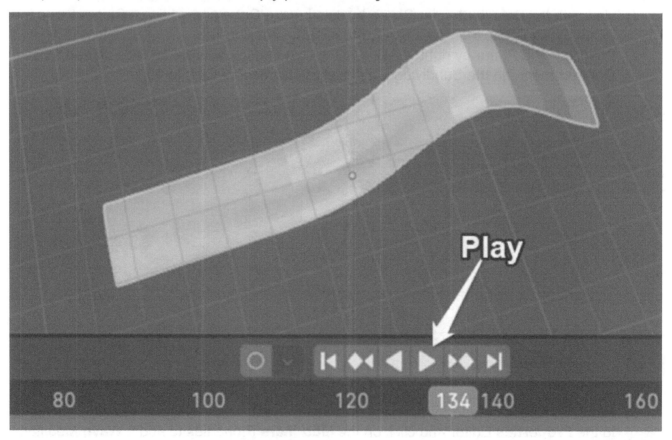

6) Deselect the **X** Axis in the **Modifier** panel and replay the animation, you'll observe a wave along the **Y** axis.

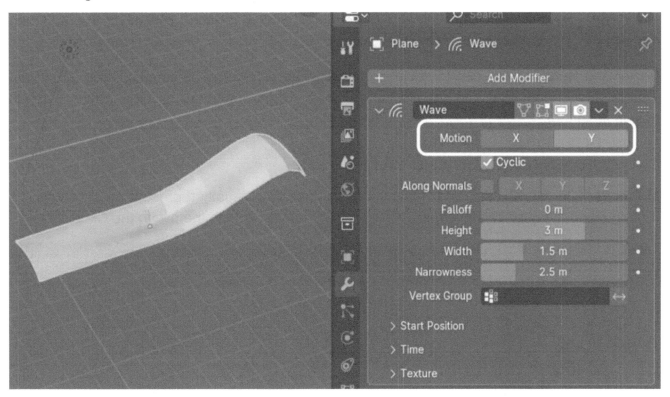

7) Expanding the Start Position and **Time** Tabs within the Modifier grants you complete control over the motion of the wave.

CHAPTER 8: EDITING WITH CURVES

In Blender, a Curve serves as a guiding line or path to manipulate the form of a mesh during modeling or direct the motion of an object in animation. There are five main types of curves available: **Bezier, Circle (Bezier Circle), Nurbs Curve, Nurbs Circle**, and **Path.**

Each type of curve initially appears as a simple line in a Blender scene in Object Mode. However, upon entering Edit Mode, control handles become visible, allowing for precise adjustments to the curve's shape. Additionally, the curve can be scaled, extruded, and further refined by adding more control handles.

Hint: a curve itself doesn't appear in the final rendered image; rather, it functions solely as a tool for editing a mesh object. While the object renders, the curve remains invisible to the rendering process.

Bezier and Nurbs curves can form closed loops when configured as circular, such as circles. This feature enables them to seamlessly en-close a region, enhancing their utility in various design scenarios.

THE CURVES, CIRCLES AND PATHS

In Blender, Curves, Circles, and Paths serve as lines that visually represent data or outline a route guiding direction or movement. It's im-portant not to confuse them with the Circle Object.

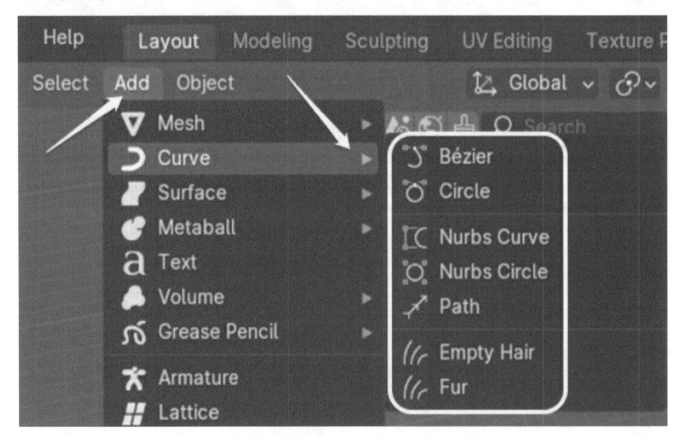

These curves are highly flexible and editable, allowing users to tailor their shape to specific needs. They play various roles in animation, such as guiding objects along a path, influencing their shape through extrusion along the curve, or duplicating objects along the curve. **Curve Circles**, for instance, are circular curves that connect at their ends, forming a continuous loop. Blender offers five fundamental curve options, conveniently accessible through the **Add** menu in the 3D Viewport Editor Header or by pressing **Shift + A** while the mouse cursor is in the 3D Viewport Editor. To explore these options, position the **3D Viewport Editor** in Top **Orthographic** View and delete the default **Cube**.

Next, we shall explore the Curves, Circles, and Paths.

PATHS

1) You can get started by selecting **Path** from the **Add> Curve** menu.

A Nurbs Path, for instance, is introduced in the 3D Viewport Editor in **Object** Mode in Top Ort ho graphic View.

2) In **Edit** Mode, the Path is highlighted in yellow to reveal its Control Points.

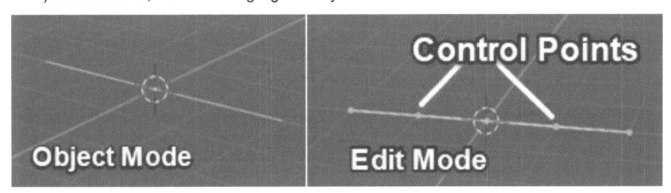

3) To begin editing, deselect the **Path** and then click the left-click a **Control Point** and move the Control Point with the **Move** tool to adjust the Control Point (when you click and move the Control Point, it changes to **white**). Alternatively, press the **G** key (**Grab**) and move the **Mouse** or activate the **Translate** Tool in the **Tool** Panel to adjust the position of the **Control Point**, thereby reshap-ing the Path to your liking.

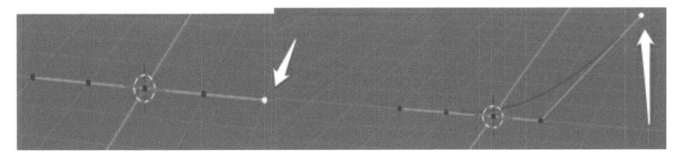

4) One practical use for a Path is to animate an object along its route. To facilitate this, users can enable **Normals** in **Curve Edit Mode Overlays**, which displays **chevrons** along the Path. These chevrons specify the direction of movement when the object is ani-mated to follow the Path.

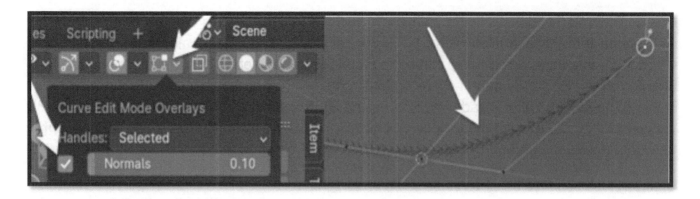

It's essential to recollect that while Paths can be scaled, rotated, and translated like any other object, they do not appear in the final render when generating images or animations. They solely serve as guides for editing and animation purposes.

THE BEZIER CURVE AND BEZIER CIRCLE

The Bezier Curve shares similarities with a Curve Pat h when reshaped, as demonstrated in the previous example. However, upon closer examination in **Edit** Mode, users will notice a more intricate control system for shaping the curve to their specific specifications.

In **Edit** Mode, with **Normals** enabled in Overlays, chevrons appear along the curve, aiding in visualization and understanding of its direc-tion and flow.

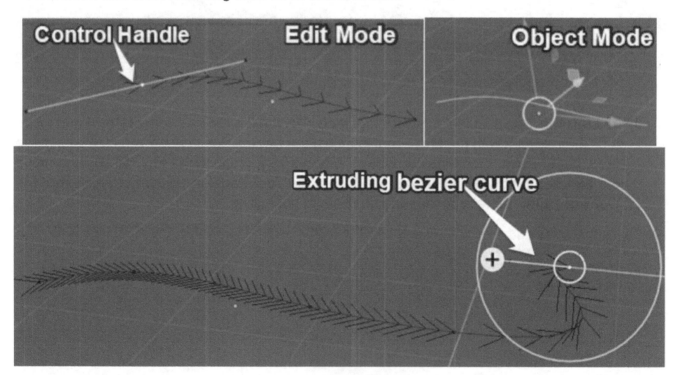

The **Bezier Circle** shares similarities with the Bezier Curve, featuring control handles positioned at the four cardinal points. To manipulate the circle, users can select a handle by right-clicking the mouse button, then use the **G** key to grab and move it to reshape the path. Addi-tionally, the **R** key can be used to rotate and flatten the curve as needed.

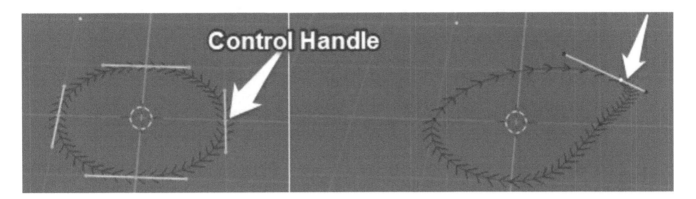

Hint: the Bezier Circle, Nurbs Path, and Nurbs Circle are all displayed and manipulated in Edit Mode.

MODELING FROM A CURVE

To model a mesh object from any curve path or circle, extrusion can be utilized.

1) Begin by entering a **Bezier Curve** in User Perspective View, then zoom in and switch to **Edit** Mode by pressing **Tab.**

Hint: the following procedure does not create a mesh object but demonstrates what occurs when the curve is extruded in **Edit** Mode.

2) When you enter **Edit** Mode, the control handles at both ends of the curve are selected.

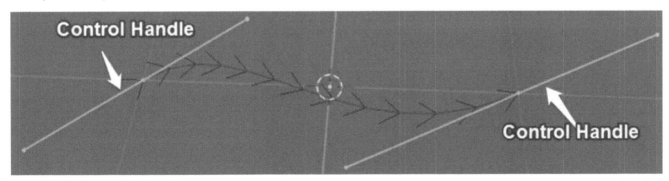

3) To extrude, move downward on the **Z**- Axis by pressing the **E** key followed by the **Z** key, then dragging the mouse.

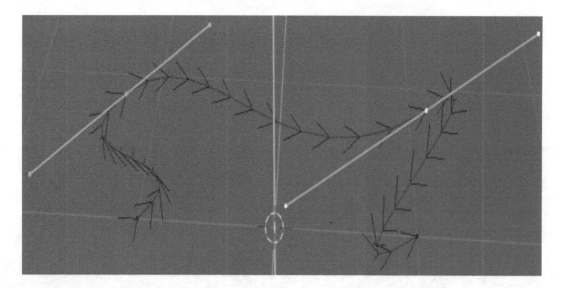

4) To create a mesh from a curve, ensure you are in **Object** Mode with the **default Bezier Curve** selected (without extrusion). In the **Properties** Editor, navigate to **Object Data Properties, Geometry** Tab, and adjust the **values** as shown below. Finally, rotate the 3D Editor Viewport.

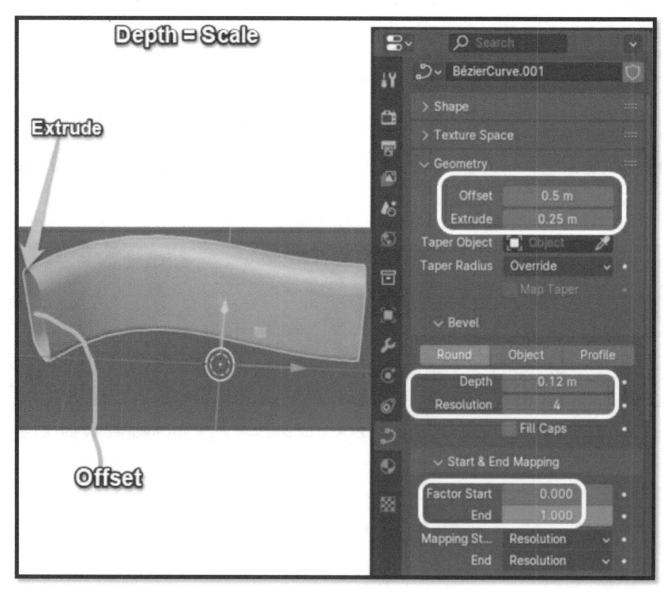

5) When the **mesh shape** is generated, switch to **Object** Mode and navigate to the **3D Viewport Editor** Header. Click on **"Object"** and choose **"Convert - Mesh"**.

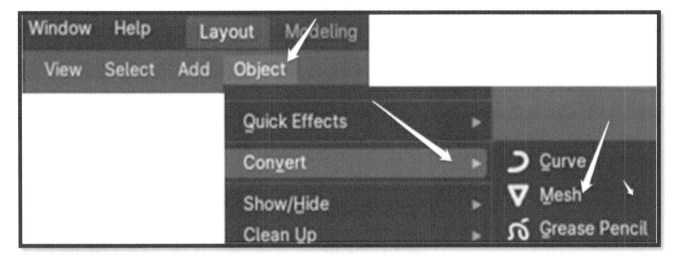

6) Upon conversion, switch to **Edit** Mode to observe the creation of **vertices, edges**, and **faces**.

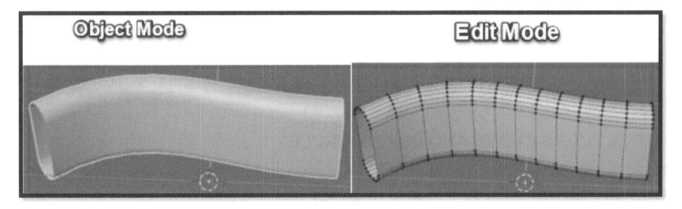

Before converting to a mesh, while still in Edit Mode, users have the option to select the control handles on the original Bezier Curve and adjust the object's shape accordingly. However, it's crucial to Hint: once converted to a mesh, the original curve is deleted.

CLOSED LOOPS

Bezier and Nurbs circles are examples of closed loops, allowing them to serve as foundations for creating tubular objects or establishing uninterrupted paths for animations. Additionally, any curve or path can be converted into a closed loop.

1) To illustrate, consider adding a curve path in **Edit** Mode with the right-hand control point moved and extruded **three times**.

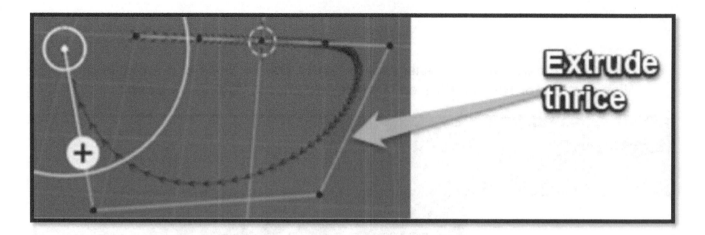

2) While still in **Edit** Mode, navigate to the header and click on **"Curve"** then select **"Toggle-Cyclic"** to create a closed loop.

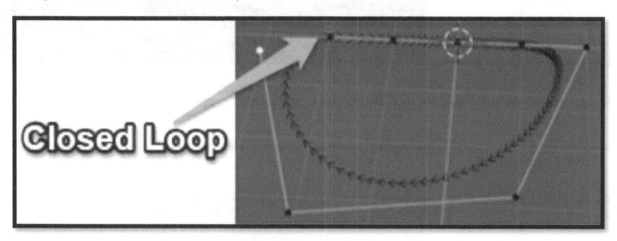

USING NURBS CURVE AND NURBS CIRCLE

To use Nurbs Curves in Blender, access them in the 3D Viewport Editor by either pressing **Shift+A** or clicking **"Add"** in the 3D Viewport Header and selecting from the displayed menu. You'll find two options: **Nurbs Curve** and **Nurbs Circle**.

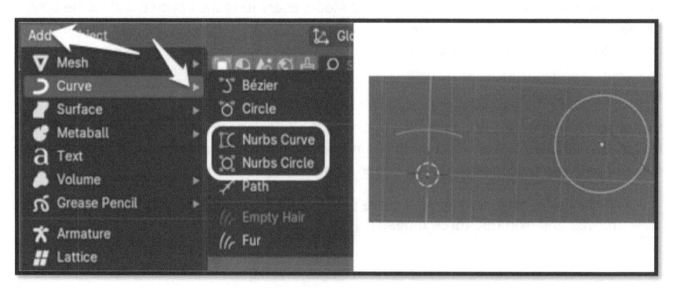

1) Position the 3D Viewport Editor in Top Orthographic View. In Edit Mode, both Nurbs Curves and Circles are equipped with control handles that allow users to manipulate their shape with precision.

Additionally, chevrons are visible along the curve, indicating their suitability for use as animation paths.

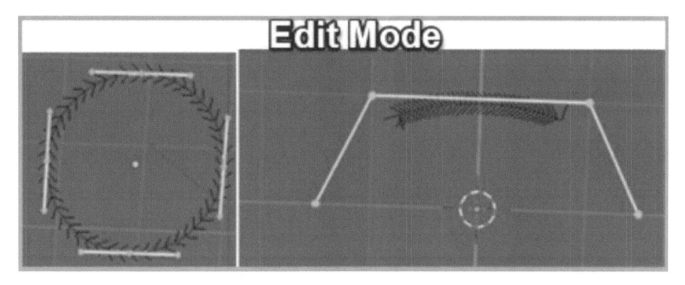

2) A Nurbs Circle in the illustration below displays a selected control point being moved along the **X**-axis. Then, tilt the 3D Viewport into a User Orthographic View

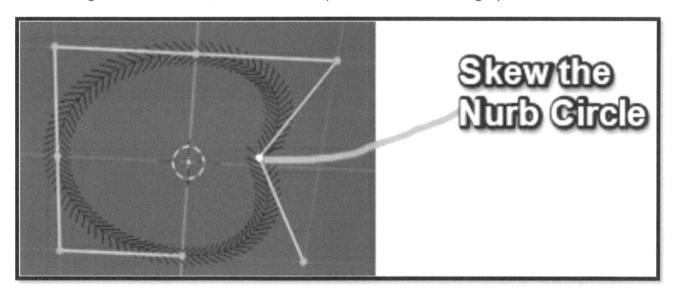

3) When the Nurbs Circle is selected in **Object** Mode, its shape can be adjusted by modifying settings in the **Properties** Editor, in the **Object Data Properties** under the **Geometry** Tab.

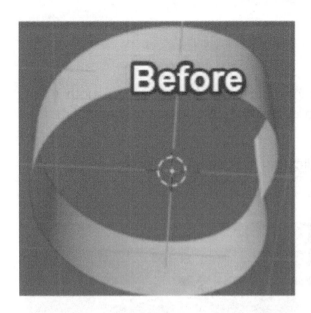

Before

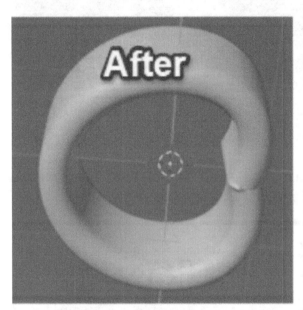

After

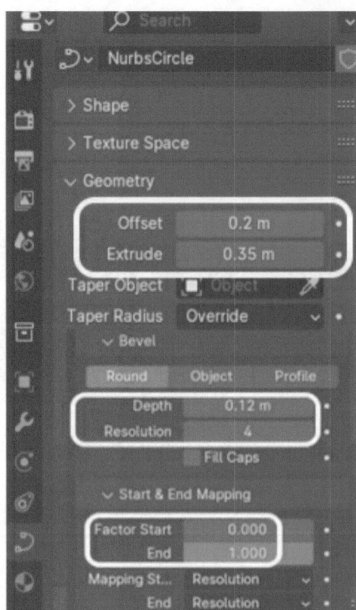

NurbsCircle

> Shape

> Texture Space

∨ Geometry

| Offset | 0.2 m |
| Extrude | 0.35 m |

Taper Object   Object

Taper Radius   Override

∨ Bevel

| Round | Object | Profile |

| Depth | 0.12 m |
| Resolution | 4 |

Fill Caps

∨ Start & End Mapping

| Factor Start | 0.000 |
| End | 1.000 |

Mapping St...   Resolution

End   Resolution

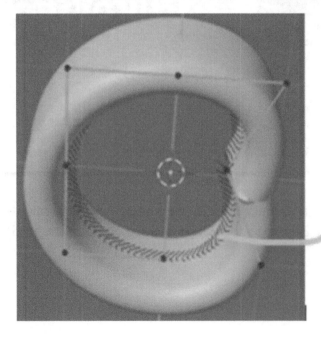

Control Points available in Edit Mode

4) After expanding the circle and selecting it in Object Mode, you can convert its shape into a mesh object. To do this, navigate to the header, click on **"Object,"** then select **"Convert to - Mesh from Curve•.** This will display the **object** in **Edit** mode, revealing its ver-tices, edges, and faces.

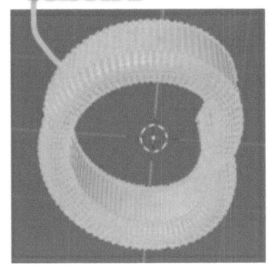

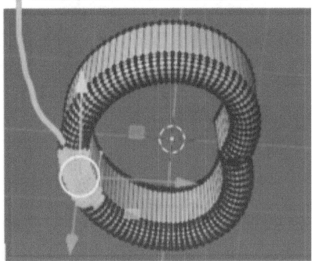

Hint: once the object is converted to a mesh object, the ability to utilize the settings in the **Properties Editor's Data** buttons, in the **Geome-try** tab, becomes unavailable.

To manipulate the shape further, deselect the vertices and then individually select the desired vertices for adjustment. This process demonstrates that by converting one type of object to another, users gain access to different options for shape manipulation.

The **Nurbs Curve** offers another avenue for generating shapes, objects, or animation paths.

1) In **Edit** mode, the curve is presented alongside control handles and control points. Users have the flexibility to select individual points or multiple points and then apply **Move, Rotate, or Scale** operations to sculpt the curve to their liking.

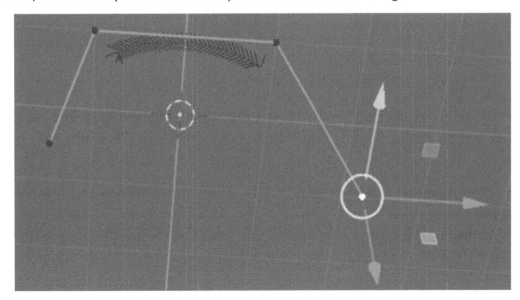

2) Users can further refine the curve's shape by adjusting settings in **Object** Mode within the **Properties** Editor, in the **Object Data** Properties under the **Geometry** Tab.

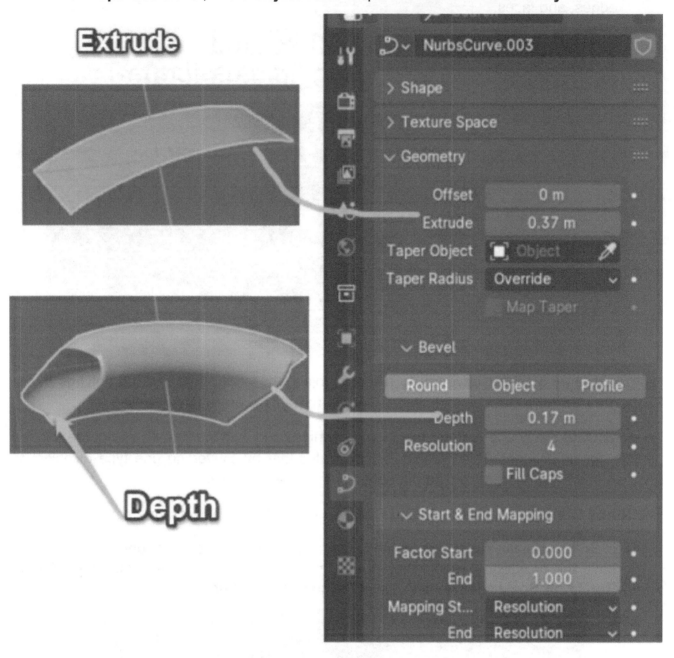

LOFTING

Lofting, sometimes known as Lathing, involves creating shapes using curves, which are then converted into mesh objects. To illustrate this process, we'll use a Bezier Circle along with a Bezier Curve.

1) Open a new Blender scene and delete the default **Cube.** Then, add a **Bezier Circle** to the scene.
2) After deselecting the **circle,** add a **Bezier Curve.** Zoom in on the 3D Viewport Editor for a closer look.

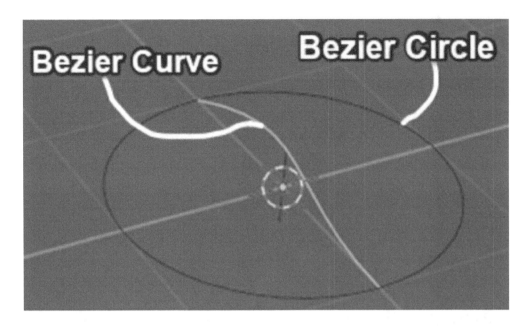

3) Next, deselect the curve and select the circle. In the **Properties** Editor, navigate to **Object Data Properties**, then the **Geometry Bevel** Tab. Click on **"Object"** and select the **Bezier Curve.** Make sure to check **"Fill Caps".**

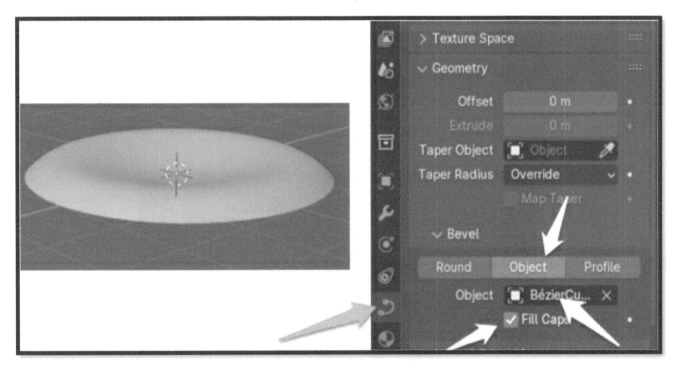

4) This generates a shape in the 3D Viewport Editor. To better understand what's happening, switch the 3D Viewport Edit or to **Wire- frame Viewport Shading** Mode (**Z** key + Num Pad 4).

Additionally, select the **Bezier Curve** by clicking on its name in the **Outliner** Editor.

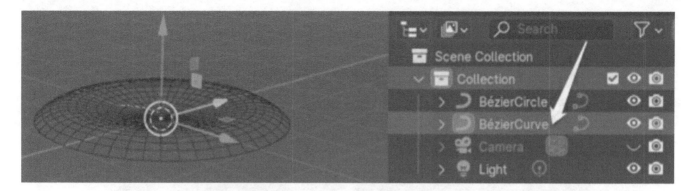

For clearer visibility, consider turning off the grid and floor display in the Viewport Overlays.

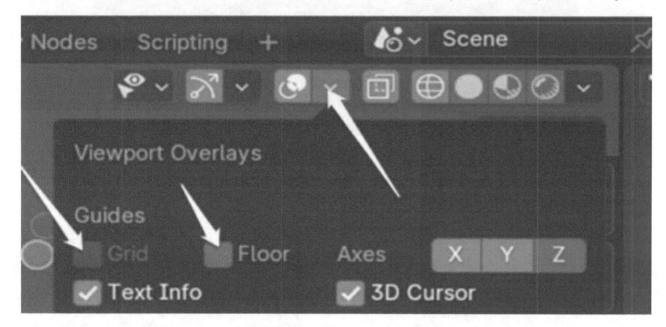

5) Next, switch to Front Orthographic View and translate the curve to match it with the profile of the generated shape.

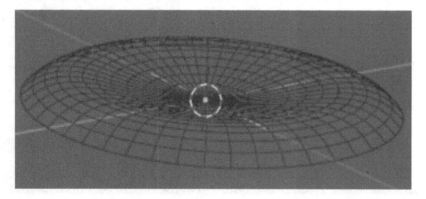

By adjusting the 3D View Editor's perspective, users can observe that the shape is created by extruding the curve profile through 360° as shown here.

6) While the Bezier Curve is still selected, switch to Edit Mode by pressing **Tab** to see the control handles at each end of the curve. By selecting the control handle at the center of the shape and translating it along the **X-axis** towards the outside, users can in- crease the inner diameter of the shape. In the same way, translating the control handle at the outer diameter adjusts the outer diameter.

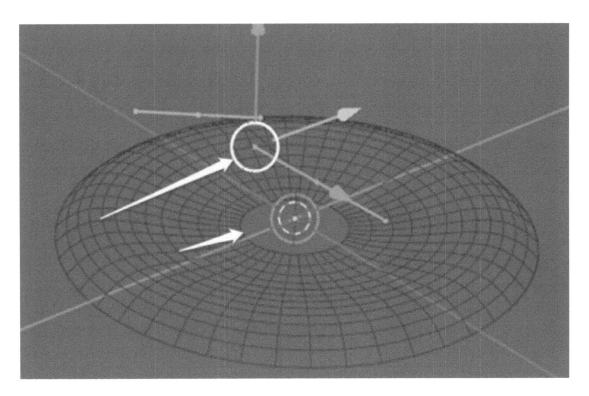

7) To alter the shape further, shift-select both control handles, then press **R + Y + 90.** This flips the Bezier Curve up on its edge and then adjusts the shape into a form resembling a pot as shown below.

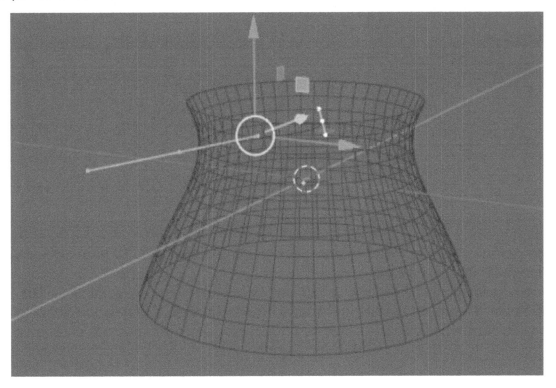

8) By manipulating the control handles, users can further adjust the shape. Selecting both control handles and subdividing (right- click in the editor and select **"Subdivide"** from the **Curve Context** Menu). This adds a third control handle as shown here.

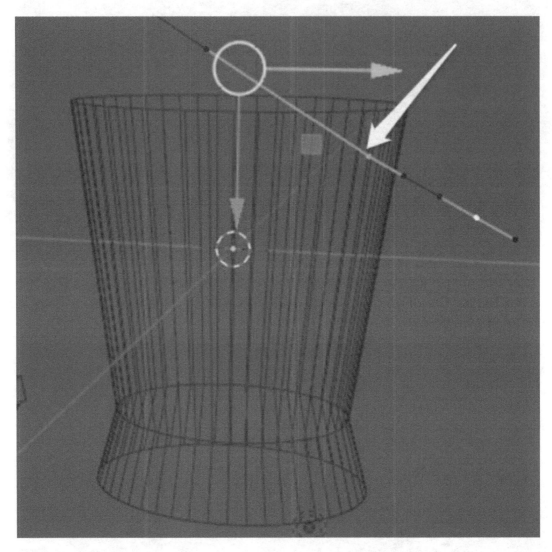

9) With the newly added control handle selected, pressing the **V** key displays **the Handle type** menu. Choosing **"Vector"** from this menu enables users to produce sharp corners when the handle is rotated.

10) Once the shaping process is finished, switch to **Object** Mode by pressing **Tab**. Deselect the **Bezier Curve** and select the **shape** it se lf. Change the viewport shading mode to Solid as shown here.

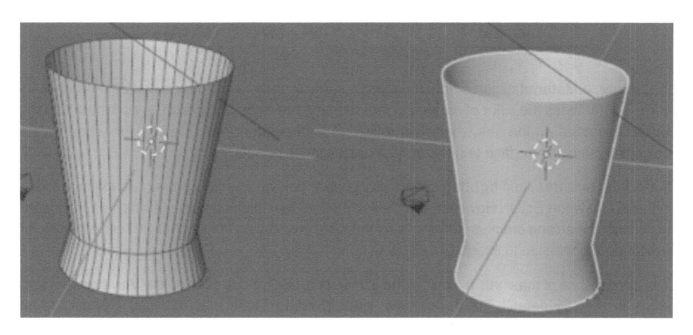

11) In the **Properties** Editor, navigate to **Object Properties** (NOT **Object Data**), then the **Viewport Display Tab.** Tick or select the "**Wireframe**" option to view the subdivisions that will be created when the shape is converted to a mesh object
Users can adjust the subdivisions by modifying values in the **Properties Editor** under the **Object Data** buttons, within the **Shape Tab** under **Resolution.**
12) Once satisfied with the shape, click on **"Object"** in the Header and select "**Convert to Mesh from Curve".** To add **thickness** to the **shape**, apply a **Solidify** Modifier and increase the Thickness value accordingly.

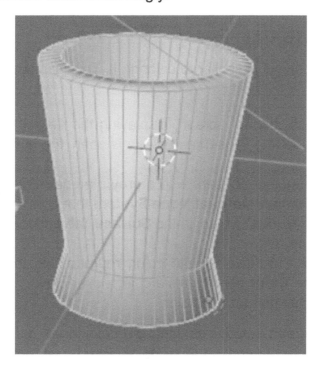

CHAPTER 9: APPLYING MATERIALS

In Blender, a **Material** dictates how an object's surface appears on the computer screen. At its core, it determines the color of an object, representing how light reflects off its surface within the visible spectrum. In the real world, this reflection is dependent on certain factors such as the object's base color, surface texture, and ambient lighting effects.

Materials, textures, and **lighting** collectively govern how an object is presented within a scene in the 3D Viewport Editor. However, the Viewport offers four distinct display modes, each tailored to simplify the editing process, whether it's modeling, previewing color schemes, or preparing for rendering (conversion to image or video).

The appearance of materials (colors) in the 3D Viewport Editor depends on the Viewport Shading Mode in use. By default, the **Solid View- port Shading** Mode is used when Blender is first opened, primarily serving modeling purposes. In this mode, materials (colors) are not essential for basic modeling tasks. Additionally, Blender's Material Node System, which offers versatile and comprehensive control over material effects, is active by default.

Hint: in the **Solid Viewport Shading Mode,** materials (colors) do not display in the 3D Viewport Editor when the Node System is enabled.

However, the **Node System** can be disabled to allow colors to display alongside the 3D Viewport in **Solid Viewport Shading Mode**.

HOW TO ASSIGN MATERIAL

Assigning a material to an object is similar to coloring it. To grasp this process within Blender 's user interface:

1) begin with the default Blender screen, displaying the default cube object within the 3D Viewport Editor. Ensure the Properties Edi- tor is open, the **Material** Properties section to be precise.
2) By default, the cube object appears with a gray material. Within the Material Properties section, there is a **Blender Material Node System** that controls the material, denoted by the highlighted **"Use Nodes"** button in the **Surface** Tab and the presence of **"Prin-cipled BSDF"** in the **Surface** bar.
3) The Base Color bar indicates a white color, representing the gray color of the cube. Clicking on this **Base Color** bar reveals a color picker circle, allowing for the selection of a different color to change material color.

However, in the default screen setup, changing the color does not reflect in the 3DViewport Editor. The cube remains gray because the **Node System** is in control, and the Viewport is in **Solid Viewport Shading Mode**.

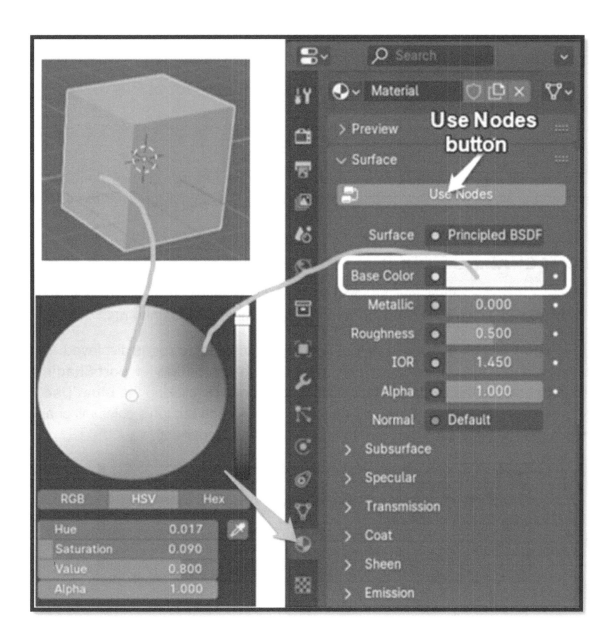

Hint: The default cube object comes pre-applied with material, as evidenced by the Material Properties display along its controls. When a new object is added to the scene, the control won't display only the **"New "** button appears in the Material Properties section.

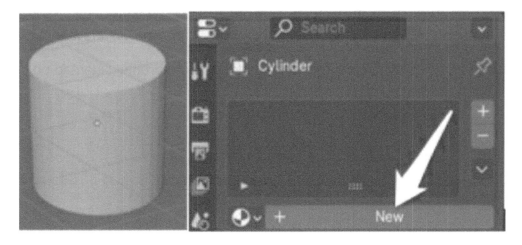

4) Clicking this **"New"** button with a new object selected will display identical material properties as those of the default cube, applying the default gray material to the new object.

VIEWPORT SHADING MODES

The 3D Viewport Editor offers four shading modes, each suited for different operations. The default mode, **Solid**, is typically used for demonstrating material assignments.

In **Solid Viewport Shading Mode,** only the default gray material (color) is displayed. To display a different material (color) within the 3D Viewport Editor while in **Solid Viewport Shading Mode**, you need to deactivate the **Node System**. This can be done by clicking the **blue "Use Nodes"** button in the **Properties** Editor, **Surface** Tab. Upon clicking, the but ton's color will change from blue to white or gray, indicating that the Node System is no longer active.

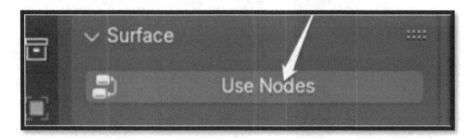

MATERIAL PROPERTIES

The application of materials is mainly handled within the **Properties** Editor under **Material** Properties, although the **Blender Material Node System** also offers control.

The screenshot below illustrates the default **Material Properties** control panel for adjusting the display of the material (color) of the de- fault cube object within the **3D Viewport Editor**.

The **Base Color** setting determines the material color of the currently selected object within the 3D Viewport Editor.

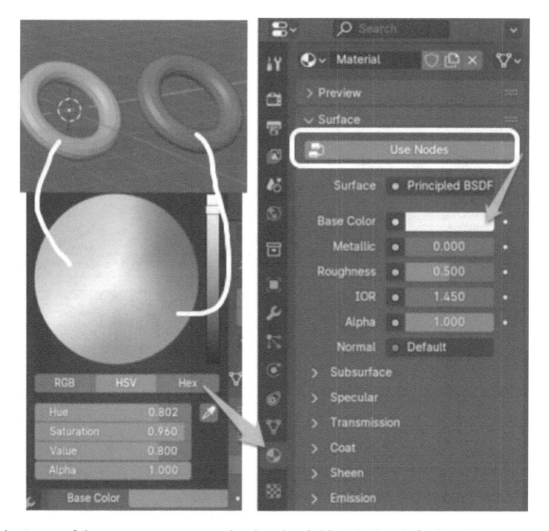

Color is just one of the numerous properties involved. Hint: in the default setting,

✓ the 3D Viewport is in **Solid Viewport Display** Mode. The material (color) of the default cube object is determined by the setting in the **Base Color** bar within the **Material** Properties. However, if you attempt to change the color by clicking the bar and selecting a different color from the color picker circle, you won't immediately seethe change reflected in the 3D Viewport.

✓ To make the new color appear, you need to click the **blue "Use Nodes"** button to deactivate the Node System.

✓ Moreover, new objects don't come with a pre-applied material. Instead, Blender displays them with the default gray color.

MATERIAL NODE SYSTEM

The Blender Material Node System functions as a visual representation of computer data or instructions organized in a pipeline to gener-ate a color display. It operates similarly to mixing colors, where the primary colors- Red, Green, and Blue- when combined in equal parts, produce white.

In the Node System, this mixing process is represented by interconnected nodes, controlling material color. These nodes can be connected, disconnected, and rearranged within the pipeline to create various visual effects.

THE DEFAULT MATERIAL NODE SYSTEM

The Blender Material Node system is visible within the **Shader** Editor. When the default cube object is selected in the 3D Viewport Editor, the Shader Editor presents a Principled BSDF Node linked to a Material Output Node.

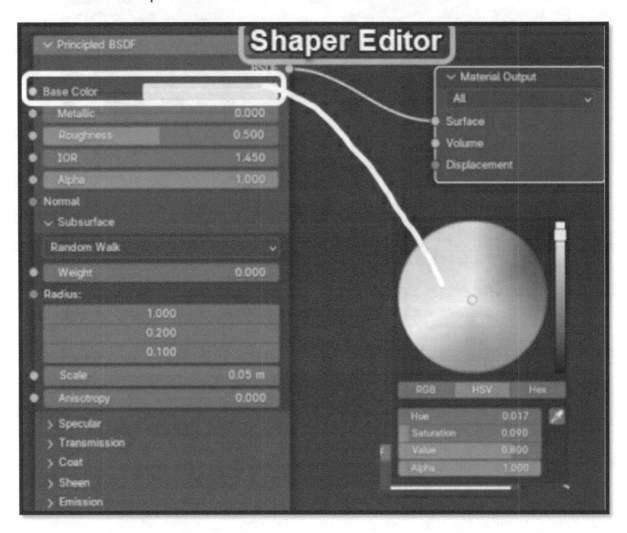

Hint: nodes do not automatically appear when a new object is added and selected in the 3D View port. However, the **Base Color** setting within the **Principled BSDF Node** governs the material (color) of the cube object in the 3D Viewport (the currently selected object).

To observe material (color) changes within the 3D Viewport using the **Node** System, the Viewport must be set **to Material Preview or Ren-dered Viewport Shading** Mode.

You might have observed that the controls found within the Principled BSDF Node can also be accessed through the **Properties** Editor under **Material** Properties. This means you can adjust settings in either location to impact the material display within the 3DViewport Editor.

With numerous controls available, there's a wide range of effects that you can achieve. Familiarizing yourself with the layout of these con-trols in the user interface will enable you to explore and follow full tutorials effectively.

Now, let's look into how the settings in the **Material** Properties are organized and how they influence the display in the 3D Viewport. The fundamental concept is that the settings found in the **Material** Properties, within the **Surface** Tab, contribute to creating a **Material** Index. This index is stored within a **Data block** in a **Material Cache** and can be retrieved for use on objects within the 3DViewport.

MATERIAL PROPERTIES EXPANDED

In simple terms, the material can be equated to color. The appearance of an object in the 3D Viewport Editor is dictated by a collection of data known as a **Material Index.** In the default Blender scene, the color of the default cube object is controlled by a Material Index, result-ing in the cube being displayed with its default gray color.

- ✓ The default cube comes with a pre-applied default gray **Material Index,** as indicated by the presence of controls within the **Proper- ties** Editor under **Material** Properties. However, this pre-application only applies to the default cube.
- ✓ Any additional objects added to the scene do not automatically have a Material Index assigned to them. In the **Material** Properties section, you'll only find a **New Button** until a **Material Index** is created.
- ✓ Before clicking the **New** Button, Blender utilizes the default Material Index behind the scenes to render the object in the **3D View- port Editor**, resulting in the default gray color.
- ✓ Clicking the **New Button** applies the default **Material** Index, as indicated by the updated controls in the **Properties** Editor. Hint: the Blender Node System remains active, with the **Use Nodes** button highlighted in blue.

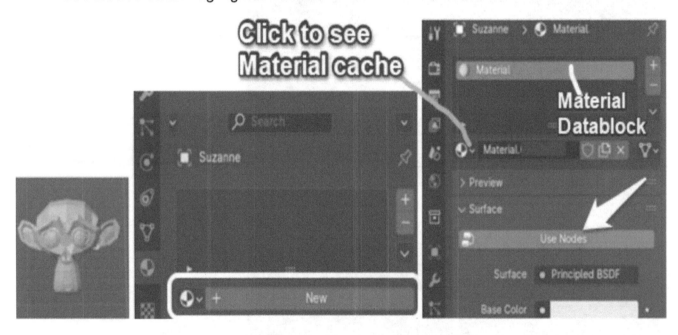

To deactivate the **Node System**, simply click the **Use Nodes** button, causing it to turn **white**.

In the screenshot above, you'll observe a new object, **Suzanne (Monkey Object)**, introduced into the scene.

For a deeper comprehension of the components within the **Material** Properties, it's recommended to start a new Blender file with only the default cube present in the 3D Viewport.

PROPERTIES ASSIGNMENT COMPONENTS

The screenshot below illustrates the components involved in the Properties assignment.

The data responsible for controlling the material display of the currently selected object in the 3DViewport Editor is known as the **Mate-rial** Index. This **Material Index** is encapsulated within a **Material Datablock**, which is stored in a cache known as the **Material Cache.** In the default scene, there exists a single data block stored in the cache, containing the Material Index.

When you select the datablock within the cache (clicking to highlight it in blue), it gets transferred to the **Material** Properties, where it's assigned to the **Material** Slot. This, in turn, assigns the **datablock/Material** Index to the selected object in the 3D Viewport.

Hint: while this analogy may not perfectly reflect the details of programming, it serves to explain data assignment within the user interface.

The term **"Material Slot"** originates from the action of clicking the plus (+) sign next to the **Active Material Index**, which adds a new **Material Slot.**

ADDING MATERIALS (DATABLOCKS)

When you add material, you're essentially creating a new datablock that contains a material index. In the screenshot below, you can see the default **Material Datablock** that exists when you open the default Blender scene, containing the default cube object. This data block is simply named **"Material".**

Now, let's say you add a new object to the scene, such as an **Ico Sphere.**

1) In the **Material** Properties section, you'll initially only see the **New** Button. Clicking this button generates a new datablock named **"Material.001."** Both the **"Material"** and **"Material.001"** Datablock results in the default gray color being applied.

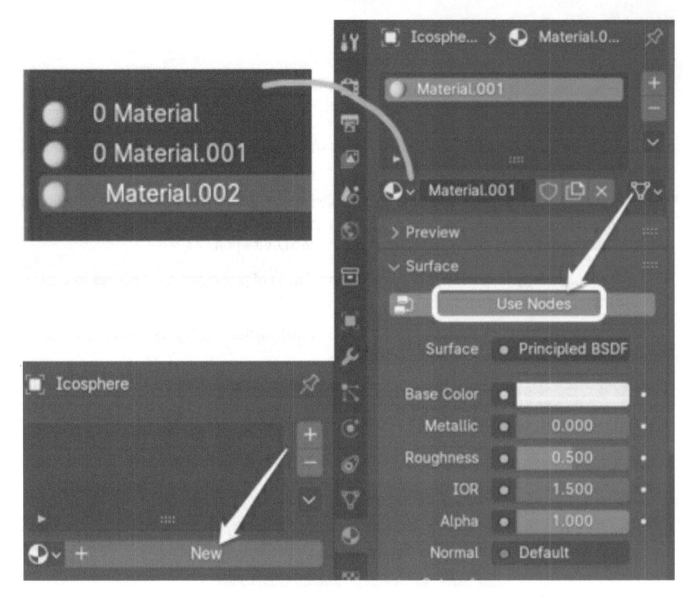

2) recall that to view color in the 3D Viewport when in **Solid Viewport Shading** Mode, you need to deactivate the **Node** System.

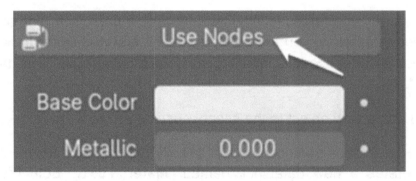

The previous discussion has shown that when a new object is added to the scene and the **New** Button in the **Material** Properties is clicked, a new **Material Datablock** is automatically generated. However, you can also manually create new **Material Datablocks** by selecting either the Cube or the UV Sphere in the 3D Viewport.

3) Hint: you need to have an object selected in the 3D Viewport to display **Material** Properties in the **Properties** Editor.

4) To streamline the process of manually creating new datablocks, ensure that the default Cube object is selected in the 3DViewport. This will cause the **Properties** Editor under **Material** Properties to show the default **Material Datablock** named **"Material"** as - signed to the **Material Slot**, resulting in the default gray color of the cube.

5) To manually create a new Material Datablock, simply click the **New Material** Button. This generates a **Datablock** named **Mate- rial.001**, which is then assigned to the Material Slot.

The Material Cache will display two datablocks, which are Material and Material.001 which then generate the default gray color.

6) Subsequently, clicking the **New Material** Button again results in the creation of a third Datablock, named **Material.002. Datablock Material.002** again generates the default gray.

7) To customize the color, cancel the **Node System** and select each **Datablock** from the **Material Cache.** Then, click the **Base Color** bar and select a **color** from the **color picker.**

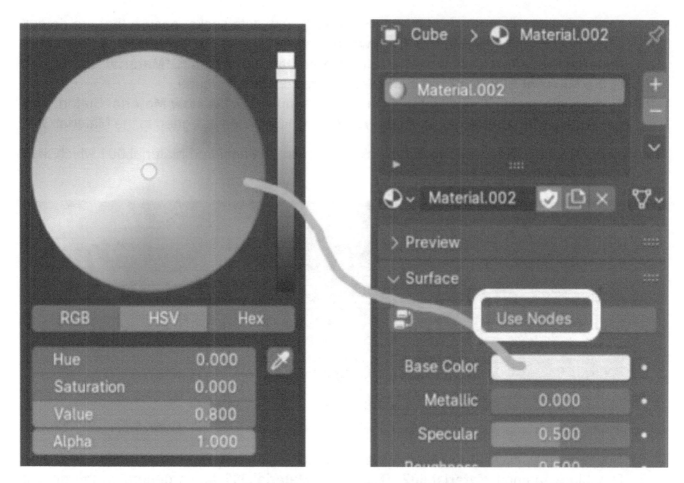

As **colors** are allocated to each Datablock, the **Cube** Object in the 3D Viewport reflects the equivalent color. When new objects are added to the scene, they originally appeared in the 3D Viewport with the default gray color. In the **Properties** Editor, **Material** Properties section, only the **New Button** is visible.

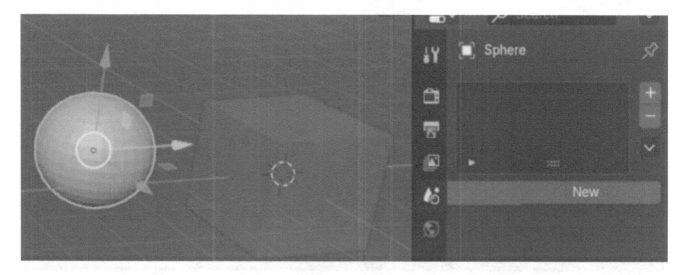

8) To assign a color without using the New Button, you can select a **Datablock** from the **Material Cache** (e.g., O **Material.001 - red**). Choosing "**0 Material.001**" generates a **Material Slot** and assigns the **Datablock** to it, resulting in the **Sphere** being colored **red**.

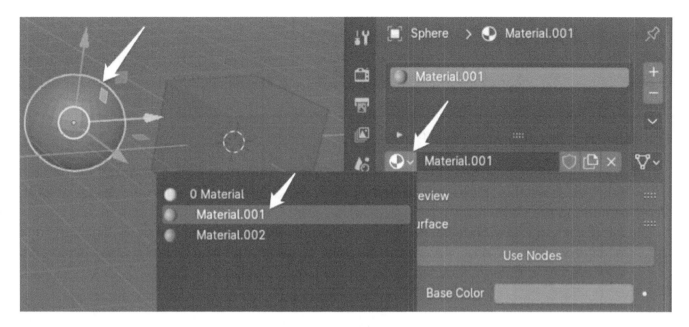

When Datablocks are created and stored in the **Material Cache,** they can be assigned to new objects added to the scene through **the Material Slot.**

Recall that the Material Cache is specific to the Blender File you're working on. Add it ion ally, each object has only one Material Slot. Select-ing a Datablock from the Cache assigns that Datablock to the Slot, thereby applying it to the selected object.

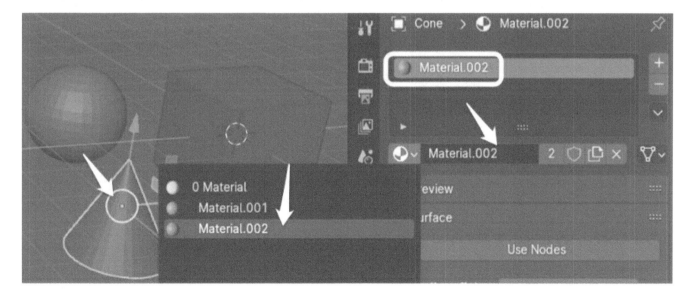

MULTIPLE DATABLOCK ASSIGNMENT

Material Datablocks stored in the Material Cache are versatile and can be applied to any object or even specific parts of an object. For in- stance, individual faces of a cube can be colored differently.

Following the previous instruction, let's say the Cube Object has been assigned the Material Datablock, Material.002, resulting in it being colored blue. Meanwhile, the Material Cache contains additional datablocks named Material (red), Material .001 (green), and Material.002 (blue).

UTILIZING MULTIPLE MATERIAL SLOTS

When datablocks are chosen from the Cache, they're allocated to a Material Slot linked with the chosen object. To incorporate multiple data blocks for diverse colors, you employ multiple Material Slots.

For instance, let's begin with a new Blender file.

1) Select the default **Cube** in the 30 Viewport. In the **Properties** Editor, **Material** Properties, you'll observe the **"Material"** datablock from the **Cache,** assigned to the **Material Slot,** rendering the **Cube** gray.
2) Next, click the **New Material** Button to create new **Material Datablocks**, and assign each a different **Base Color**. As each datablock is generated and given a Base Color, it's allocated to a Material Slot, thus altering the Cube 's color.

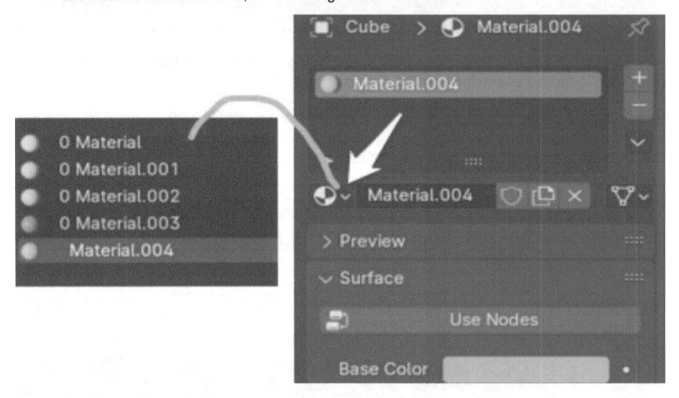

In the Cache, selecting **"0 Material"**(gray) maintains the Cube's gray color.

3) Now, switch to **Edit Mode** in the 30 Viewport Editor. With the **Cube** selected, deselect all **vertices** (left-click in the Viewport), and in the Viewport Header, switch to **Face Select** Mode.

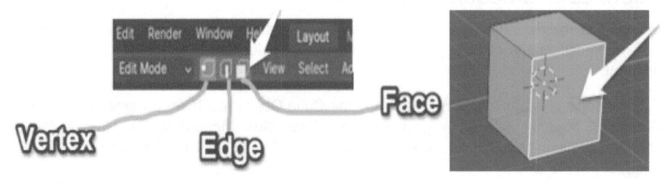

4) In the **Properties** Editor, **Material** Properties, try to create a new **Material Slot.** With the Slot selected, open the **Cache** and choose a **Datablock.**

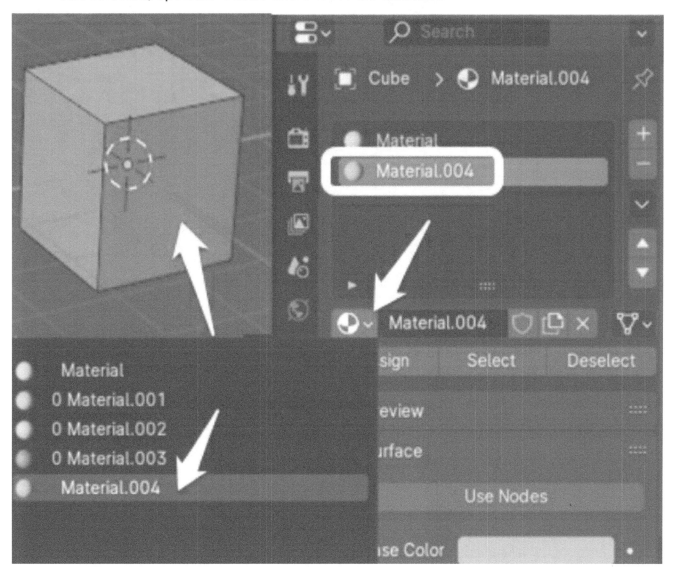

VERTEX GROUP MATERIALS

You can use multiple Material Slots to apply colors to specific areas on the surface of an object, defined by Vertex Groups.

1) For instance, in a new Blender file, you can delete the default Cube Object and add an **IcoSphere.**
2) in **Edit** Mode with **Face Select** enabled you can select faces on the Ico Sphere.
3) Next, in the **Properties** Editor under **Object Data** Properties, you can click the **Plus** Sign to create a **Vertex Group Slot** and then click **"Assign."**

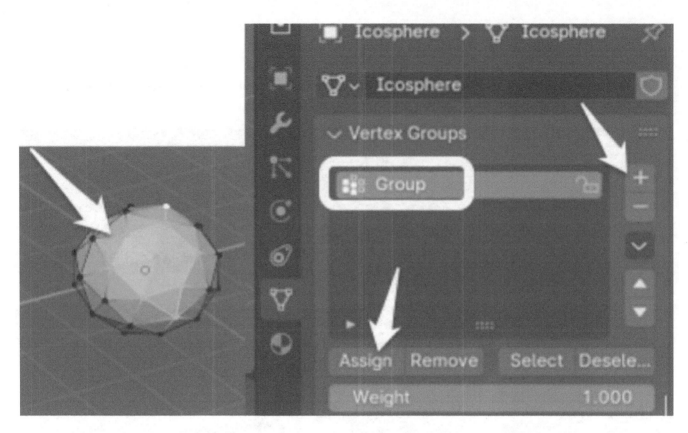

4) In **Object** Mode, with the UV Sphere selected, navigate to the **Properties** Editor and access the **Material Properties** section. Here, you can add a new material with a different base color, as shown below.

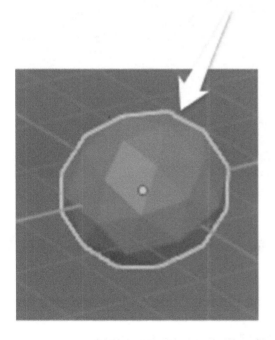

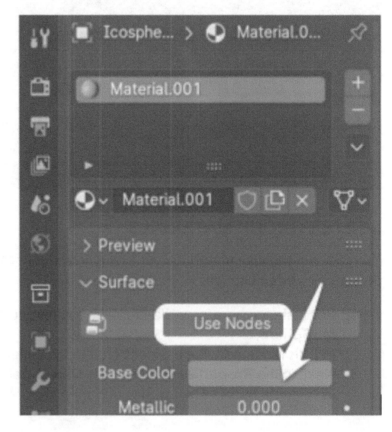

5) Recall to view color in the 30 Viewport, ensure you're in **Material Preview or Rendered Viewport Shading** Mode. Alternatively, you can cancel the **Node System.**

6) Create a new **Material Slot** and allocate a new **Material** with a different **Base Color**. Then, switch to **Edit** Mode. With the **Vertex Group** selected in the **Object Data** Properties and the newly created **Material Slot** selected in the **Material Properties**, click the **Assign** Button to apply the Material from the new Slot to the Vertex Group.

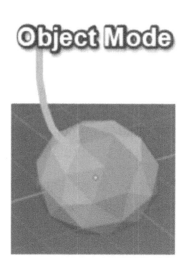

MATERIAL NODES

Hint: to simplify the previous instructions and enable colors to display in the 30 Viewport Editor while in **Solid Viewport Shading Mode**, the **Node System** was sometimes canceled in certain cases.

You can still follow the same method for creating new **Material Datablocks** even with the **Node System** active. However, to observe the color changes in the 30 Viewport, you'll need to switch to Material Preview Mode or Rendered Mode.

To illustrate this, if your focus is just on the **Base Material Color,** you can swap out the default **Principled BSDF Node** in the **Shader Editor** with the **Diffuse BSDF Node.**

Hint: when you replace the **Principled BSDF** Node with the **Diffuse BS**DF Node, the Base Color in the **Surface** Tab is renamed to **"Color".**

CHAPTER 10: WORKING WITH CONSTRAINTS

Constraints are tools that dictate an object's properties like its position, location, and size by linking it to another objector by targeting an

object to another object within a scene. This linkage allows them to function as a cohesive unit while still retaining their traits. Essentially, constraints establish connections between objects.

For instance, consider the **Track to Constraint** applied to a camera object. By setting a target as another object in the scene, this constraint ensures that the camera consistently points toward the designated object, regardless of its movement. Similarly, the Child of Constraint, when assigned to one object (the child) with another object specified as its target (the parent), causes the child to mimic the movements of the parent object. Utilizing a Child of Constraint establishes a parent-child relationship, particularly useful in animating characters.

To apply constraints in Blender, navigate to the **Properties** Editor, under the **Object Constraint** Properties. From there, click on **"Add Ob-ject Constraint"** and select the desired constraint from the dropdown menu.

Blender categorizes constraints into four distinct groups. Throughout this chapter, we'll provide concise definitions of constraints and offer several examples to help you grasp their practical applications.

GETTING STARTED WITH CONSTRAINTS

Constraints can be found in the **Properties** Editor under **Object Constraint** Properties. Upon clicking b a menu displaying constraints across four categories will appear below.

Hint: not all constraints are compatible with every type of object.

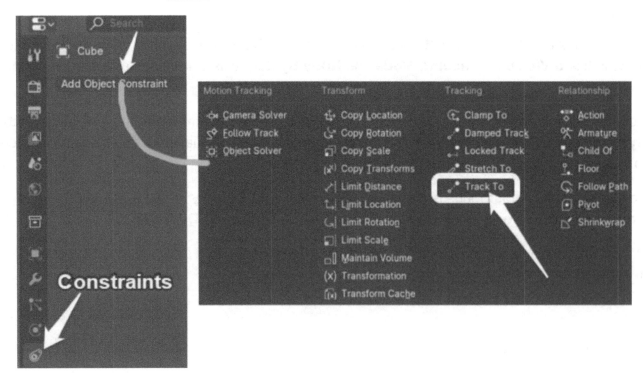

TRACK TO CONSTRAINT

The Track To Constraint serves as a practical introduction to understanding constraints and their application. In a default Blender scene, a camera object is typically aimed at a cube object, to ensure that the cube remains within the camera's view (accessible via Num Pad 0).

However, as the cube moves across the screen during animation, it may shift in and out of the camera's view. To maintain constant visibil-ity of the cube regardless of its position in the scene, the **Track to Constraint** is used, directing the camera's focus toward the cube.

Hint: the default camera is oriented and fixed to face the center of the scene (where the cube is positioned by default).

To utilize the **Track to Constraint** with the default camera, its rotation must first be unlocked. This step is specific to the default camera; newly added cameras in the scene do not require unlocking. **A" Clear Rotation**

1) To unlock the default camera, select it and press **Alt + R**. This resets the camera's rotation, causing it to point downward in the scene. **A" Clear Rotation** " panel will appear in the lower-left corner of the editor as confirmation.

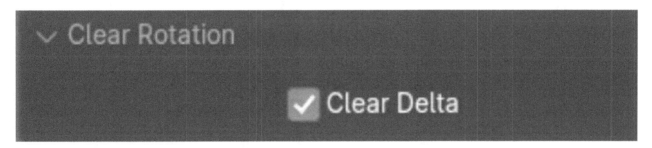

2) Additionally, if any **Delta Transform** Rotation values have been entered in the Properties Editor under Object Properties > Delta Transform Tab, ensure to check **"Clear Delta"** in the **Clear Rotation** Panel to clear any rotation adjustments.

To apply the **Track to Constraint to** the camera, follow these steps:

1) With the camera selected, navigate to the **Properties** Editor and click **"Add Object Constraint."**

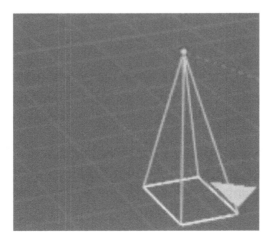

2) From the menu that appears, choose **"Track To". In** the track To panel, locate the **"Targe"** t option and select the desired target ob-ject, in this case, the Cube from the menu

3) Upon selecting the target object (Cube), you 'll see the camera reorients itself, now pointing towards the cube. A broken line connects the camera to the cube, indicating that a constraint has been applied. Pay attention to the Track Axis and Up directions speci-fied in the **Constraint Panel** (Track Axis: **-Z** and Up: **Y**)

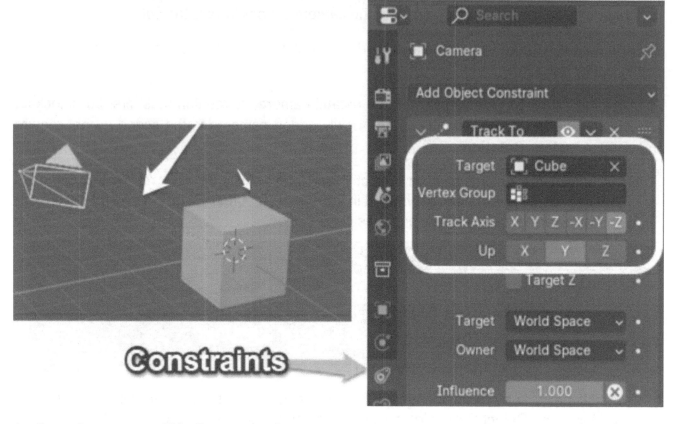

As the cube moves within the scene, the camera will consistently adjust its orientation to keep pointing toward the cube.

Remember, to associate constraints with an object, first select the **object** in the 3D Viewport Edi to r. Then, in the **Properties** Editor under **Object Constraints** Properties, click on **"Add Object Constraint"** and choose the desired constraint from the menu

CONSTRAINT STACK

In certain scenarios, it's useful to utilize more than one constraint simultaneously. When multiple constraints are applied, they form a stack arranged based on priority. This prioritization determines the order in which the constraints are executed. You can alter

1) In the Screenshot below, a **Follow Path** constraint and a **Track to** constraint are both applied to the same object. In this case, the **Track to** constraint takes precedence over the **Follow Path** constraint. To adjust the precedence, simply click, hold, and drag the **dimple** button up or down within the stack.

When working with constraints, it's common to input control values into the **Constraint** Panel to control their functions. You'll find a brief overview of constraint functions in the subsequent sections of this chapter. While many constraints are self-explanatory, detailed expla-nations will be provided for common constraints or where clarity is needed.

TRANSFORM CONSTRAINTS LIST

- ✓ **Copy Location:** causes the object with the constraint to assume the location of the target object.
- ✓ **Copy Rotation:** causes the object with the constraint to replicate the rotation of the target object. As the target rotates, so does the object.
- ✓ **Copy Scale:** Makes the object with the constraint replicate the scale of the target object.
- ✓ Copy Transforms: Function s similarly to the copy location constraint.
- ✓ Limit Distance: Confines the object within a specified distance from the target object, creating a spherical field around the target.
- ✓ **Limit Location:** Confines the object's movement within minimum and maximum distances along a specified axis, relative to either the world center or a parented object.
- ✓ **Limit Rotation:** Restricts an object's rotation around a specific axis within defined limits.
- ✓ **Limit Scale:** Controls the object's scale within defined limits along a specified axis.
- ✓ **Maintain Volume:** Ensures the dimensions of an object remain consistent along a specified axis.
- ✓ **Transformation:** This shows **Properties** Editor using the **Blender Light Preset** Theme.
- ✓ **Transform Cache:** search for the transform matrix from an external file.

163

THE TRANSFORMATIONCONSTRAINT

The Transformation Constraint enables you to govern the location, rotation, or scale of one object, or a segment thereof, by manipulating the corresponding attributes of another object. These attributes can be configured to operate within specific ranges. The object subject to control is termed the Source, to which the constraint is applied, while the other object serving as the controller is referred to as the Target.

✓ To illustrate this, let's consider a scenario with a Cube object and an Ico Sphere positioned within the 3D Viewport Editor, set in Top

Orthographic View (Num Pad 7 for Top Orthographic).

✓ In this setup, the cube will function as the Source object, regulated by the Target sphere. To endorse this, add a **Transformation Constraint to** the cube.

To implement the transformation constraint, follow these steps:

1) Select the **Source** object (the **Cube)**, go to the **Properties** Editor, and access **Object Constraints** Properties.
2) Click **on "Add Object Constraint "** and choose **"Transformation"** under the **Transform** section. Enter the Target object as **"Ico Sphere"**

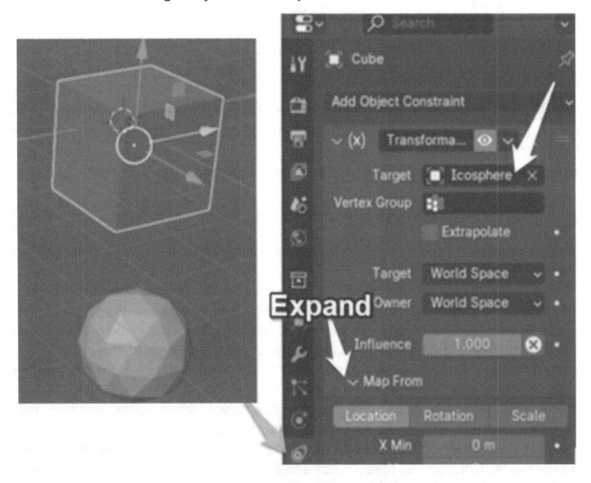

Note the default **Map from** and **Map to Location** options. When Location choices are selected, the principle of operation is to map the sphere's location relative to the cube's location within the specified axis range set in the **Map from** and **Map to** tabs.

3) In this illustration, translating the **Target Sphere** between **Om** and **6m** along the **X**-axis of the scene will influence the translation (location) of the **Cube** between **Om** and **3m** along the **X**-axis. You can observe this effect in the screenshot below.

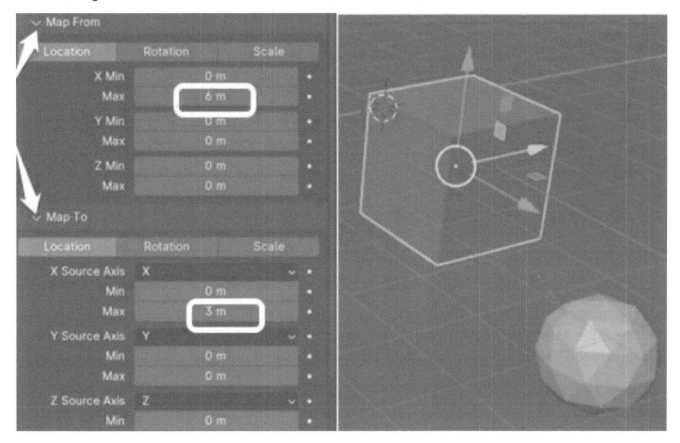

As the Sphere undergoes translation along the **X-**axis, it adheres to the constraint, ensuring that it follows suit. This translation is limited to occurring only when the Sphere is moved within the range of Om to 6m along the X-axis, while the Cube's movement is constrained within the range of Om to 3m.

By specifying the Map from and Map to values in the **Constraint** Properties, the movement of one object is influenced by the movement of another.

Let's consider the example provided:

4) Given the initial setup we used previously and with adjustments made to the values in the **Map from** and **Map to** tabs as shown below. a specific behavior unfolds when the Target Sphere is translated between Om and **6m** along the X-**axis** and the Source Cube shifts in a negative direction towards the X-axis of the scene. When the **Sphere** undergoes translation, the **Cube** shifts to- wards the X-axis of the scene. Note that the Max value is negative **(-3).**

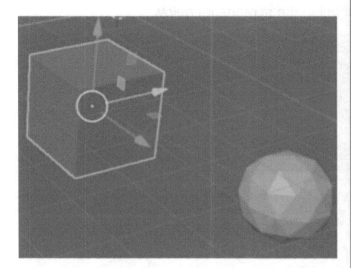
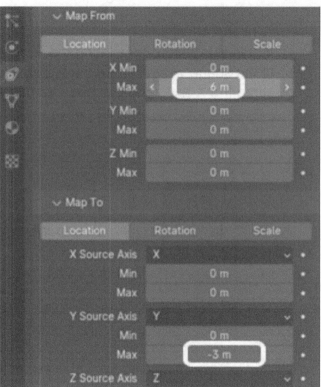

In this adjustment, the **Map From** Location values remain consistent with the previous example. However, the **Map To** Location values are modified, specifically, the Y-axis of the Source is changed to the X-axis, with a minimum of 0m and a maximum of-3m.

To grasp the procedure logically, consider that the **Map from** values dictates the behavior of the Map to values.

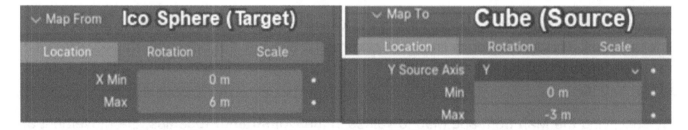

To activate a constraint, you have to input minimum and maximum range values for Location, Rotation, or Scale in both the **Map from** Axis and Map to Axis channels.

As shown above, a range of Min 0m to Max 6m is specified in the Map from Location channel. In the Map to section, a range of Min 0m to Max **-3m** is entered in the **Y**-axis of the Source object, with the crucial distinction that the Y-axis is controlled by the X-lo cat ion channel. Let's further solidify the concept by illustrating how the translation of the Sphere influences the rotation of the Cube.

5) Hint: the screenshot below displays the objects in **Top Orthographic** View, where the **Z**-axis of the scene is perpendicular to the computer screen. The **Cube** rotates around its **Z**-axis.

6) The **Map from** Location range is configured for the **Y-axis** of the Target **Sphere (**Min Om - Max 4m), indicating that the Sphere must undergo translation along the **Y-axis** of the viewport.

7) Conversely, the Map to range is set for rotation around the **Z-axis** of the Source **Cube**, with the rotation being controlled by the val-ues specified in the **Map from the Y-**axis range. Rotation: (O to **45**).

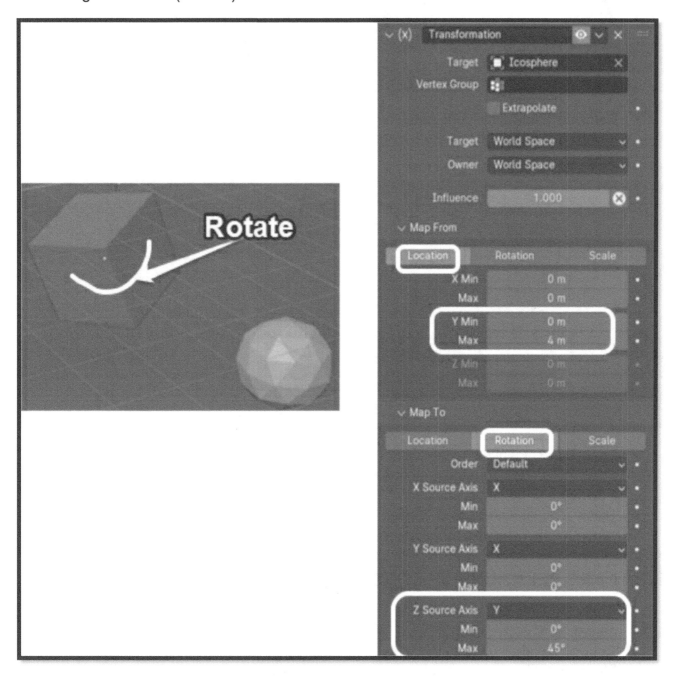

Please note the utilization of both positive and negative values when configuring range limits.

EXPLORING TRACKING CONSTRAINTS

✓ **Clamp To:** This constraint locks the object's position to a designated curve. By pressing **G** and moving the mouse, you can shift the **cube** along the curve.

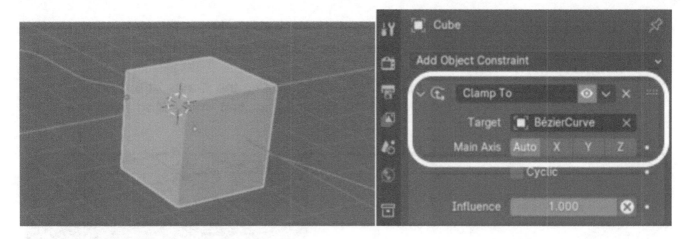

✓ **Damped Track:** This constraint ensures that one local axis of the object consistently aims toward the target object. For example, the local Z-axis of the cone points towards the cube.

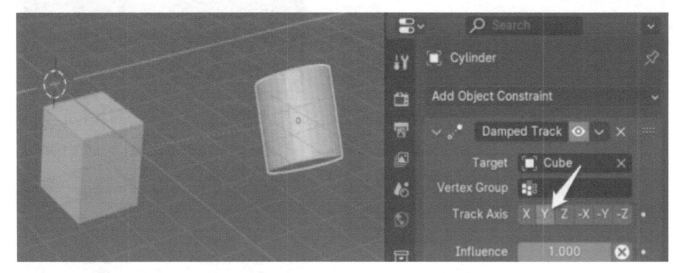

✓ **Lock Track**: Identical to the Damped Track Constraint, but with more axis control.
✓ **Stretch To:** This constraint elongates the object toward the target object or compresses it away from the target.
✓ **Track To:** As introduced earlier, the Track to Constraint ensures that the object continuously faces the target object, regardless of their respective positions.

WHAT ARE RELATIONSHIP CONSTRAINTS?

✓ **Child Of:** This constraint forces an object to follow a not her object designated as its parent.
✓ **Action:** We shall discuss this later
✓ **Floor:** Permits the target object to block the movement of the object. For instance, a sphere descending in a scene won't pass through a plane set as the target object.
✓ **Follow Path:** Animates the object to follow a nominated curve path as the target. This constraint also incorporates the feature to rotate and bank as it follows the curve. It can also duplicate objects along the curved path.
✓ **Pivot:** Makes the object leapfrog to the opposite side of the target object along an axis between them. When you enter **Offset** values, it can adjust the location on either side of the axis.

✓ **Shrink wrap**: Locks an object onto he surface of another mesh object that has been set as the target.

THE ACTION CONSTRAINT

The Action Constraint enables you to control one object's action by manipulating another object's action. An action can involve **transla-tion, rotation, or scale**. For example, the rotation of a sphere controls the translation of a cube.

To demonstrate, animate the cube to move from minus three Blender units to plus three units on the **X**-axis within **100** frames. You can do that with the listed steps:

✓ Enable the **Auto keying** button and then press **Spacebar** and G to move the cube from left to right within the 3D Viewport Editor.
✓ Restrict the movement within **-3 to 3** within X-Axis.

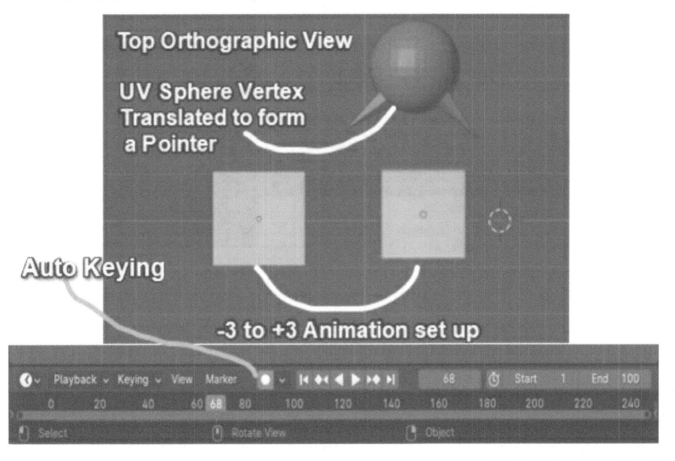

Place the animation at **Frame 1**, then, select the **cube** and add a **Relationship Constraint** of **type Action** in the **Properties** Editor under **Constraints** Pro per ties. Configure the values using the Constraints panel as shown below.

Note: When setting the action as **"CubeAction"** in the **Action** Tab, the cube jumps from minus three to minus six. During playback, the cube moves from minus six to the center of the scene. Rotating the sphere about the Z-axis translates to the cube. The Z-rotation of the tar- get (UV sphere) dictates the cube's action within the limits of the animation, with the Z-rotation (target range) constrained from 0 to 90°.

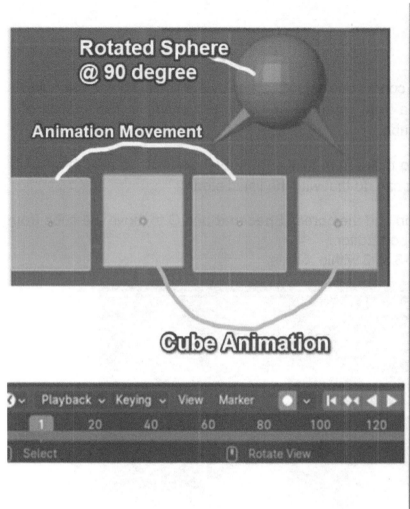

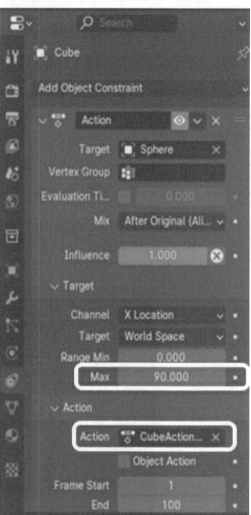

The action range spans from Frame **1** to Fra me **100** of the animation. Upon applying **the Action Constraint**, the cube animation adjusts to range from minus 6 to O in the 30 Viewport Editor.

Additionally, you can set an animation to rotate the UV Sphere. Consequently, when the cube is translated (moved), the sphere rotates accordingly.

THE SHRINKWRAP CONSTRAINT

The Shrinkwrap Constraint might be better termed as the **Mesh Surface Lock**, as long as the object locks to the surface of another mesh object designated as the Target.

It's important to differentiate this constraint from the **Shrinkwrap** Modifier. To illustrate how the constraint operates.

1) Within the default Blender scene, In the Front Orthographic view **(Num Pad 1),** add a **UV Sphere** and an **Icosphere.** Scale the UV Sphere down significantly and arrange the objects as shown below.
2) Zoom in on the view toob serve a close-up of the UV Sphere and the surface of the Icosphere.

170

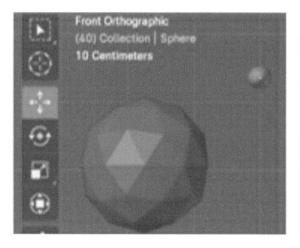 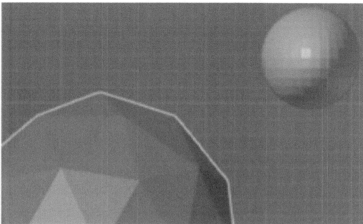

3) Select the **UV Sphere**, go to the **Properties** Editor, and access **Object Constraints** Properties. Add a **Shrinkwrap Constraint**.

4) In the **Shrinkwrap Constraint** panel, click on the **Target** selection bar and choose the **Icosphere** as the Target. Hint: the default Mode in the **Shrinkwrap** pan el is set to **"Nearest Surface Point."**

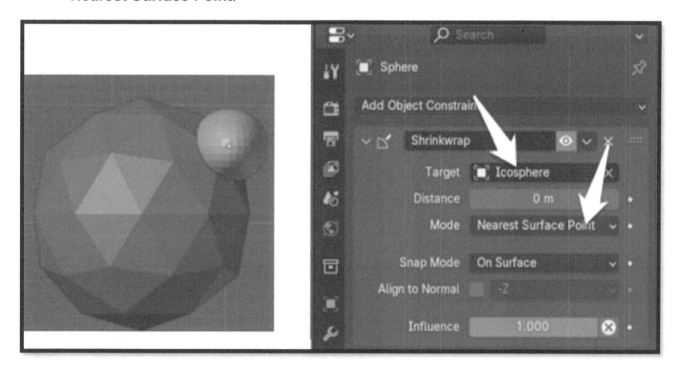

With the Mode set to **"Nearest Surface Point"** and the **Target** set to **Icosphere,** the UV Sphere moves to the surface of the Icosphere at the nearest point to its original position as shown above. The **"Nearest Surface Point"** mode is one of four available options.

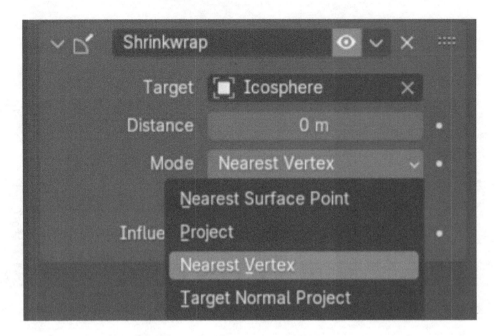

5) When **"Project"** mode is selected, the Constraint panel includes buttons for **Axis X, Axis Y, and Axis Z**, they include both positive and negative values.

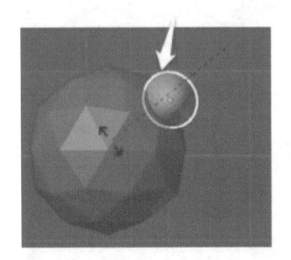

In the Shrinkwrap Constraint Properties, Note that the Mode is set to **"Project"** and the Space is set to **"Local Space"**

In this context, **"Local Space"** implies that the projection is dependent on the local axis of the selected object.

The illustration below displays the disparity in the local axis of the UV Sphere when it is rotated. Since the local **Minus- Z-Z Axis** is desig-nated as the **Project** Axis in the **Constraint** Properties, the sphere is projected to the nearest point on the target projection plane along its Minus-Z Axis.

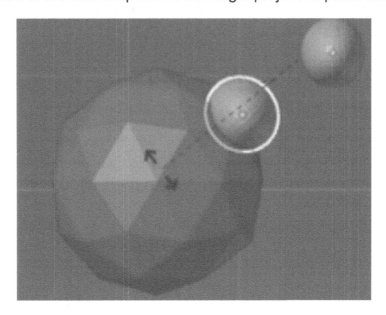

6) When you press the **R** key and rotate the sphere, the direction of the **Minus Z** Axis changes, causing the sphere to move along the surface of the target projection plane.

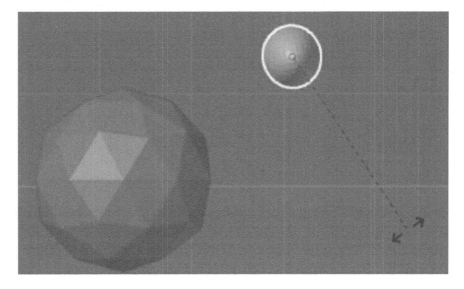

FOLLOW PATH - EXTRUDE/BEVEL

The Follow Path Constraint enables an object to trail along a Curve Path that is designated as Target when animated. This constraint in-cludes a "Follow Curve" option, causing the object to rotate and bank as it travels along the path during animation.

Moreover, the Follow Path Constraint can be used to produce shapes by extruding a profile along the length of a Curve Path. You should understand that a three-dimensional shape is defined by its cross-section profile and the curvature of its length.

See Chapter 6, specifically the section on **Modeling** from a Curve, which involves a manipulation of a Bezier Curve to generate a Mesh Ob-ject, resulting in a regular shape. This procedure demonstrates how irregular shapes can be formed by generating a profile along a curved path.

THE CROSS-SECTION PROFILE AND LENGTH

The illustration below shows a cross-section profile and a length curve.

✓ The Cross Section Profile is a Nurbs Circle, which has been reshaped in Edit Mode. Similarly, the Length Curve is a Bezier Curve, which has been scaled up and reshaped in Edit Mode (as discussed in Chapter 6). The Length Curve(**Bezier Curve**) will act as the centerline of the extrusion.

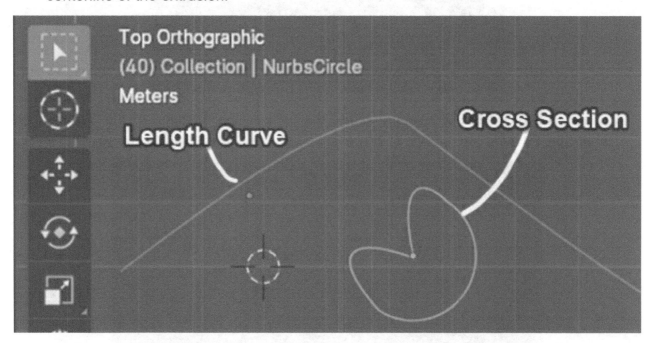

✓ To execute the extrusion along the Length Curve, the Cross Section must be properly oriented and positioned at the beginning of the Length Curve. Notably, the illustration above displays the 3DViewport Editor in **Top Orthographic** View (Num Pad 7), aligning the Local Axis of the Profile with the Global **XY Axis** of the Scene.

To orient and position the Cross Section for extrusion, follow these steps:

1) Select the **Cross Section** (Nurbs Circle - Modified), and in the **Properties** Editor, **Object Constraint** Properties, add a **Follow Path** Constraint. Designate the **Target** as **Bezier Curve.** Consequently, the Cross Section moves to the start of the Bezier Curve

174

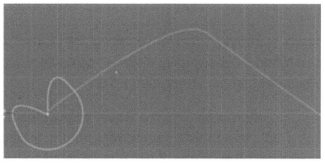

In the **Follow Path** Constraint, the default **Forward Axis** is **Y** (highlighted in blue), while the **Up Axis** is **Z**, aligning with the **Local Axis** of the **Cross Section**. To achieve proper extrusion along the Length Curve, the Cross Section must be positioned at right angles to the Length Curve.

2) To rotate the Profile, go to the **Properties** Edi to r, then the **Follow Path Constraint** section. Change the **Forward Axis to Z** and the **Up Axis to Y**. However, this adjustment doesn't affect the orientation until you enable **"Follow Curve"** in the Constraint panel.

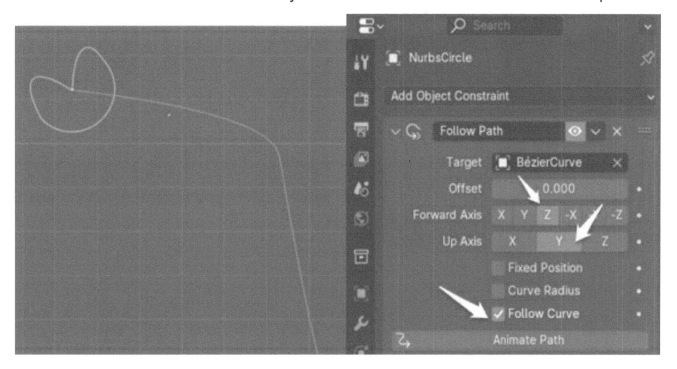

When "Follow Curve" is enabled, you'll notice the Profile positioned at the end of the Curve Path. Its Local Axis aligns with Y Up and Z For- ward, approximately in line with the Curve Path.

Hint: extruding the Profile along the Curve to create the 3DShape is unconventional. This operation is essentially a Bevel operation con- ducted within the Bezier Curve's Object Data Properties in the Properties Editor.

3) Before applying the **Bevel** to the **Bezier Curve**, ensure to scale down the **Nurbs Circle**. It's important to acknowledge the disparity in orientation between the Nurbs Circle Profile and the profile of the final object.

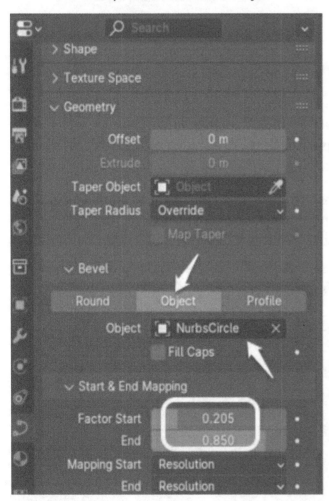
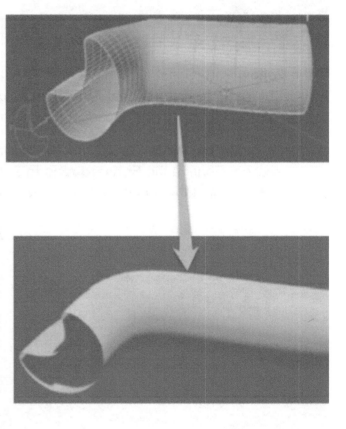

CHAPTER 11: SHAPE KEYS AND ACTION EDITORS

The Shape Keys and Action Editors are tools that allow for precise control over the shape of an object or the pose of a character. By inserting key frames in the animation timeline, users can easily adjust these aspects. While armature control handles are useful for posing char-acters broadly, finer details like facial expressions or finger movements require more detailed control. Considering the complexity of manipulating individual vertices throughout an animation, the Shape Key and Action Editors offer slider controls for efficiently managing mesh shapes or character posing. Specifically, the **Shape Key** Editor facilitates the manipulation and animation of vertices, while the **Ac-tion Editor** enables the creation of object movement and scaling animations.

SHAPE KEYS EDITOR

In the Shape Key Editor, you can manipulate vertices or vertex groups. You can find the Shape Key Editor in the header of the Dope Sheet Editor.

To illustrate its functionality,

1) begin with the default Blender scene, delete the **cube,** and introduce a **basic plane** object consisting of four vertices. Then, position the scene in the top orthographic view (Num Pad **7**) and zoom in for better visibility.
2) Beneath the **3D Viewport** Editor lies the **Timeline** Editor. Alter the **Timeline** to the **Dope Sheet** Editor. Within the **Dope Sheet** Editor, locate the **dropdown** menu in the header labeled "**Dope Sheet**" and switch it to "Shape Key Editor". The **summary** is only visible when you change back to the Dope Sheet from the Shape Key Editor.

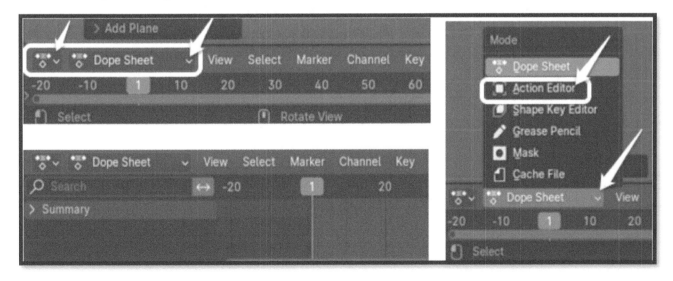

When the Shape Key Editor is selected, it functions similarly to a basic animation timeline, it has frame numbers along the top horizontal bar. Additionally, a vertical blue line represents the time line curs or within the editor.

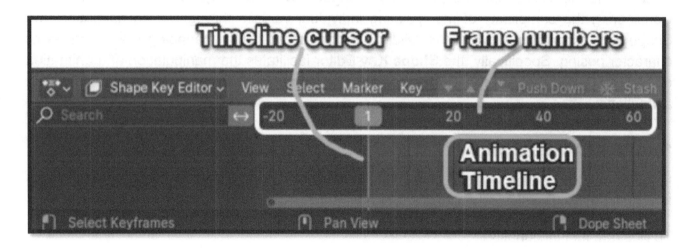

In the Shape Key Editor, you'll find key sliders that enable you to adjust the shape of an object within the 3D Viewport Editor. These sliders constrain the movement of the object's vertices within set minimum and maximum limits. By manipulating the vertices using these slid-ers at different frames along the animation timeline, you can create a dynamic shape-change animation for the object.

These key sliders are specific to the currently selected object. To begin, you'll need to establish a basis key in the Properties Editor within the **Object Data** Properties under the **Shape Keys** tab. This basis key serves as the foundational master key or data block for subsequent keys associated with the selected object.

ADDING A BASIC KEY AND KEY 1

To add a basis key:

1) choose the **plane** in the 3D Viewport Editor. Then, navigate to the **Properties** Editor and access the **Object Data** Properties tab. Within this tab, locate the **Shape Keys** section and click on the **plus** sign icon as shown below.

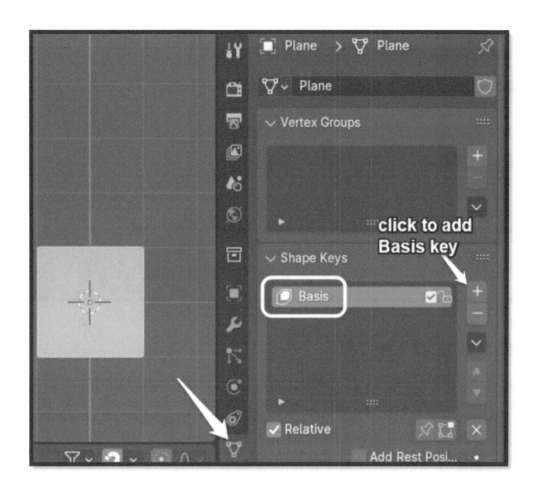

This action will expand the tab, revealing the insertion of a basis key. As a result, the Dope Sheet Summary will be visible in the Shape Key Editor at the bottom of the screen.

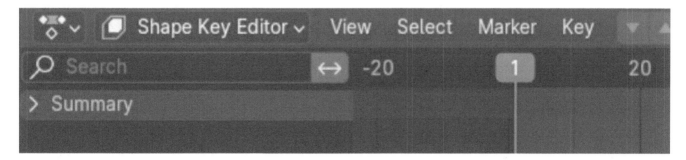

2) To include a key slider, navigate to the **Properties** Editor and access the **Shape Keys** tab in the Object Data Properties, then click on the **plus** sign icon again, and **Key 1** will be generated. Subsequently, in the **Dope Sheet Summary**, you'll observe the display of Key 1.

SETTING MOVEMENT LIMITS

To create movement limits, begin by placing a key slider. Then, define the boundaries for control.

1) In the 3D Viewport Editor, position the mouse cursor and switch to Top Orthographic View (Num Pad 7). Enter Edit **Mode** by press-ing Tab.
2) Deselect **vertices** by clicking in the viewport. Choose a **single vertex** and relocate it by dragging it using the **G** key and **mouse** (this marks the maximum movement limit, as shown below.

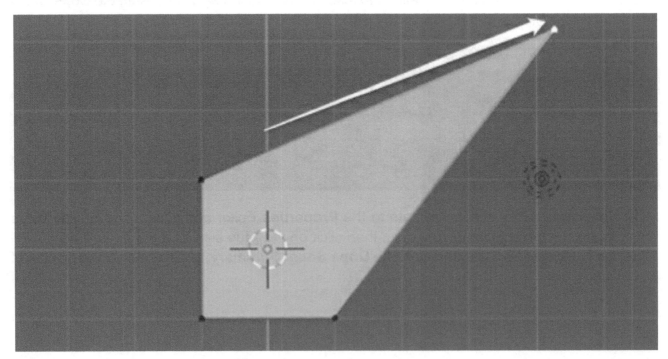

3) Return to **Object** Mode by pressing **Tab**. The vertex will revert to its original position, shifting the vertex in **Edit** Mode effectively establishes the movement limits.

4) Next, in **Object** Mode within the **3DViewport** Editor, manipulate the **Key 1** Slider in the **Dope Sheet** of the **Shape Key** Editor. Slide it to the right (**0.000 to 1.000**), as shown below, then revert it to **0.000**. Observe the plane's shape alteration in response within the 3D Viewport Editor.

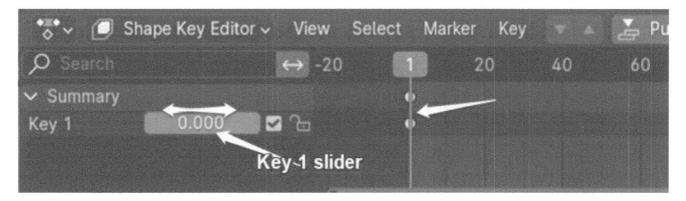

INSERT KEYFRAMES

To insert key frames, simply drag the slider within the Shape Key Editor and return it to the position of 0.000. This action automatically creates a key frame in the timeline. The key frame appears at the location of the timeline cursor (represented as a blue line in Frame 1) and is denoted by small orange diamonds as shown above (**in the Setting Movement Limits section**). These key frames are visible both in the Shape Key Editor and the Timeline Editor.

Hint: dragging the slider only moves the selected vertex within the predefined limits that were specified. The slider value ranges from 0.00 to 1.000, representing the initial position to the maximum limit of movement.

To insert a second key frame, follow these steps:

1) First, navigate the blue line **cursor** within the **Shape Key** Editor to another frame, such as Frame **40**.

2) Adjust the **Key 1** Slider until the vertex in the 3DViewport Editor reaches the desired position (in this case, **0.818**). Once positioned correctly, release the mouse button to set the key frame as shown below. Maintain the slider at the chosen value for the second key frame. Return the blue line cursor to **Frame 1.**

As you move the blue line cursor, you'll notice the shape of the plane in the 3D window transforming, with the vertex shifting from its initial position to the designated location at Frame **40**.

Sometimes achieving the precise vertex position can be challenging when dragging the key slider. It requires a delicate touch to reach the exact location you desire.

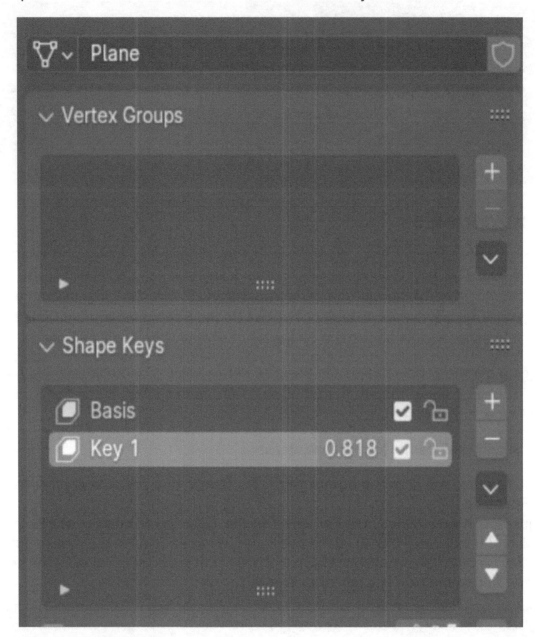

DELETING KEYFRAME

To delete a key frame and start afresh,

1) position the blue cursor within the Shape Key Edi to r at the desired frame in the Timeline.
2) Right-click on the value bar within the Properties Editor under **Object Data** Properties within the **Shape Keys** tab. From the menu that appears, select **"Delete Key frame."** It's worth noting that the relative value bar imitates the Key 1 slider.

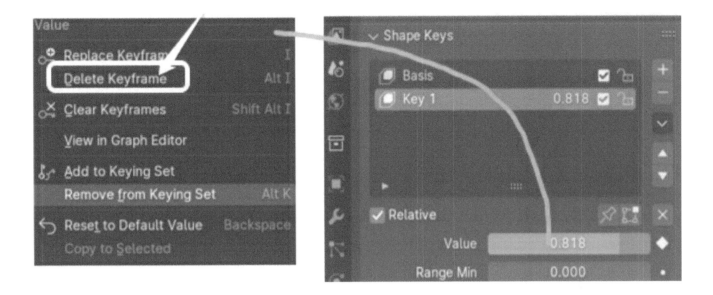

ADDING A NEW KEYFRAME

To add a new key frame,

1) simply adjust the **Key 1** slider once more. For precise values, double-click on the **slider** and input the desired **value** manually.

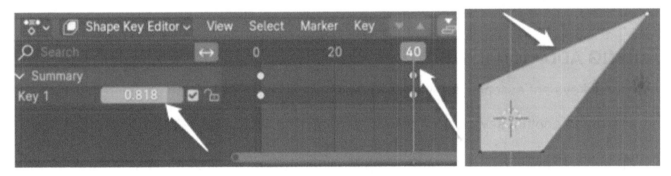

2) After inserting a key frame, there's no need to return the timeline cursor to frame **1**. Instead, move it to another frame, adjust the Key **1** slider accordingly, and another key frame will be automatically added. Repeat this process as needed for multiple key frames.

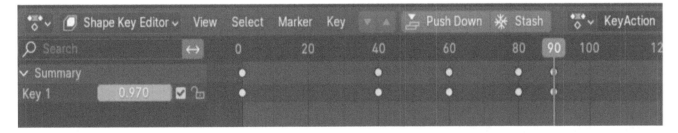

EXPLORING ANIMATION

So far, key frames have been incorporated within the **Shape Key** Editor Timeline. You can navigate the timeline by dragging the **blue line** cursor to observe the corresponding shape changes in the 3DViewport Editor. To view the animation playback, access the **Timeline** Editor and hit the play button as shown below.

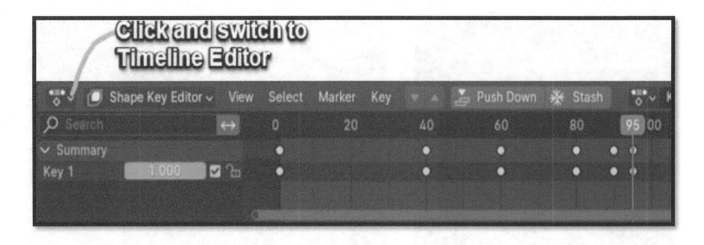

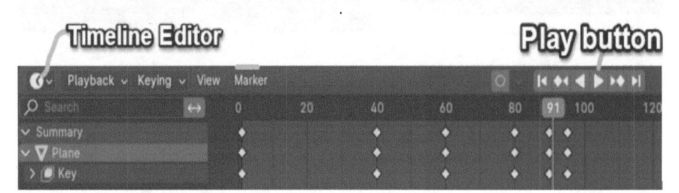

ADDING ADDITIONAL KEYS

Additional keys are essential for animating other parts of the mesh, such as different vertices.

1) To add another key, position the cursor within the **Shape Key Editor** Timeline at Frame **1.**
2) In the **Properties** Editor, under **Object Data** Properties within the **Shape Key** tab, click on the plus sign (+) to introduce **Key 2.**
3) Next, switch to **Edit** Mode within the 3D Viewport Editor, select a **distinct vertex** on the plane, and relocate it to define its move-ment limit.
4) Return to **Object Mode**, and you'll notice that **Key 2** has been added to the Dope Sheet Summary.

Repeat this key framing process using Key 2 for the new vertex.

5) After inserting **key frames** for the new vertex controlled by Key **2,** adjusting the timeline editor cursor or playing the animation will display both vertices moving simultaneously as the animation plays.

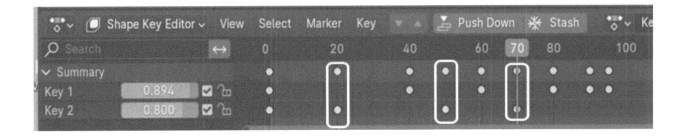

USING ACTION EDITOR

The Action Editor facilitates control over the translation, rotation, and scale of the object in general.

1) Start by selecting the **object i**n the 3D Viewport Editor. From the default screen layout, having the 3D Viewport Editor and Timeline Editor positioned at the bottom of the screen, switch the **Timeline** Editor to the **Dope Sheet** Editor.

2) To illustrate this transition, change the **Dope Sheet** mode to the **Action Editor** mode as shown below.

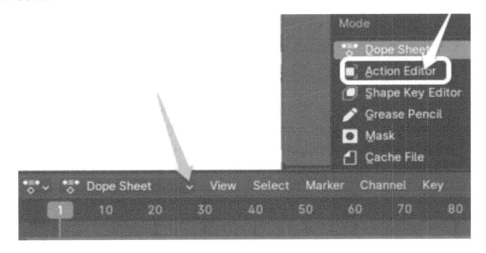

3) Within the 3D Viewport Editor, press Num Pad **7** to change to **Top Orthographic**, and click to choose the default **Cube**. With the mouse cursor positioned in the 3D Viewport Editor, press the I key and select **"Location, Rotation & Scale"**.

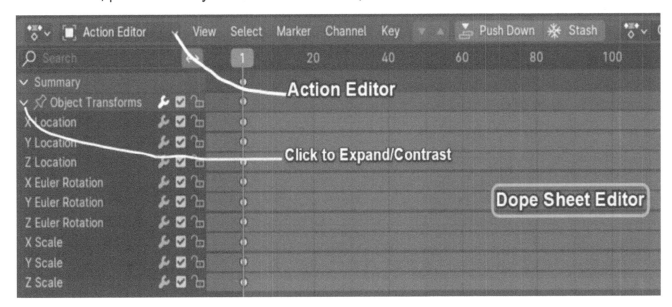

185

This action inserts a key frame at **Frame 1** and generates an object transforms summary in the **Action** Editor.

4) Click on the **disclosure triangle** icon preceding "**Object Transforms**" to reveal the key frame entries for **X, Y,** and **Z** locations, rotations, and scales. In the **Action** Editor header, click on "**View**" and enable "Show Sliders". This action displays sliders for each key frame component.

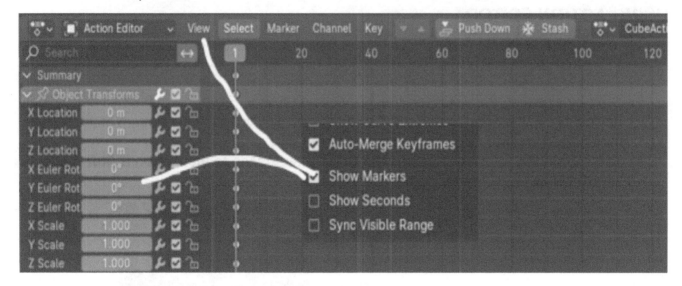

5) To manipulate the **cube** in the 3D Viewport Editor, adjust the **sliders** by repositioning the cursor (represented as a blue line) in the **Action** Editor to a different frame as shown below. Once you've moved the slider to the desired position, right-click on the new value and select "**Replace Key frame**." This action ensures the changes are applied to the specific frame.

When you position the cursor at another frame and modify the slider values, new key frames are automatically inserted. This process re-sults in the creation of an animation, as each key frame represents a different state of the cube over time.

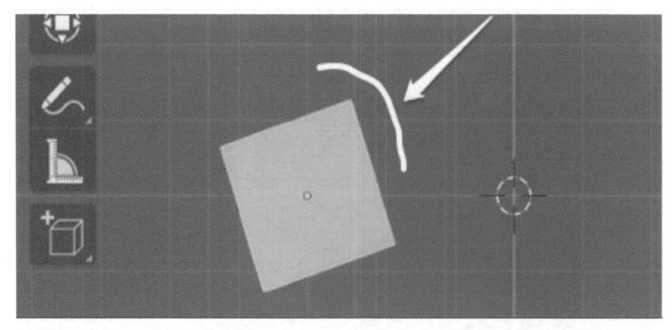

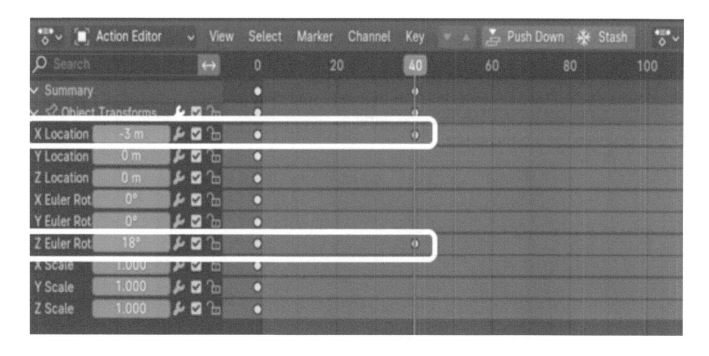

PUTTING THE SHAPE KEYS AND ACTION EDITOR INTO USE

The previous examples introduced the basic functionality of Shape Keys and the Action Editor, but they may not seem particularly thrilling, leaving you wondering about their practical applications. To explore further into these topics, let's embark on the following exercise:

1) Start by creating a new Blender scene. Remove the default **cube** and add a **monkey** object, often referred to as **"Suzanne"**.
2) Press Num Pad **1** to position the scene in **Front Orthographic** view and zoom in to focus on **Suzanne's** head, filling the 3D Viewport Editor.
3) Switch to **Edit** Mode and carefully select the **vertices in the face**, following the visual guidance provided in step **(4).**
4) Adjust the **Timeline** Editor to the **Dope Sheet** Editor mode, then switch to the **Shape Key** Editor mode. In the 3D Viewport Editor, position the **monkey** object to ensure the **mouth** is visible.

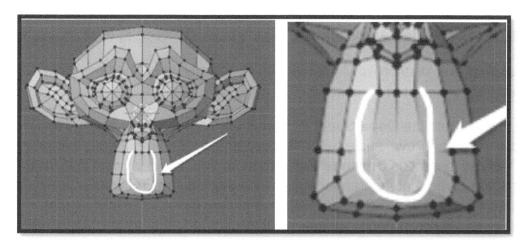

5) Switch to **Object** Mode, go to the **Properties** Editor, navigate to **Object Data** Properties, and access the **Shape Key** t ab. Click on the plus sign to introduce a **Basis** Key. In the

Action Editor header, click **"New"** to generate a summary in the **Dope Sheet**. Additionally, click on the plus sign (**+**) again within the **Shape Keys** t ab to insert Key 1.

Now, imagine Suzanne's laughter coming to life. While in the 3DViewport Editor,

6) press Num Pad 3 to switch to **Right Orthographic** View and enter **Edit** Mode. Utilize the widget to manipulate the selected **vertices**, moving them to the left to create a slight protrusion of Suzanne's lips.

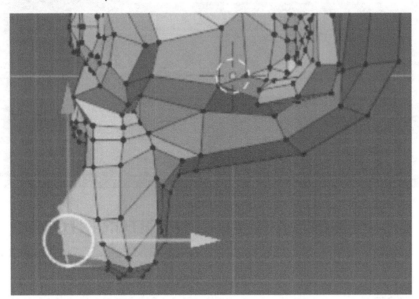

7) Next, switch to **Front Orthographic** View and scale the selected vertices up along the **Z** axis and slightly along the **X** axis. Using the widget, move the vertices upward.

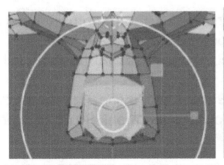 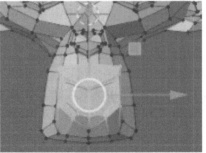

Finally, switch back to **Object** Mode, **observing** the vertices revert to their original location.

During the scaling and location adjustments, you've effectively defined the movement limits for **Key 1** for each of the selected vertices.

8) Now, switch from the **Dope Sheet Action** Editor to the **Shape Key** Editor. In the editor's header, click on **"View"** and enable **"Show Sliders**. "Expand the summary and move the **Key 1** slider to witness **Suzanne's mouth** in motion. Keep in mind that moving the slider inserts a key frame at the frame number indicated by the timeline cursor's position in the animation timeline (Frame 1), as illustrated in step (9).

9) If you prefer **Suzanne** not to begin laughing immediately at the start of the animation, simply move the cursor down the track in the **Timeline** before adjusting the slider (around Frame 20 as shown below.

Keep in mind that Blender defaults to a 250-frame animation in the Timeline. If you position the Shape Key Editor cursor beyond this range, it won't have any effect unless you adjust the **End Frame** value in the Timeline Editor Header.

10) To add a **series** of key frames to the animation, move the cursor to Frame **40**. Adjust the key **slider** and leave it in position; this action inserts a key frame at Frame **40**. Then, move the cursor to Frame 50 and repeat the process as many times as desired as shown below. Return to **Frame 1** in the **Timeline** Editor and play the animation. You'll observe Suzanne's mouth moving as the animation unfolds.

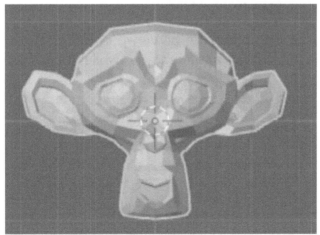

To add more dynamic action to the animation, let's have Suzanne turn her head while she laughs.

11) First, zoom out in the 3D Viewport Editor and press Num Pad 2 to switch to User Perspective View. In the **Action** Editor Header, click the **"New"** button. With the timeline cursor positioned at **Frame 1,** press the **I** key and select **"Location, Rotation & Scale"** to insert action key frames.

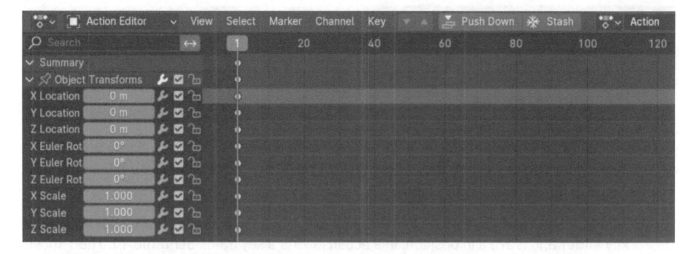

12) Next, move the cursor to Frame **100**, coinciding with the end of the **Shape Key** animation. Adjust the **Z Euler Rotation** slider to **45** degrees (keep in mind that Blender measures rotation in Euler units).

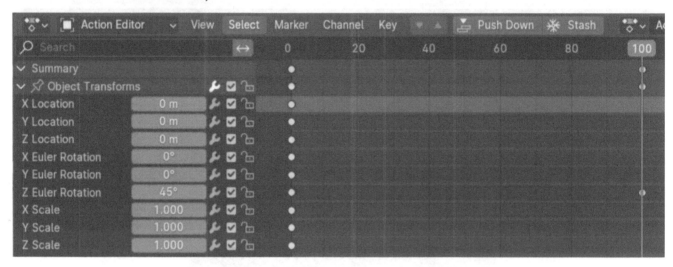

13) Now, press **Num Pad 0** to place the 3DViewport Editor in **Camera View** and play the animation. You'll see Suzanne's mouth moving while she turns to face the camera.

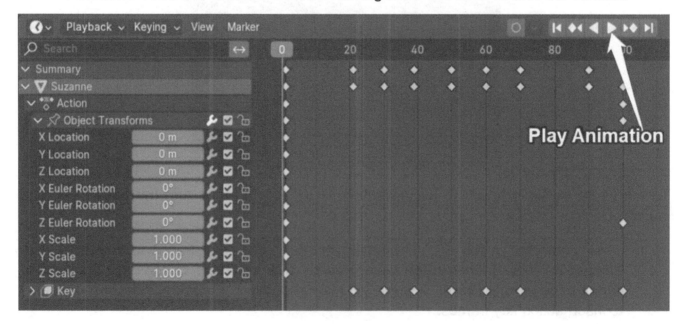

Play Animation

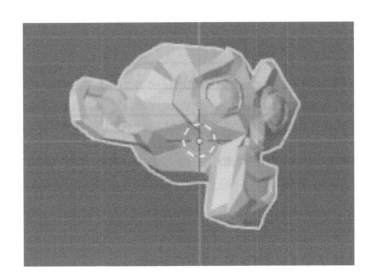

CHAPTER 12: INTRODUCTION TO PARTICLE SYSTEMS

Particle Systems serve as versatile tools for simulating various effects such as dust, fire, clouds, and smoke, as well as for generating hair, grass, fur, and other strand-based objects. When applied to an object, a Particle System prompts the object to generate and emit particles.

These particles can be configured to display in numerous ways, allowing for the creation of static and animated patterns or even models of characters. For instance, a swarm of insects or an army of soldiers can be used to simulate.

In Blender, particles manifest as small spheres on the computer screen, emitted from an object. To emit particles from an object, a particle system is added to it, followed by running an animation sequence.

When a particle system is added to an object, it comes with default settings that allow it to function independently. However, to create specific particle effects, one needs to adjust the settings.

Particles essentially represent points on the computer screen that can be customized to appear in various ways. However, these particles, or points, do not render when the scene is rendered. Instead, they are reconfigured to display as other objects in the scene, which are then rendered.

Typically, a particle system is employed to generate multiple particles. In fact, it's common to create thousands of particles, probably orig-inating from various objects within the scene.

Next, we shall show you a few straightforward instructions for running a particle system.

SETTING UP DEFAULT PARTICLE SYSTEM

To begin setting up a default particle system, start by opening a new scene in Blender.

1) Remove the default cube object and replace it with a **UV sphere**.

Particles can be emitted from the vertices, faces, or volume of a mesh. Opting for a UV sphere offers a suitable number of vertices and faces from which particles can be emitted. Maintain the default values for the sphere as they appear in the Properties Editor.

2) With the **UV sphere** selected, navigate to the **Properties** Editor and access the **Particle** Properties. Click on the plus (+) sign to add a particle system as shown below.

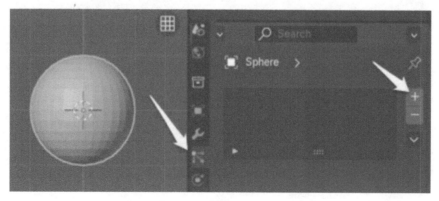

The Particle Properties panel opens, revealing the tabs that control the system. Blender automatically generates a default particle system for the UV sphere, as illustrated below.

Take note of the default type, which is set to **"Emitter"** under Particle Settings. An alternative system, **"Hair"**. The **"Hair,"** type offers unique functionality, which will be explored further in this chapter.

Hint: when a particle system is created, it is specific to the selected object in the 3D View port Editor.

3) The order of **tabs** in the **Properties** Editor, such as the **Emission** Tab panel, is simply for convenience. There is no specific order of priority. Tabs are organized vertically on the left-hand side of the panel. You can adjust the order of **tabs** by clicking and drag-ging the dimpled area in the upper right-hand corner of each tab.

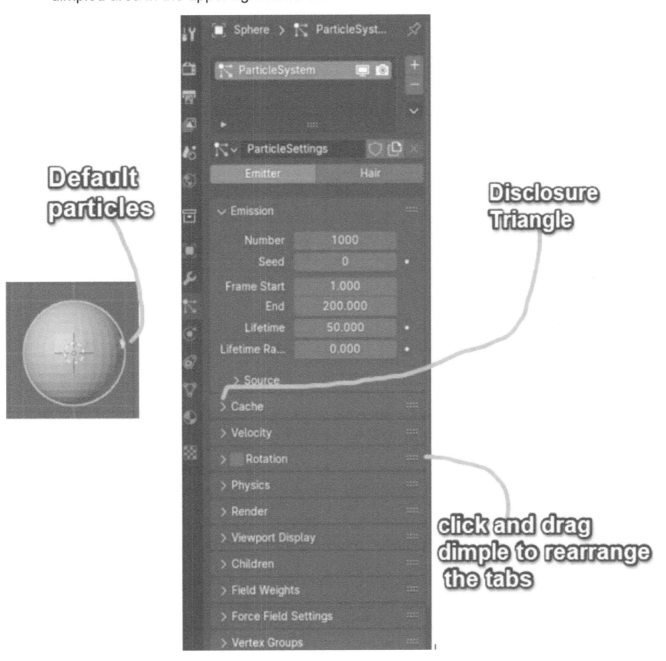

Particles will only be visible in the 3D Viewport Editor when an animation sequence is initiated

193

by activating the **"Play"** button in the **Timeline** Editor or by dragging the **timeline cursor** (the vertical blue line) to a frame in the animation. By default, particles are repre-sented as small white spheres.

4) To witness the default particle system in operation, simply press the **"Play"** button in the Timeline Editor to initiate an animation sequence. The screenshot below displays particles being generated.

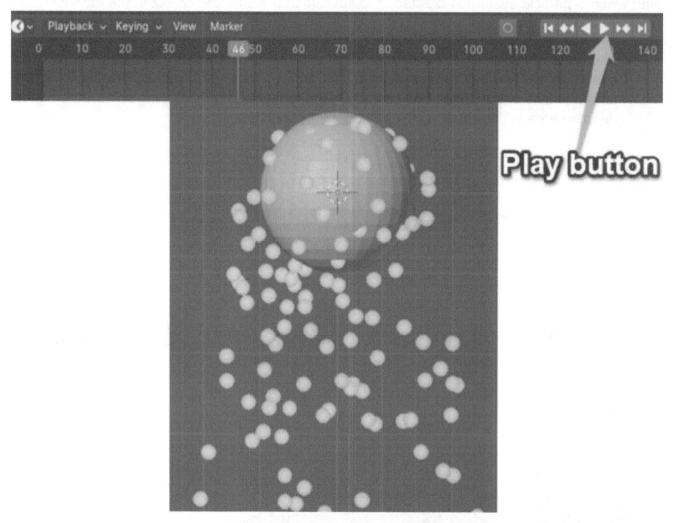

Hint: The **Timeline** Editor is typically displayed across the bottom of the screen, The blue line, known as the Timeline Cursor, moves as the animation progresses.

With the **Emitter** object selected (in this case, the UV sphere), the animation will play, revealing particles as small white spheres being emitted and descending toward the bottom of the screen as shown above.

5) In the Timeline Editor, the animation runs for **250frames** before looping. Press the **"Esc"** key to stop the animation.

6) To shift the animation to Frame 46, use the right arrow keys on the keyboard (with the mouse cursor positioned in the **Timeline** Editor), or click and drag the blue line cursor in the Timeline Editor, or right-click on Fra me 32 in the Timeline Editor. This will display the particles as they appear in Fra me 46.

The provided example illustrates the application of a simple particle system. The particles emitted from the UV sphere descend down- wards due to the gravitational effect applied.

7) You can observe this effect by accessing the **Scene** Properties in the Properties Editor. In the **Scene** Properties under the **Gravity** tab, click on the checkbox next to **"Gravity"** to toggle off the gravitational effect, as shown below.

8) position animation in the **Timeline** Editor to Frame **1** and replay it, simply navigate back to **Frame 1** and press play. When you replay the animation, you'll observe particles emitted from the UV sphere dispersing in all directions away from the sphere as shown below.

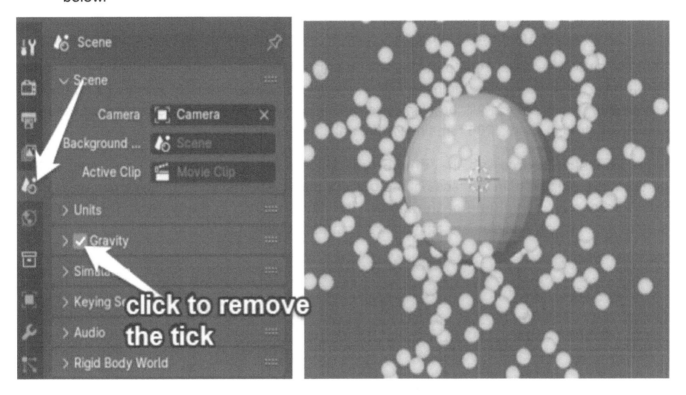

Hint: the particles have a set duration of display, known as the **"Lifetime,"** before they disappear. This time is configured in the Emission Tab, as shown below.

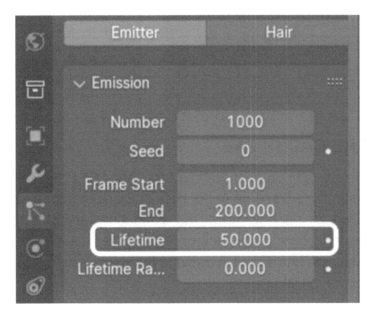

195

EXPLORING EMISSION AND EMISSION SOURCE TABS

Let's consider the details of the Emission Tab first

- ✓ **Number**: Specifies the total number of particles to be emitted throughout the animation.
- ✓ **Seed:** Introduces randomized emission variations.
- ✓ **Frame Start:** Determines the frame number at which particle emission begins.
- ✓ **End:** Specifies the frame number at which particle emission ceases.
- ✓ **Lifetime:** Sets the duration in frames for which emitted particles will be displayed. The default value is 50 frames.
- ✓ **Lifetime Randomness**: Introduces random variations in the lifetimes of particles.

With the default settings, **1000** particles will be emitted throughout the animation, which spans **250** frames as shown in the Timeline Editor. Particle emission starts at Frame **1** and ends at Frame **200**. Each particle will be displayed for a lifetime of **50** frames, ensuring that the last particle emitted at Frame **200** remains visible until the end of the animation.

In the **Emission Source** Tab, the "**Emit From**" option is set to **"Faces."** This means that particles are emitted from the faces of the object's mesh. Alternatively, particles can be emitted from **vertices** or the **volume of the mesh**. The other settings in the **Source** Tab control the se-quence in which particles are emitted, as illustrated below.

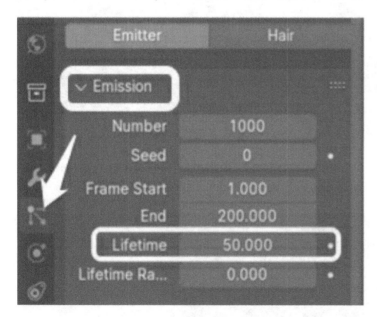 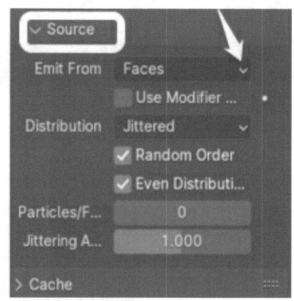

WORKING WITH THE CACHE TAB

In the Cache Tab, there's a vital process outlined for managing particle system data. When a particle system is played for the first time in the default Blender Scene, the computer computes the necessary information for each frame of the simulation (animation) and stores it in RAM (memory). Upon subsequent plays, the computer re computes the information, incorporating any changes made to the settings, and stores it again in RAM. However, if the Blender file is closed without saving, this information is gone.

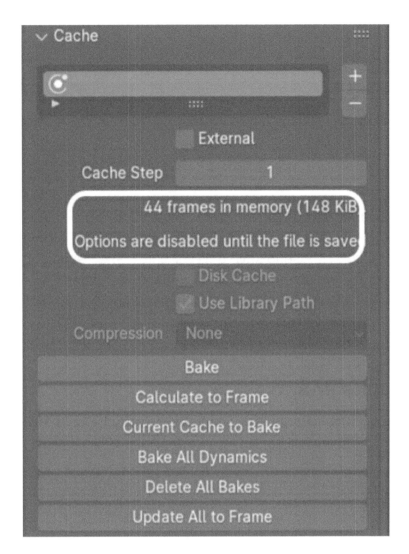

For complex particle simulations, storing data in RAM can consume a significant amount of memory, impacting computer performance. Thus, it's advisable to save the Blender file as soon as you can. Once saved, you have the option to save the simulation to a cache, freeing up memory.

Hint: the options in the **Cache** Tab are disabled until the file is saved. Essentially, this means you cannot save to the cache until you have saved the Blender file. Once the file is saved, check the "**Disk Cache**" option, which saves the data to the cache using the **Library (Lib)** Path.

When you play the simulation with **Disk Cache** enabled, a blendcache_Cache file is created and placed in the same directory as the. blend file. After enabling **Disk Cache** and saving the file, you'll notice a red line at the bottom of the Timeline Editor, indicating the saved data. With default settings, playing the simulation generates a solid line, as data is recorded for each frame of the default 250 frames. In the di- rectory where the Blender file is saved, you'll find the blendcache_Cache folder holding 250 BPHYS files.

In the default simulation with 250 frames, there are 250 BPHYS files. The number of files increases with the length of the simulation. To conserve space in the cache, especially for lengthy simulations, you can choose to save data for only some frames by adjusting the **Cache Steps** value. Increasing this value, such as to 10, means that data is recorded for every tenth frame. Therefore, for the default 250-frame simulation, the number of BPHYS files in the cache would be reduced to 26 (25 divisions, with a frame at each end). While increasing the Cache Steps saves space on the hard drive, it may result in a decrease in simulation quality.

USING THE VELOCITY TAB

In the Velocity Tab, you'll find settings that dictate the direction and speed of particle emission, as shown below.

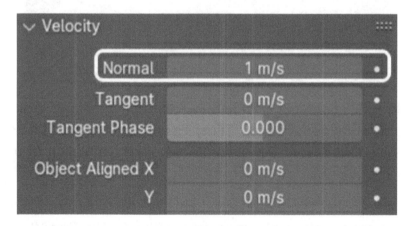

- ✓ **Normal** This provides particles with an initial velocity that is perpendicular (at right angles) to the point of origin.
- ✓ **Tangent:** Sets the velocity to be parallel to the face.
- ✓ **Tangent Phase and Object Alignment:** Both control the emission direction between normal and tangent orientations.

PARTICLE DISPLAY

A particle usually appears as an object added to a scene. To illustrate this,

1) Place a plane object and a mon key object in the scene in the User Perspective. Scale down the monkey object significantly and posi-tion it to one side as shown below.

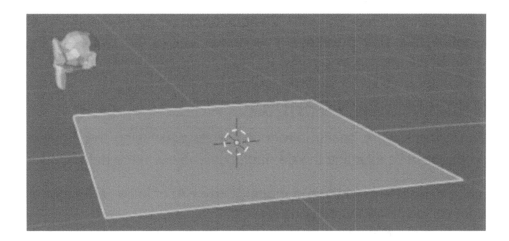

2) Select the plane object in the 3D view port editor and apply a **Particle System**. Disable **gravity** in the **Scene** settings.

3) In the Emission tab, reduce the number to 5 (emitting only 5 particles) for the particles of the plane, and adjust the end value to **10** (the **5** par tic les will be emitted within **10 frames)**.

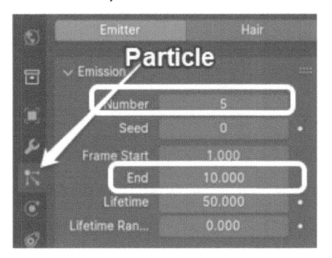

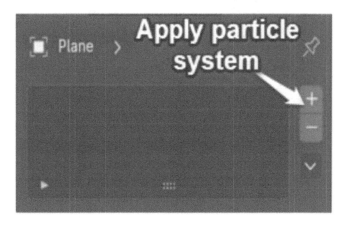

4) In the **Render** tab, modify the **Render As** to **"Object"**. Selecting" **object**" introduces an object tab. Click **on 'instance object** ' and choose **'Suzanne'** (the m**onkey**).

5) Play the animation in the timeline editor (you can stop at frame **50** since the particles will only display for 50 frames).

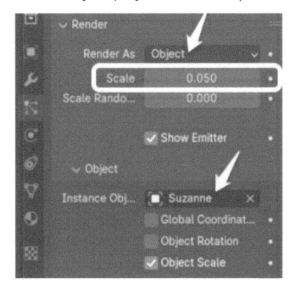

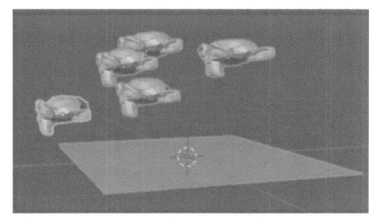

6) Position the timeline cursor at frame 30and zoom in on the plane. If you observe closely, you will notice **five tiny monkeys** posi-tioned above the plane. In the **Render** tab, increase the Scale section as desired.

USING PARTICLE EMISSION OPTIONS

Particle Emission options were briefly introduced while discussing the Source Tab. To gain clarity on these options, let's examine the de- fault cube object in the default 3D viewport editor.

1) Set the cube to display in wireframe mode (**Z** key + **4**) or lo ca t e the button in the header (upper right-hand side of the screen).
2) Access the **Particle Emission** options in the **Properties** Editor, in the **Particle** buttons under the **Source** Tab as shown below.
3) You will see the default cube with the default particle system applied at **Frame 1**, showing one particle. The default setting for Emit From in the Source Tab is set to Faces.

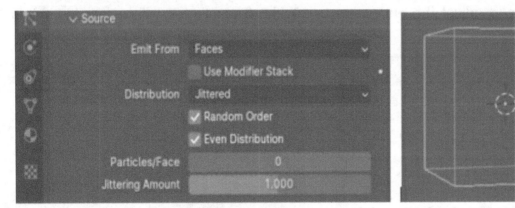

4) The screenshot below shows various Emit options from Faces, to Verts and Volumes.

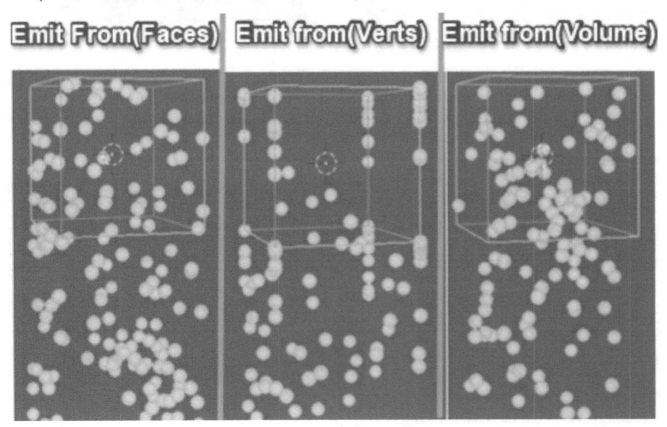

5) When in **Wireframe** Display Mode, particles are emitted from the **volume** with a **Velocity** normal set to **0.00** and **Gravity** disabled. These particles gather within the volume of the cube as shown below.

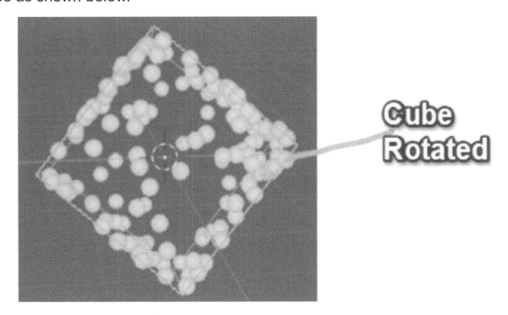

To further buttress emission options,

1) let us start by replacing the default **cube** in the 3D viewport editor with a **UV sphere.** The sphere offers a significantly greater num-ber of vertices and faces from which to emit particles. Disable **Gravity** in the scene settings.

The order of particle emission is managed in the **Properties** Editor, in the **Particle** buttons under the **Emission Source** Tab (Hint: the **Source** Tab only appears when the Emission Tab is opened).

2) By default, particles are configured to emit from faces in a random order(distribution).

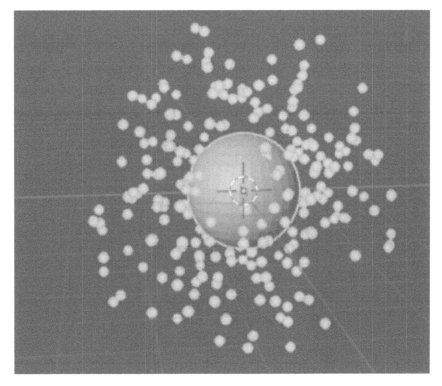

3) In the **Source** Tab, deselect **"Random Order"** and play the animation again.

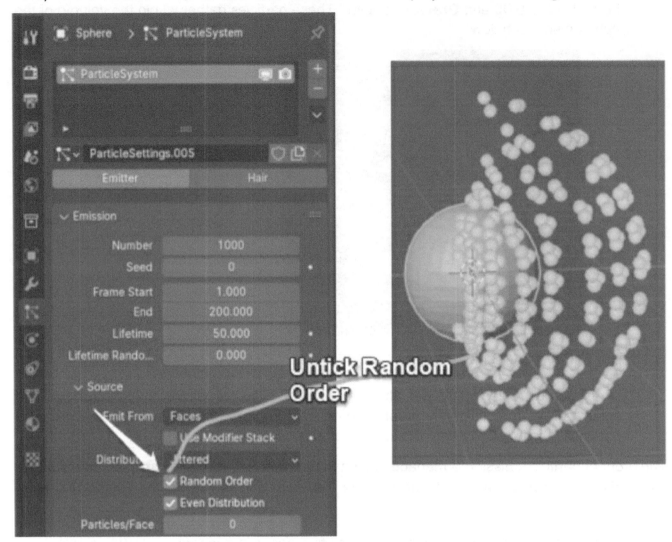

4) Since the 3D viewport editor defaults to the **User Perspective** view, it might be challenging to discern the effect of removing the random option. Press 7 to switch the view to the **Top Orthographic** view, then press 1 to switch to the **Front Orthographic** view. With the timeline editor cursor shift to frame **50**, you'll observe an organized arrangement of particles. In both views shown below, the particles are emitted from faces.

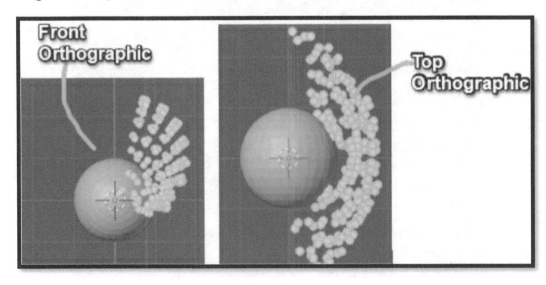

5) By changing **Emit From** to Vertices in the **Source** Tab at the same **frame 50**, the array of particles becomes even more orderly.

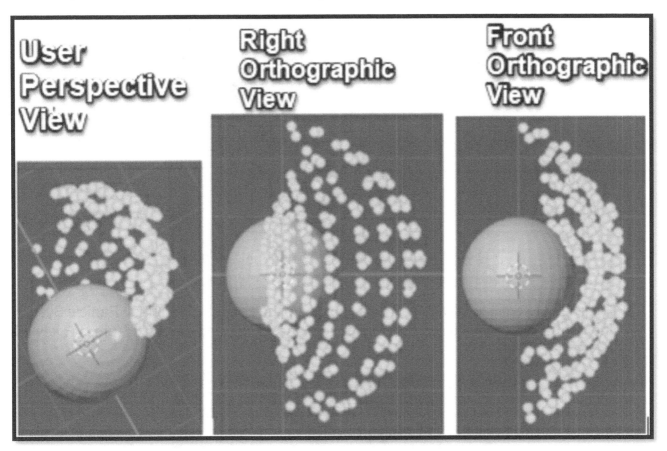

Occasionally, you might want to restrict particle emission to a specific area of an object's surface. In such cases, particles would be emitted from an area defined by a vertex group.

USING NORMALS

Particle effects can be achieved by using various shaped objects as particle emitters and adjusting the **Normal** values in the **Particle** prop-erties, as discussed when we are examining (The **Velocity** Tab- **Normals**).

1) Start with a **plane** object in the **3Dview port** editor and apply a **Particle System.** When the animation plays in the timeline editor, particles are emitted from the face of the plane and descend in the scene because of the gravitational force.
2) In the **Velocity** tab, extend the normal value to **5.000** and replay the animation. You'll notice that the particles go up from the sur- face of the plane before descending.

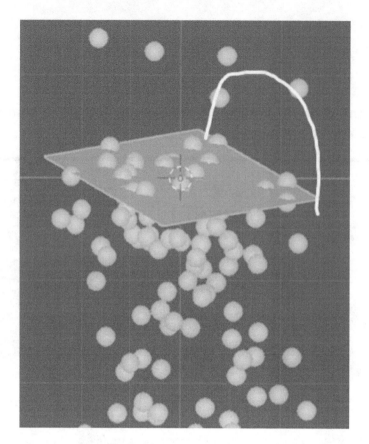

3) Particles are emitted from the surface **Normal** to the **Face**. In the default Particle System, the normal direction is upwards. Rotate the plane **45°** around the X axis (press **R** key + **X** key + **45**).

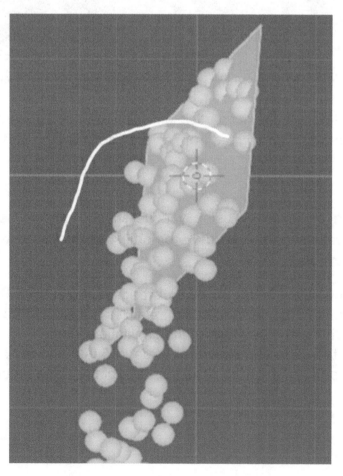

Even with the plane rotated, the particles continue to be emitted normally to the face of the plane. The direction of the **Normal** is relative to the **Face.**

You can visualize the direction of **Normals** in two ways.

- ✓ In **Object** Mode, click on **Overlays** in the header and enable **Face Orientation**. In the default scene, the upper surface of the plane displays blue, indicating the positive direction for emission. By rot at in g the view, you'll notice that the underside of the plane is displayed red, indicating the negative direction (Keep in mind that you can input positive and negative values in the Velocity Tab, which alters the emission direction. However, this doesn't change the color display on the surface.

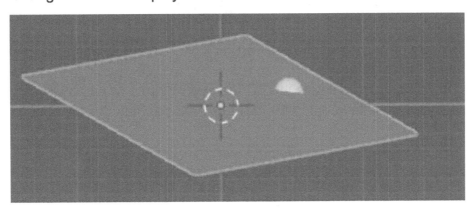

- ✓ In **Edit Mode Overlays** (located at the bottom of the panel), you'll find **Normals** as shown below. Click to toggle the hide and display of normals in the 3D View Editor. Use the Size slider to adjust the size of the normal display

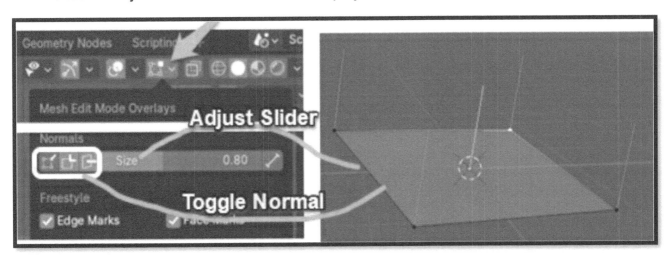

Note: Changing the Size value doesn't affect the velocity for emission.

Understanding how particles will be emitted from an object allows you to set up a particle display. For example, create a flat disk object as illustrated in the screenshot below:

1) Selecting a **Circle** Object in **Edit** Mode. Press the **E** key (**Extrude but DON'T move the mouse**). This duplicates the vertices. Then, scale the duplicated vertices inward.

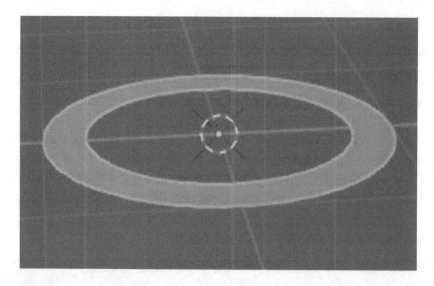

2) Disable **Gravity** by accessing the **Properties** Editor, then navigating to the **Scene** buttons and selecting the **Gravity** tab.
3) With the **Disk Object** selected in the 3D Viewport Editor, switch to **Object** Mode and add a **Particle System** while keeping the de- fault values. Play the animation in the Timeline Editor.

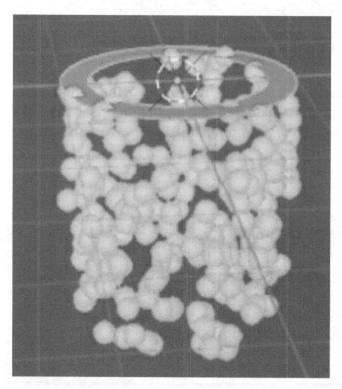

Particles will be emitted from the faces of the disk and descend along the bottom of the screen, even though gravity is turned off. Particles are emitted with a default starting velocity of **Normal = 1.** You can view the **Velocity** value in the **Particle** Proper ties under the Velocity Tab.

4) When you enable **Normal** visualization, as explained earlier, you'll notice that the Normal direction points downward, indicating the descent as shown below. If you need to change the direction swiftly while in **Edit** Mode, head to the **Screen Header**, click on the **Mesh** Button, then choose **Normals**, and **Flip** as shown below. Keep in mind, that you cannot play the **Animation** in Edit Mode.

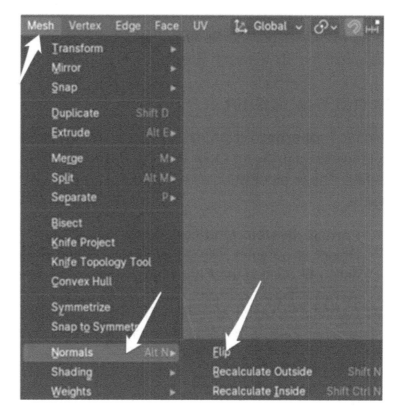

Here's how to create a Particle Effect:

5) Begin with the disk illustrated above, Flip the **Normals** upward to ensure proper orientation.
6) In **Object** Mode, navigate to the **Source** Tab and switch **Emit From**: from **Faces** to **Vertices**. Ensure that **Random Order** is unchecked.
7) Adjust the **Lifetime** value to **200** under the Emi ss ion Tab. When you replay the animation, you'll observe the Particles being emitted progressively from the mesh Vertices, coiling around the disk, eventually forming a spiral pattern. These **Particles** are arranged in short columns.
8) In the **Velocity** Tab, set **the Emitter Geometry' s Normal** to 0.000 and **Object Alignment Y** to **1.000.**
9) If you re play the animation again, you'll see the Particles spiraling along the **Y**-Axis within the Scene as shown below.

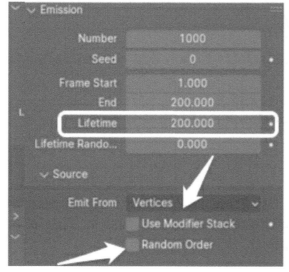

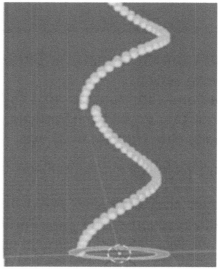

Hint: up to this stage, the Particles have been represented as small white spheres in Object mode within the 3D Viewport Editor.

PARTICLE MODIFIER

Within the **Properties** Editor, navigate to the **Modifier Properties Selection** menu, where you'll encounter two significant modifiers: the **Particle System Modifier** and the **Particle Instance Modifier.** These modifiers play a crucial role once you have a basic understanding of Particle Systems.

- ✓ **Particle System Modifier:** When you apply a Particle System Modifier to a selected Object, it automatically generates a default Particle System. Essentially, it mirrors the action of clicking the **Plus Sign** (+) within the **Particle Properties** panel. Once applied, you can fine-tune the settings to achieve your desired outcome.
- ✓ **Particle Instance Modifier:** The Particle Instance Modifier allows you to replicate an array of Objects to mimic the array of Particles being emitted.

For a practical demonstration:

1) Set up a **Scene** in the **Top Orthographic** View (Num Pad **7**), comprising a **Circle** Object and a scaled-down **UV Sphere** Object, posi-tioned according to the layout shown below.

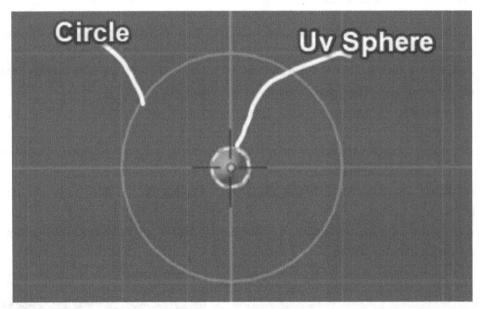

2) Disable **Gravity,** ensure the **Circle** is selected, then add a **Particle System** with the following settings:
- ✓ **Emissions Tab: Number: 10, Lifetime: 200**
- ✓ **Source Tab: Emit From: Vertices, Uncheck Random Order**
- ✓ **Velocity Tab: Normal: 0 .25 m/s.**

Avoid playing the animation at this stage.

3) Deselect the **Circle** and select the **UV Sphere**. Within the **Properties** Editor, go to **Modifier** Properties and add a **Particle Instance Modifier**. Specify "**Circle**" as the Object (the one with the Particle System applied).

4) Play the animation in the Timeline window to witness an array of Spheres forming in a spiral arrangement, replicating the spiral pattern of the Particles as illustrated below.

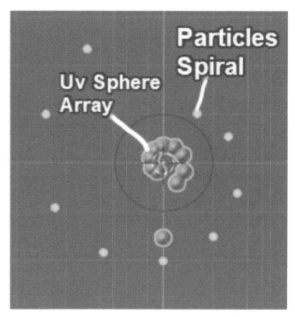

HAIR PARTICLES

Hair particles are utilized to generate various elements such as grass, hair, fur, or whatever that can simulate surfaces with fibrous strands.

Unlike other particle types, **Hair Particles** are an except ion- they render directly in the 3D Viewport Editor without needing to be config-ured as instance objects for rendering.

To illustrate the creation of hair particles:

1) begin by deleting the default **Cube** object in the 3D Viewport Editor and adding a **Plane**, then zoom in for a closer view.

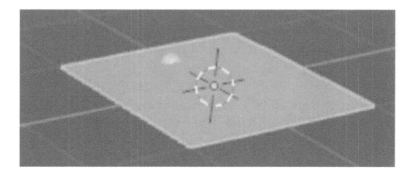

2) Next, with the **Plane** selected, navigate to the **Properties** Editor and access the **Particle** Properties. Within the top panel of the Par-ticle Edi tor, select **"Hair"** as shown below.

3) When the Hair Particle is applied to the Plane in the 3D Viewport Editor, long strands protrude from the surface. By adjusting the **Hair Length** value in the Emission Tab, you can control the length of these strands.

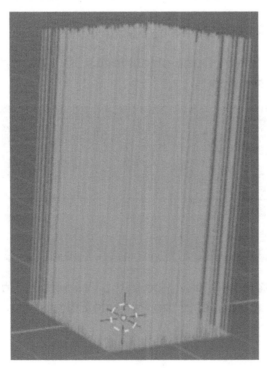

Hint: hair particles render directly in the 3D Viewport Editor and inherit the color of the emitter object.

When hair particles are emitted from the **Plane** and a **material** is added to the **Plane** in **Material Preview Viewport Shading Mode**, they take on the appearance of the material.

While adding a hair particle system to a **Plain** object is appropriate for producing surfaces with fibrous strands like a doormat or patch of grass, a more compelling application is to add hair to a character's head, creating a more dynamic effect.

ADD HAIR TO A CHARACTER

Let's add hair to Suzanne the Monkey Mesh Object to demonstrate this feature.

1) Begin by opening a new Blender file and deleting the default **Cube**. Then, add a Monkey Object (Suzanne) to the scene. With **Suzanne** selected in the 3D Viewport Editor, add a Hair Particle System.

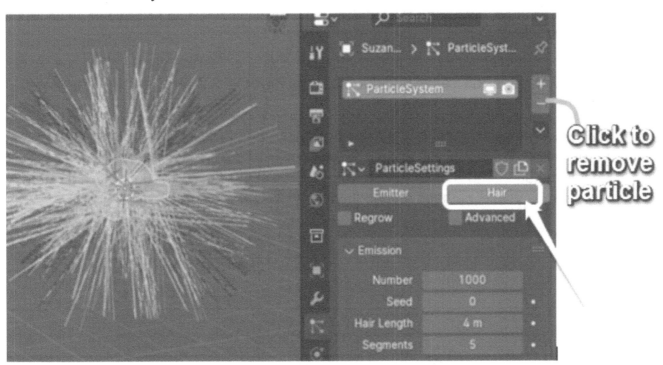

Introducing a **Hair Particle** System to Suzanne results in a monkey with hair protruding in all directions, giving her a hairy-headed appearance.

2) At this initial stage, take note that the **Particle System** is named **"ParticleSystem"** with associated settings named **"ParticleSetting"** as shown above. While this may not seem significant now, it will become relevant as you progress.

3) If you prefer a more polished look, remove the **Particle System** by clicking the minus (-) button as shown in the above screenshot. To precisely control where the hair grows, designate a **Vertex** Group. Switch to **Top Orthographic in Edit Mode**, then create a **Vertex Group** on the top of **Suzanne 's head** and name it **"Hair"**.

In the **Object Data** Properties section of the **Properties** Editor, you've designated a specific area on the **monkey's head** by selecting a group of **vertices**. However, there's no hair yet.

4) While still in **Edit Mode**, navigate to the **Particles** Properties and add a **new Particle System.** Change the **Type** from **Emitter** to **Hair.** Since you're in **Edit** Mode, there won't be any visible change in the 3D Viewport Edi to r.

It's worth noting that Blender names the new Particle **System "ParticleSystem"** as before, but since you're working in the same Blender file, new **Particle Settings** named "**Particle Set tings.001"**are linked as shown below.

5) Switch to **Object** Mode in the 3DViewport Editor in the **Right Orthographic view**, and you'll notice an abundance of hair- every- where. To adjust this, navigate to the Hair Length parameter in the **Emission** Tab and decrease the value until the hair strands appear reasonable, perhaps around **0.650.**

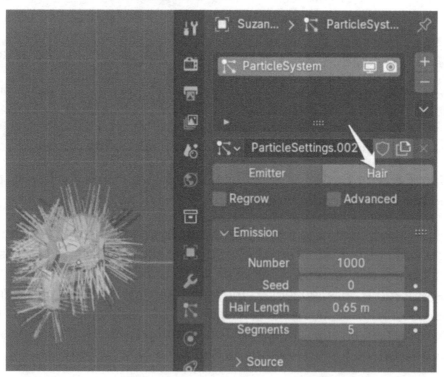

6) While still in the **Particles** Properties, scroll down to the **Vertex** Groups Tab. In the panel beside **Density**, click and select **"Hair"** from the displayed menu as shown below. This ensures that hair only appears on the selected **area** (the Vertex Group).

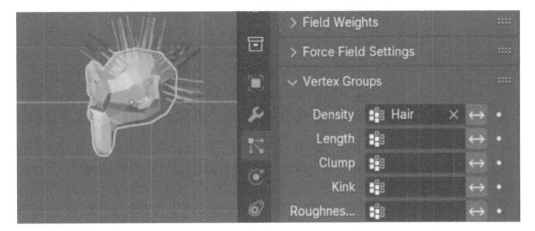

7) Press **Num Pad 3** for a side view. To enhance the appearance, navigate to the **Children Tab** in the Particle Properties and select "**Simple**" to achieve a bushier, Mohawk-like look as shown here.

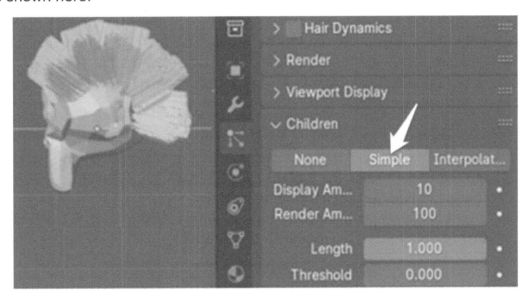

Suzanne is starting to resemble a cool character from a cartoon, but she could use a bit more personality. Adding a beard might just be the solution.

ADD A BEARD

To incorporate a beard, you'll need to create a new **second Vertex Group** and apply a new **Hair Particle System** to that group.

The initial Hair Vertex Group was formed by selecting vertices in Edit Mode. To change things up, you can create the new Vertex Group using the **Weight Paint** Method.

1) When **Hair Particles** are allocated to the Vertex Group named **"Hair,"** switching the 3DViewport Editor to **Weight Paint** Mode reveals Suzanne's face turning blue with a splash of colored scalp amidst the hair. This coloring reflects the Hair Vertex Group that has been established.

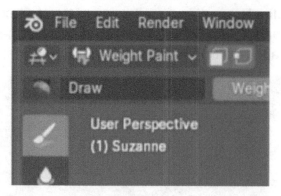

2) In **Weight Paint** Mode, the 3D Viewport Editor Cursor transforms into a **Paint** Brush. To select **vertices** for a new **Vertex** Group, simply drag the **Paint Brush** (Cursor) over the surface of the **object(Suzanne)**. As you drag, the surface changes color, indicating the selection. The color gradation indicates the strength of the selection, with light **blue** representing partial selection and **red** indicating full selection.

Caution: At this stage, **Suzanne** is selected in **Object** Mode with the **Vertex** Group named **"Hair"** activated in Edit Mode. The Hair Particle System with **ParticleSettings.001** is applied.

Dragging the Brush over Suzanne's chin will allocate new vertices to the Hair Vertex Group, thereby applying the Hair Particle System to that region. This results in hair being added to the chin with the same properties as the scalp. preferably, you'd want different properties for the chin hair, necessitating the use of a separate Vertex Group. Next, we will create a new vertex group

3) To create a new Vertex Group for Suzanne's beard, first, ensure that the 3D Viewport Editor is in **Edit** Mode and that all **vertices** are deselected. Then, navigate to the Properties Editor and access the **Object Data** Properties for **Suzanne**. Here, you'll find the previ-ously created Vertex Group named **"Hair"**.

4) Click on the **plus** sign (+) to generate a new   **Vertex Groups** lot. By default, it will be named **"Group,"** butyou should rename it to **"Beard"**.

Now, with the new Beard Vertex Group established, you can create a new Particle System that will be tailored for the beard. This will grant you full control over the properties of the beard, allowing for a customized appearance.

5) To create a new Particle System, head to the **Properties** Editor and navigate to **Particle Properties**. Click on the **plus** sign (+) to initi-ate a new Particle System and ensure to set the **Type** as "Hair".

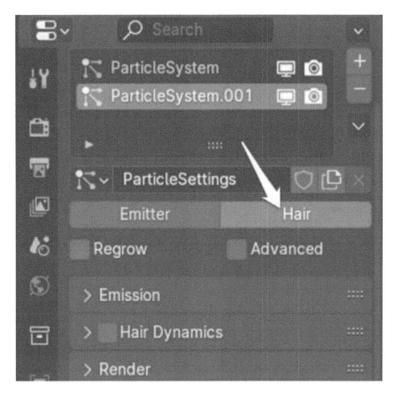

By default, the new system will be named **"ParticleSystem.001**," but you have the option to rename it to something more descriptive like **"Beard Particles"** and "**Hair Particles** "for clarity.

6) After setting the new Particle System to **Type: Hair**, Suzan ne once again appears entirely covered in hair. To rectify this, navigate to the **Vertex** Group Tab and enter "**Vertex Group Beard"** in the **Density** Slot. This removes the excessive hair, preparing for vertex selection through painting.

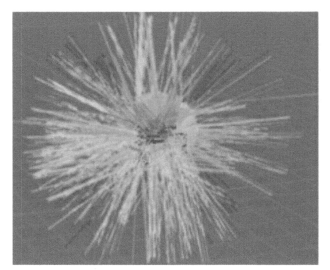

7) Switch the 3D Viewport Editor to **Weight Paint** Mode and pain t over Suzanne's chin to select the **vertices** for the beard. In the **Parti-cle** Properties section of the **Properties** Editor, navigate to the **Emission** Tab and decrease the **Hair Length to 0.3m.**

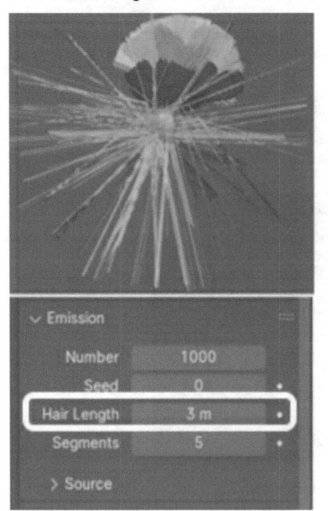
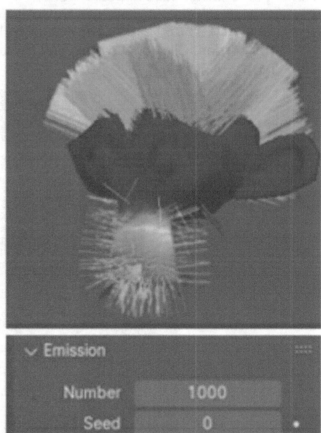
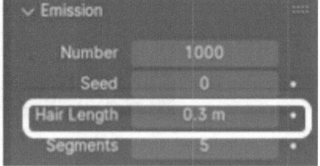

8) In the **Children** Tab, change the type from **None** to **Simple.**

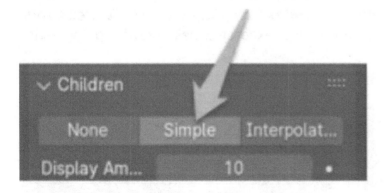
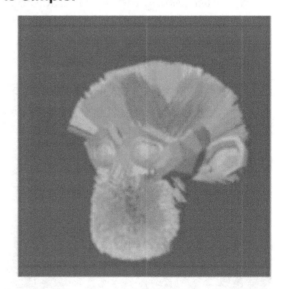

In **Object** Mode in the 3DViewport Editor, you'll see Suzanne with a **gray** monkey with a **gray beard** and **gray hair**. While this is accept- able, it lacks excitement. Elevate the appearance by adding different materials to Suzanne's surface, creating distinct skin and hair colors. In Object

Mode, Suzanne appears complete with hair, sporting the default gray color. The hair particles, or strands, inherit the material color of the emitter object, which in this case, is Suzanne with the default gray hue.

To introduce color to the hairy, the vertex groups. you'll need to create **Material Datablocks,** which represent different colors, and assign these datablocks to the vertex group.

In the Material Properties section, you may find additional Material Datablocks if there are other objects present in the 3D Viewport. Each object typically has its own Material Datablock.

Hint: this procedure is described with the Blender Node System deactivated. This deactivation allows Materials (colors) to be displayed directly in the 3D Viewport Editor, in Solid Viewport Shading Mode.

Material Datablocks can be created independently of objects in the 3D Viewport Editor. These datablocks can then be assigned to any object present in the scene or vertex groups on an object's surface. However, there's one caveat: Material Proper ties will only be visible in the Prop-erties Editor if there is an object present in the 3DViewport Edi to r.

Let's assume you've selected Suzanne in the 3D Viewport and applied a material to color her face. Additionally, you've created a vertex group to designate where you want to place the hair and beard.

9) To create Material Datablocks, with **Suzanne** selected in **Object** Mode, create two new Material Datablocks named **"Hair"** and **"Beard**. "Assign a **material (color) to** each datablock. Ensure to disable the **Node** System to allow materials to display in the 3D Viewport Editor when in Solid Viewport Shading Mode.

10) With **Suzanne** selected in **Edit Mode** and the **Vertex** Group **"Hair"** selected in the Properties Editor under **Object Data** Proper- ties, navigate to the **Material** Properties. Select the **"Hair"** Datablock and click the **"Assign"** button.

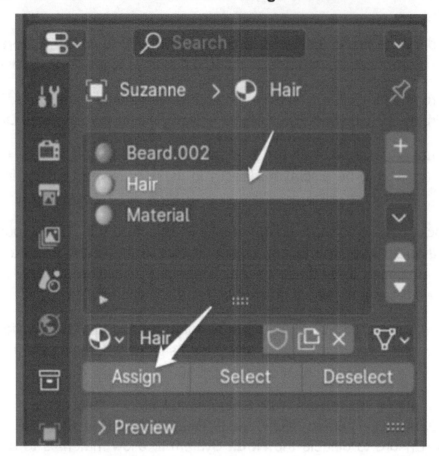

11) With **Suzanne** selected in **Edit Mode** and the Vertex Group **"Beard"** selected in the Properties Editor under **Object Data** Properties, navigate to the Material Properties. Select the "Beard" Datablock and click the **"Assign"** button.

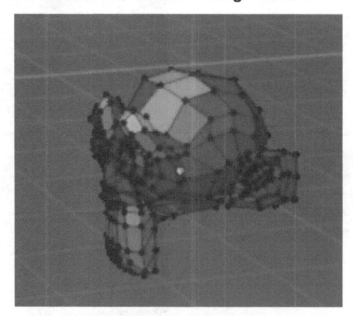

These Material Datablocks control the appearance of the hair particles, adopting the color assigned to the corresponding Vertex Group as shown below.

PARTICLES FOR ARRAYS

Particles emitted from an animated object can be utilized to craft intriguing arrays, such as a spiral.

1) To construct the spiral, include a **Plane** Object in the scene as the **Emitter Object**, with an **IcoSphere** designated as the **Rendered Object**.

2) When adding the **IcoSphere** you'll notice **the Add IcoSphere** panel appearing in the lower left-hand corner of the screen. Click on the panel to access the settings, where you'll find **"Subdivisions: 2"**as the d e fault setting. Decrease this value to **"Subdivisions: 1"**to minimize the vertex count on the surface of the IcoSphere. Though it's not essential for this task, it's a good practice, espe-cially in simulations where minimizing vertex count is advisable.

3) Position the **IcoSphere** off to the side of the screen or consider placing it in a separate collection to hide it from view. Apply a vibrant material to the **IcoSphere** to enhance visibility. Ensure that the **3DViewport Editor** is set to **Material Preview Viewport Shading**.

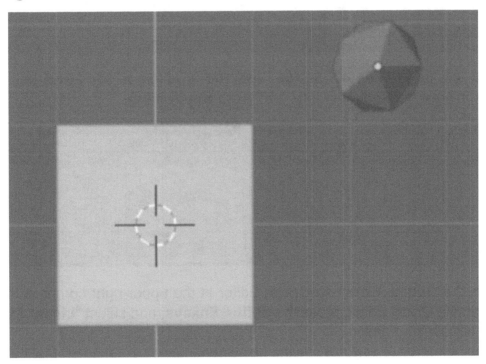

Let's bring some life to the plane by making it rotate.

4) First, select the plane you want to animate and ensure your **Timeline Editor Cursor** is at Frame 1, then switch **"on" Auto Keyfram-ing**.

5) Press the **"I"** key and choose **"Rotation "** from the **Keyframe** menu. This manually inserts a keyframe at **Frame 1** in the **Tirneline** Editor.

6) Now, with the **Tirneline** Cursor at frame **20** and your Mouse Cursor in the 3D Viewport Editor, press the **"R + K + 90 + Enter"**.

219

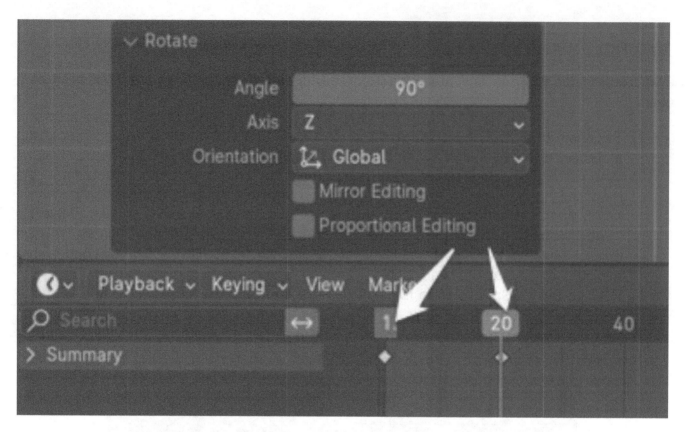

7) Repeat this for Frames **40, 60, 80**, and **100** to automatically insert keyframes. Once you've finished, remember to turn **"off" Auto Keyframing.**

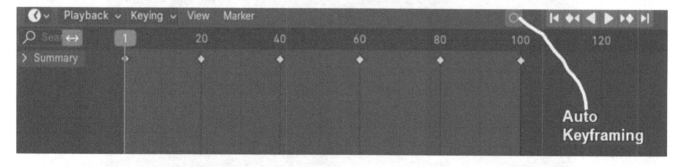

Auto
Keyframing

8) **Switch the Outline Editor to Graph** Editor at the upper right corner, with your mouse cursor in the Graph Editor, press the **Shift + Enkeys**, and select **"Linear Extrapolation"** to smooth out the rotation.

9) Play the animation, and you'll see the plane continuously rotating around the Z-Axis. Let's add some flair with a particle system to our plane using the subsequent steps.

10) Add a Particle System to the Plane. In the Particle System settings, under the **Source** Tab, choose **"Vertices"** as the Emission source. Then, under the **Render** Tab, select **"Object "**as the rendering method, and choose "IcoSphere" from the **Object** Tab as the **Instance Object.** Experiment with the Scale and Randomness settings to get the desired effect.

11) Increase the **Lifetime** of the particles to **250**, and in the **Source** Tab, uncheck **"Random Order"** to control the emission pattern. Make sure to turn off **Gravity** to pre vent the particles from falling.

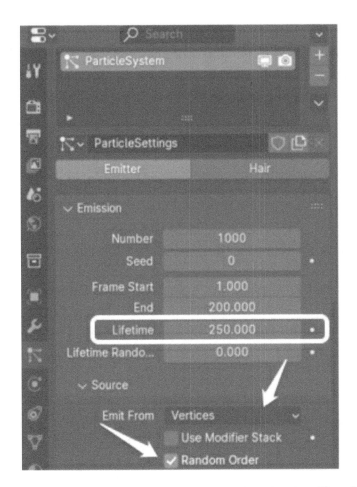

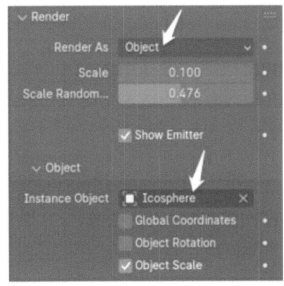

12) When youp lay the simulation in the Timeline Editor, you'll see particles displayed as **IcoSpheres** being emitted and rising in spirals as the Plane rotates, you may need to change to the User Orthographic view.

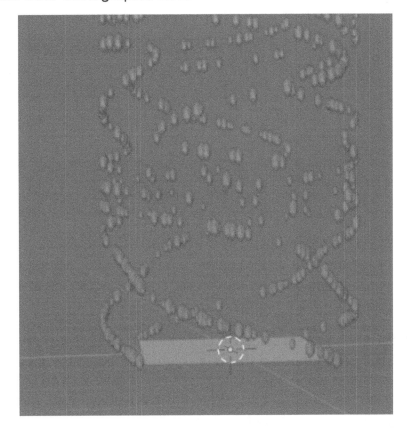

This exercise reveals how different particle settings can be combined to create effects. There are no strict rules to follow; the key is to experiment until you achieve the desired result. Remember to save your work and take note of your results for future reference. You can further enhance the effect by exploring different combinations of settings.

EXPLORE MORE ARRAYS

The versatility of particle arrays is limited only by your imagination and understanding of the tools at your disposal. This illustration will serve as a guide.

1) In the default Blender scene, swap out the default **Cube** with a **UV Sphere** to act as a Particle Emitter. Introduce an **IcoSphere** to serve as the Rendered Object (instance object).
2) Apply **Smooth Shading** to the **IcoSphere** (right -click and select **Smooth Shade**) and then position it to one side of the scene. Scale it down to around 0.250. This **IcoSphere** will be the instance object, meaning Particles generated by the **UV Sphere** will display as this object.
3) Enhance the scene's lighting by adding lamps (locate the **Light** menu in the **Add** menu and select **Ligh**t).

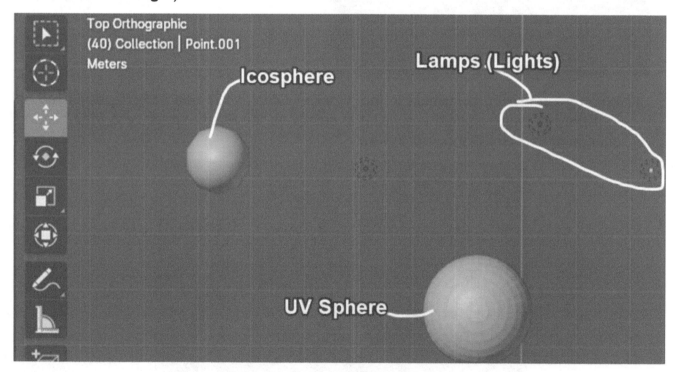

The goal of this exercise is to create an array of small objects that would represent a swarm of insects around the UV Sphere to a distant galaxy's star cluster. Let your imagination run wild. For practicality, you would create detailed models for each object in the array, but for simplicity, we'll stick with the IcoSphere.

4) Disable **Gravity** in the scene settings to allow the Particles to disperse freely in 3Dspace.
5) Select the **UV Sphere** and add a **Particle System** to begin the creative process. When you play the animation at the stage with the default Particles, you will see particles being emitted as tiny circles that drift away from the **UV Sphere** and vanish after **50 frames** from their stage of creation (**50.00 Lifetime**).

Let's enhance the animation by tweaking the particle system for a more dynamic effect. You can do that with these steps: Emission Tab:

- ✓ Increase the **Number** of particles to **28,000.**
- ✓ Set the **Lifetime** to **900** (essentially indefinite).
- ✓ Keep the Start at **1**and End at **200.000.**
- ✓ Adjust the **Lifetime Randomness** to **0.700** for variation.

Render Tab:

- ✓ Change the **Render As** option from Halo to **Object**.
- ✓ Maintain the **Scale at 0.050.**
- ✓ Adjust the **Scale Randomness** to **0.070** for variation.

Render Object Tab:

- ✓ Click on **Instance Object** and select the **IcoSphere.**

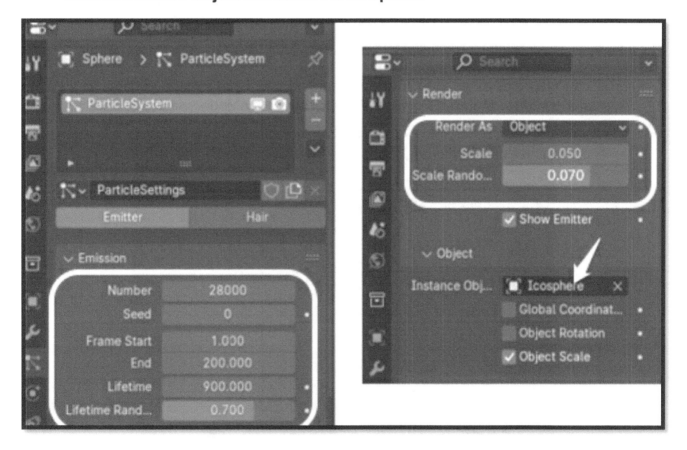

6) Go to the Timeline Editor, play the animation, then navigate the **Timeline** Cursor to Frame **110** and rotate the Viewport to observe the changes.
7) Viewing the scene in **Rendered Viewport Shading** Mode, you'll see an array generated with particles radiating out from the UV Sphere, resembling scattered lines. Zooming in on the 3D Viewport Editor reveals that each particle is an instance of the Ico-Sphere placed in the scene.

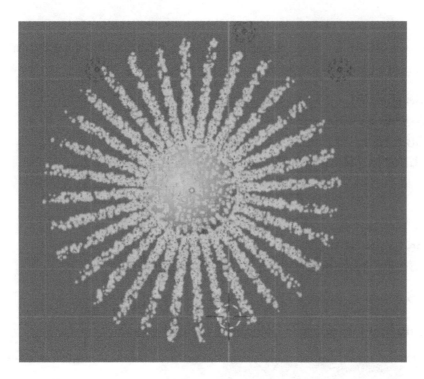

From here, you can continue adjusting settings to modify the appearance of the array.

8) You can also add material to the **IcoSphere** for additional visual effects. To view the material, switch to **Material Preview Viewport Display** Mode.

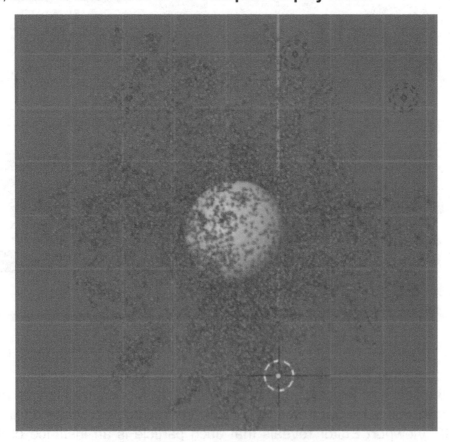

9) Then, deselect the **UV Sphere** and add an **Empty Object**. Activate a **Force Field** of type **Turbulence** with a Strength of **4** in the Physics Properties.

10) Play the animation to see the movement of Particles. As particles disperse due to the force field, a screenshot at approximately Frame 110 is shown below.

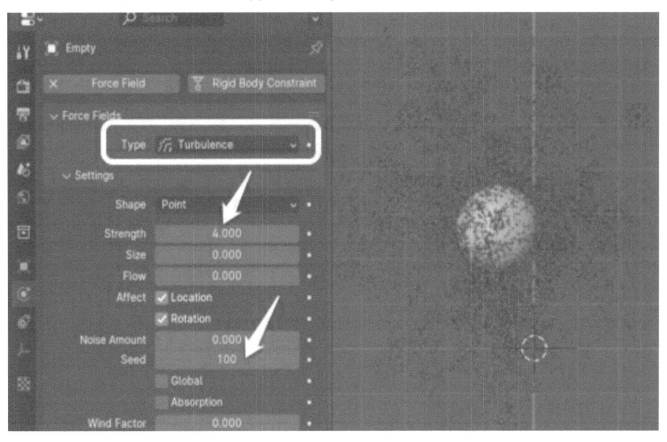

11) Next, select the **UV Sphere** and change the **Particle System** to **Emitter** Type: **Hair**. In **Frame 1** of the animation in the **Time- line** Editor, the **UV Sphere** appears as a speckled orange/yellow disk.

12) In the Particle System's **Render** Tab, switch **Render As** to **Path**. Then, in the **Children** Tab, select **Simple** for a different array effect as shown below.

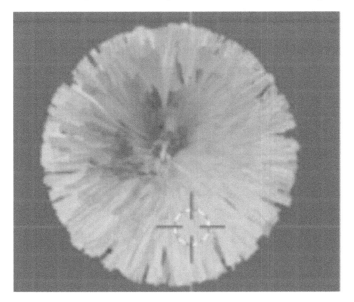
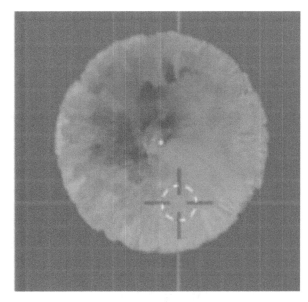

CHAPTER 13: BASICS OF PHYSICS AND SIMULATION

Within the scope of animation, simulation mirrors real-world dynamics through animated sequences. These sequences mimic physical events governed by the laws of physics. In computer animation, characters and objects move and interact as though they are subject to the same forces and principles observed in reality. The law of gravity dictates how characters leap and fall to collisions with obstacles and each other, these actions emulate real-world physics, though sometimes exaggerated for dramatic effect. Blender, for instance, uses modifiers to replicate how characters and objects adhere to these laws within the virtual environment.

In the context of Particles and their Effects, concepts like Wind Force and Gravity come into play. When objects emit particles, these par-ticles descend as if influenced by Gravity and can be affected by wind forces if applied. Gravity itself can be adjusted or negated through controls found in the Scene Properties editor, allowing for fine-tuning of gravitational effects. Similarly, Wind Forces and other Physics Simulation effects are managed through the Physics Properties editor.

Physics Properties act as modifiers, essentially code that generates specific effects, and are applied to selected objects within the 3D view- port editor. Once applied, these properties grant access to controls for fine-tuning the physics behavior of the object, all accessible within the Physics Properties section of the Properties editor.

APPLYING AND ERASING PHYSICS

To add physics to an object,

- ✓ first, select the **object** within the 3D Viewport Editor. Then, navigate to the **Physics** Properties in the **Properties** Editor and click on the desired **physics type** within the **Physics** Properties section.
- ✓ Once applied, you'll notice the icon preceding the physics type changes to a **cross (X)**, indicating that physics has been activated.
  Controls specific to the chosen physics type will then become available in the editor.
- ✓ To remove physics from an object, simply click on the **cross (X}** icon associated with the physics type.

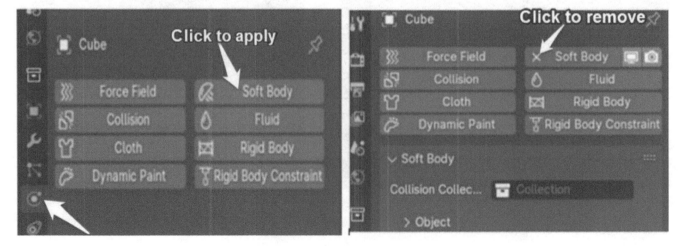

In certain instances, physics can also be applied via the Modifier Properties within the Properties Editor. Hint: some modifiers are accessi-ble in both the **Physics** Properties and the **Modifier** Properties sections.

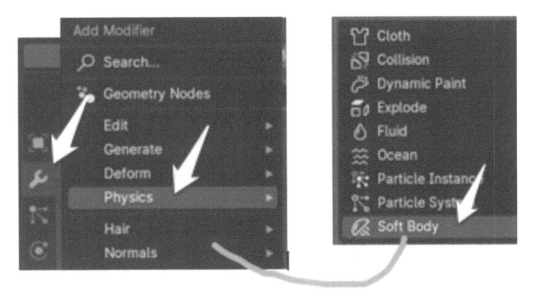

When applying a **Physics** property from the **Modifier** Properties, a panel will appear, guiding you to the **Physics** Properties section for fur-ther adjustments and controls.

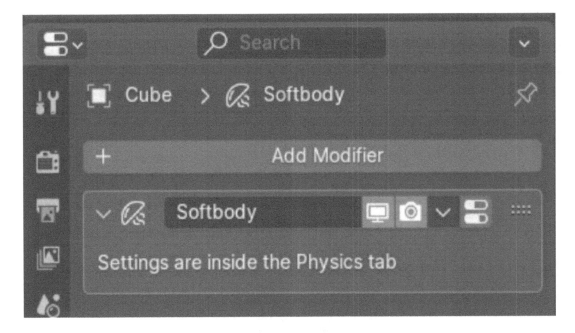

UNDERSTANDING THE REAL-WORLD PHYSICS

In **Chapter 10**, you likely noticed that particles generated from a default object descend on the screen when an animation sequence is acti-vated. The emitter object itself stays in place unless animated to move.

Imagine the default Blender Scene as a glimpse into a 3D world. While there's a gravitational force present, objects placed within the scene typically won't react to gravity until Physics is applied to them. However, particles are an exception to this rule, as they inherently adhere to **Newtonian physics by default.**

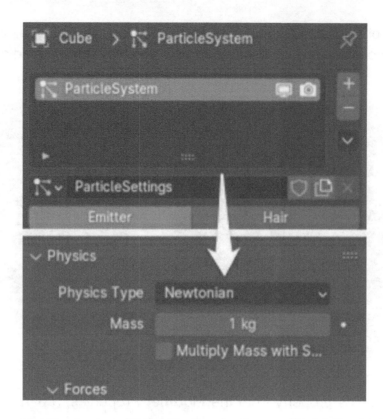

Real-world physics, also known as **Rigid Body** physics or **Rigid Body Constraint**, involves objects being considered as rigid bodies.

1) In the screenshot below, there's a **UV Sphere** placed above a Plane that's rotated on the **X-Axis** to create an incline. The Sphere has a particle system applied to it.

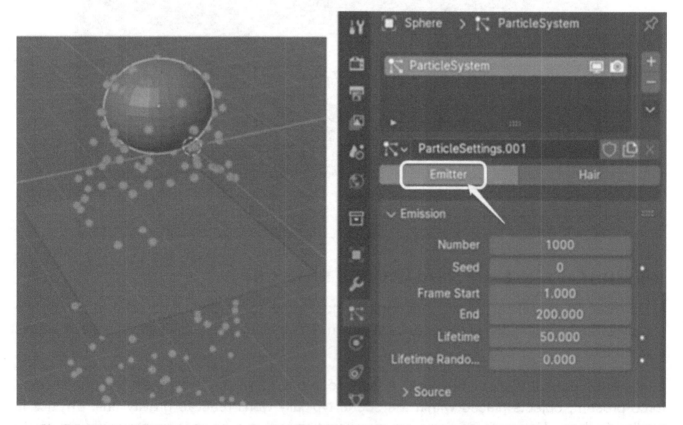

2) During animation playback in the **Timeline** Editor, particles emitted from the sphere fall through the Plane, while both the Sphere and the Plane remain stationary.

3) To change this behavior, you can enable **Physics** for **collision** on the **Plane** in the **Properties** Editor's **Physics** Properties section, as shown below.
Consequently, when the **animation** is replayed, particles will bounce off the plane, as illustrated here.

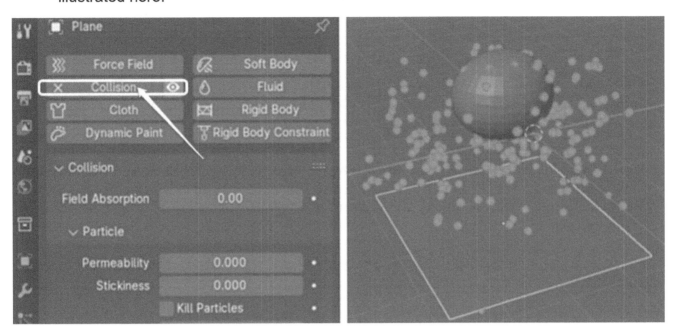

4) Within the **Physics** Properties section, controls become available once physics is enabled. These controls allow for adjustments to achieve desired effects, as demonstrated below.

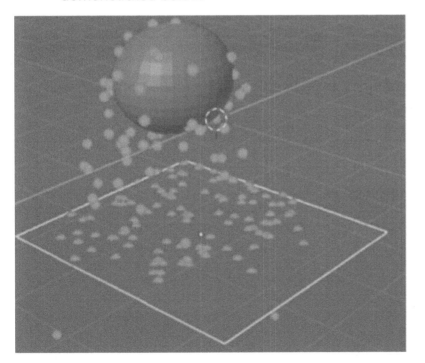
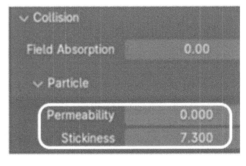

You might be curious as to why particles fall due to gravitational effects while the **UV Sphere** and **Plane** stay put. By default, a particle sys- tem is assigned a Physics type: **Newtonian,** causing particles to behave as they would in the real world under the influence of gravity.

5) To observe **Newtonia**n physics for particles, navigate to the **Particle** Properties section within the **Properties** Editor, in the **Physics** tab. Meanwhile, Gravity settings can be found in the **Scene** Properties section of the **Properties** Editor.

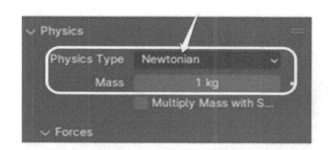 

6) To make the Sphere descend and roll down the plane, apply **Rigid Body** Physics to both the **Sphere** and the **Plane**. In the **Rigid Body** Tab, set the **Type** to "**Active**" for the **Sphere** and "**Passive**" for the **Plane**. As a result, the Sphere will descend while the Plane remains still.

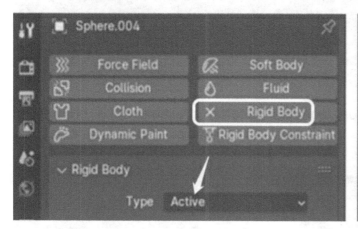 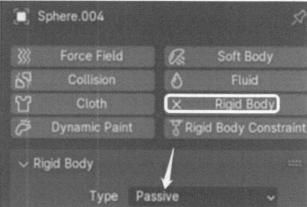

7) Click the **"Play"** button in the **Timeline** Editor Header to observe the **Sphere's** drop and rolling motion down the **Plane.**

Hint: **Rigid Body Physics** automatically encompasses **Collision** Physics, facilitating interaction between the sphere and the plane.

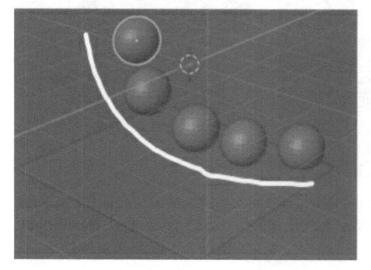 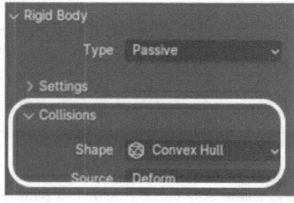

USING THE FORCE FIELD

A Force Field, such as a Wind Force, impacts the flow direction of particles within a scene. This force can be assigned to an empty object, allowing for proper positioning to achieve the desired effect. Since the empty object doesn't render in the scene, it's commonly used for this purpose. A Wind Force can be applied to any Object.

1) In the screenshot below, there is an example of a **Wind Force** applied to a **Cone** object, directing it to blow particles emitted from the **UV sphere**, as demonstrated in the previous exercise. As the sphere falls and rolls to the right down the plane, the wind force pushes the emitted particles to the left, causing them to travel back up the slope.

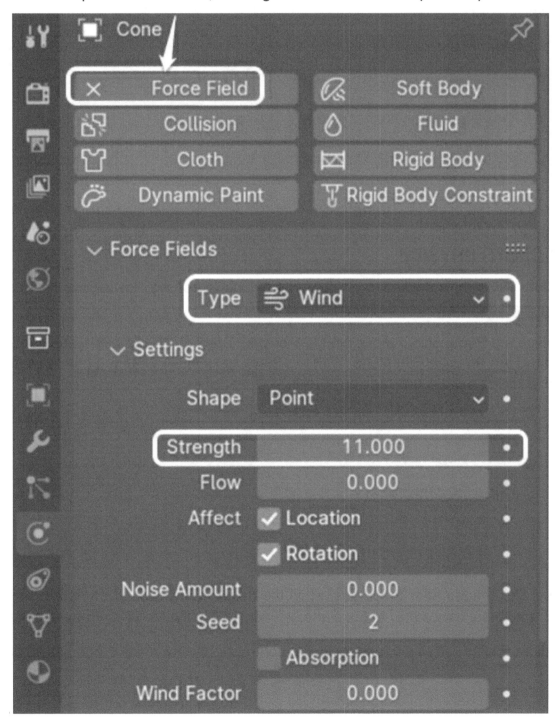

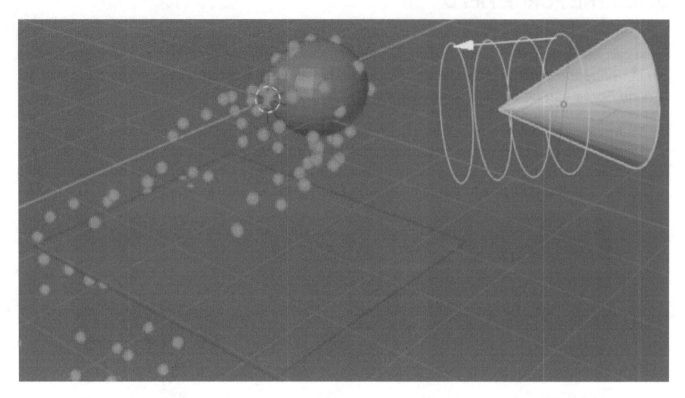

You should note the negative **Strength** value for the wind force, which influences its direction.

USING CLOTH PHYSICS

When **Cloth Physics** is applied to an object, it begins to behave like various types of fabric, exhibiting characteristics such as flexibility and draping.

1) assume a **Plane** object within the 3D Viewport Editor in **Object** Mode and subdivide the **Plane ten times** in **Edit** Mode. With the **Plane** selected in **Object** Mode, navigate to the **Physics** Properties and click on "**Cloth** ".

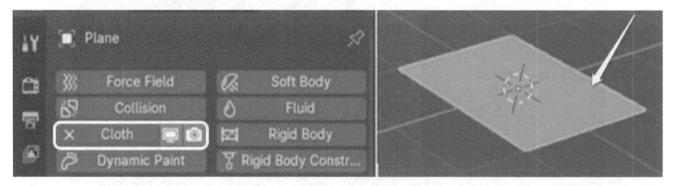

When you click the **Modifier** Properties within the **Properties** Editor, you'll notice that a **Cloth Modifier** is automatically added to the plane, as indicated in the Modifier Properties below.

This modifier directs you to the corresponding controls in the **Physics** Properties as illustrated below.

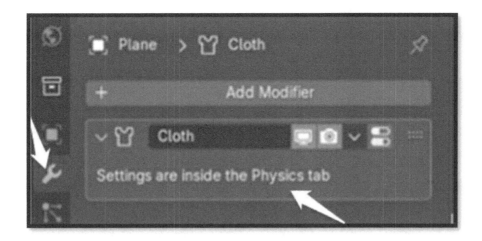

In the **Physics** Properties section of the Properties Editor, you can adjust cloth properties to simulate various fabric materials.

By default, the cloth settings emulate the characteristics of cotton fabric. However, you can modify these settings to replicate other fabric types as illustrated below.

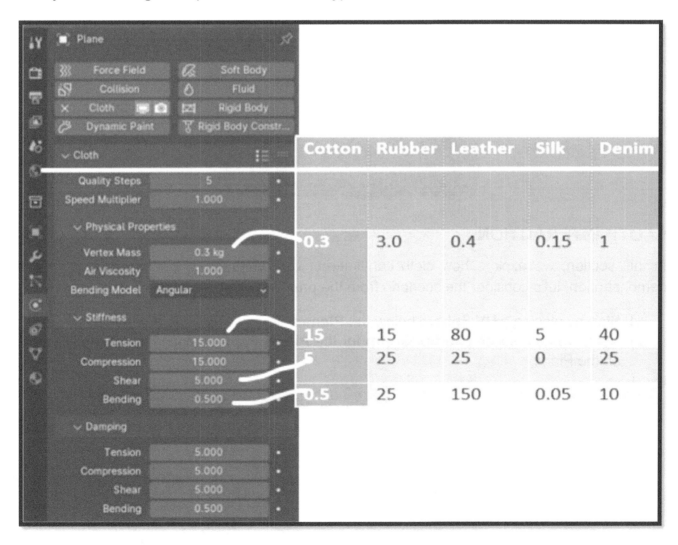

	Cotton	Rubber	Leather	Silk	Denim
	0.3	3.0	0.4	0.15	1
	15	15	80	5	40
	5	25	25	0	25
	0.5	25	150	0.05	10

1) To have the **Plane** behave as a **Cotton** fabric leave the default settings unchanged.
2) Select the **Plane** in the 3D Viewport Editor, enter **Edit** Mode, and deselect all **vertices.** Select two corner vertices and use them to create a vertex group, naming it **"Group"**.

3) In the **Physics** Properties section, expand the **Shape** Tab. Locate the **Pin Group** field and enter the name of the vertex group created earlier (Group).

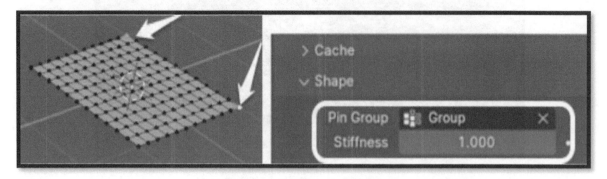

4) Playing the animation in the **Timeline** editor will demonstrate the cloth's behavior. In this scenario, the cloth, mimicking cotton fabric, swings down, pinned at the two corners, similar to securing a sheet's corners on a clothesline without the line.

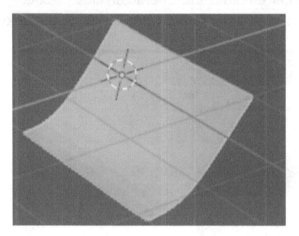

CLOTH INTERACTION

In this section, we explore how cloth can interact with other objects within a scene. As a demonstration, let's consider the scenario from the previous example.

1) Start by placing a **UV Sphere** below the **Plane** before initiating the animation.
2) Next, create a second **Vertex Group** for the **Plane**, this time encompassing all vertices on the Plane.

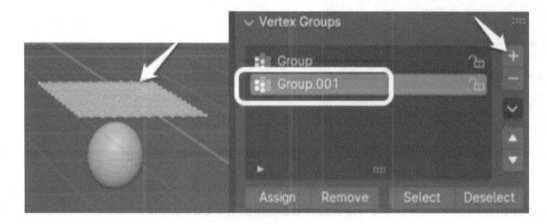

3) Then, select the **UV Sphere** and activate **Collision Physics** in the Physics Properties, keeping the default settings.
4) Select the **Plane**, go to the **Cloth Physics** Properties, and access the **Collisions** Tab.
5) Ensure that **Object Collision** is checked with the **Collision Collection** set to **"Collection"**. Similarly, make sure that **Self Collis**ion is checked with Vertex Group **"Group .001 "**specified.

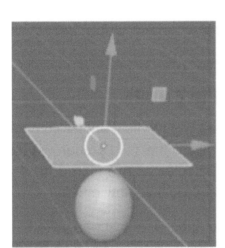
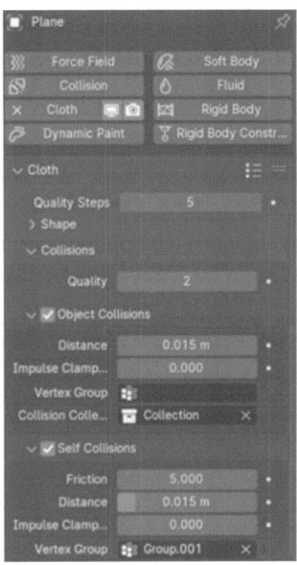

6) Now, replay the animation to observe the cloth draping over the **Sphere.**

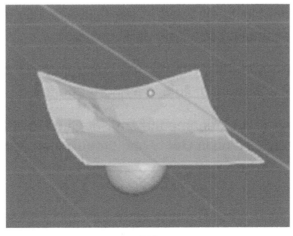

USING FLUID SIMULATION

Fluid Simulation in Blender mimics the real-world behavior of fluids, which is influenced by factors like physical obstacles, gravity, pres-sure, and the composition of the fluid itself. Essentially, the fluid's behavior adheres to the laws of physics.

In Blender, a fluid simulation creates a visual representation on the computer screen, creating the illusion of observing real fluid dynamics in an environment. However, it's important to recognize that what you see is an artistic interpretation, achieved through clever programming.

Blender uses an adaptable framework called Manta flow for fluid and gas simulations. Manta flow is an open-source framework designed for fluid simulation research in Computer Graphics. Its parallelized C++ solver core, Python scene definition interface, and plugin system enable rapid prototyping and testing of new algorithms.

UNDERSTANDING FLUID CONCEPT WITHIN BLENDER

In Blender, a fluid simulation starts with particles representing the fluid on the computer screen. These particles originate from particle systems that mimic the fluid's characteristics, which include spray, foam, and bubbles. Eventually, these particles are rendered as a mesh with materials applied to react to scene lighting, creating a realistic fluid flow effect.

To set up a fluid simulation, you will create a designated space in the scene called the Domain, where the fluid dynamics will occur. Then, you insert objects within this Domain to serve as fluid inflow sources and obstacles for controlling the flow. The Fluid Inflow Source typi-cally acts as a particle emitter object.

To illustrate this concept, let's walk through a simple exercise using the default Blender scene,

1) First, switch the 3D Viewport Editor to **Wireframe Display** Mode. Then, scale up the default **Cube** along the **Z-axis**, deselect it, and add a second **Cube**, scaling it down in size. Both cubes should be positioned at the center of the 3D World, with the smaller cube placed above the larger one. The larger Cube serves as the **Domain**, representing the mini artificial world, while the smaller Cube acts as the Fluid Emitter.

It's crucial to ensure that all objects involved in the fluid simulation remain entirely inside the Domain, without any parts protruding out- side as shown below.

When setting up the Domain and Fluid Emitter, pay attention to their relative scales. A larger emitter will generate a greater amount of fluid in a shorter period.

2) Finally, in the **Outliner** Editor, rename the smaller Cube to **"Fluid"** and the default **Cube** to **"Domain"**. This helps maintain clarity and organization within the scene.

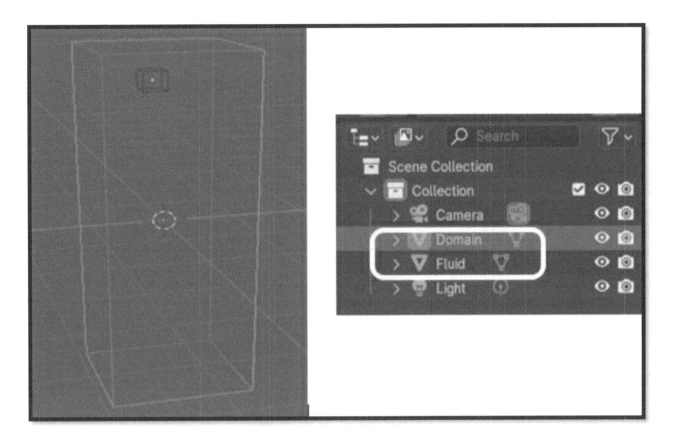

Let us look into the fluid flow within this simple demonstration. The fluid will be generated by the Emitter Object and delivered as a continuous stream. Initially, the stream will be directed along the Y-axis, where it will make contact with the side of the Domain before de-scending and filling it as if it were a container. The direction of flow is illustrated below.

To control the simulation, you'll find the necessary settings in the Properties Editor under Physics Properties. Both the Fluid Emitter and Domain require specific adjustments.

3) Start by deselecting the **Domain** and selecting the **Fluid Emitter Cube**. In the **Properties** Editor, navigate to **Physics** Properties and click on **Fluid** to access the **Fluid** Tab.
4) select **"Flow"** from the **Fluid Type** dropdown menu. Fluid Settings instantly populate the Editor.
5) Within the **Fluid Settings** Tab, select **"Liquid"** on the Flow Type menu and **"Inflow"** from the Flow Behavior menu. Ensure that **"Use Flow"** is checked (ticked) to activate the settings.

Notice:

The "Flow Behavior: "Inflow" setting configures the **Emitter** Object Cube to continuously release fluid. This fluid flow is activated when an animation is played in the **Timeline** Editor. However, Hint: currently, if the animation were to be played, no fluid would be generated.

6) The direction of fluid inflow begins along the Y-axis of the 3 D World. This direction is established by giving the fluid an initial velocity, which means to give a fluid a kick start in the **Y-direction**. To achieve this, you need to enable the **"Initial Velocity'** op-tion. Set the Initial Y value to **2 m/s** as illustrated below.

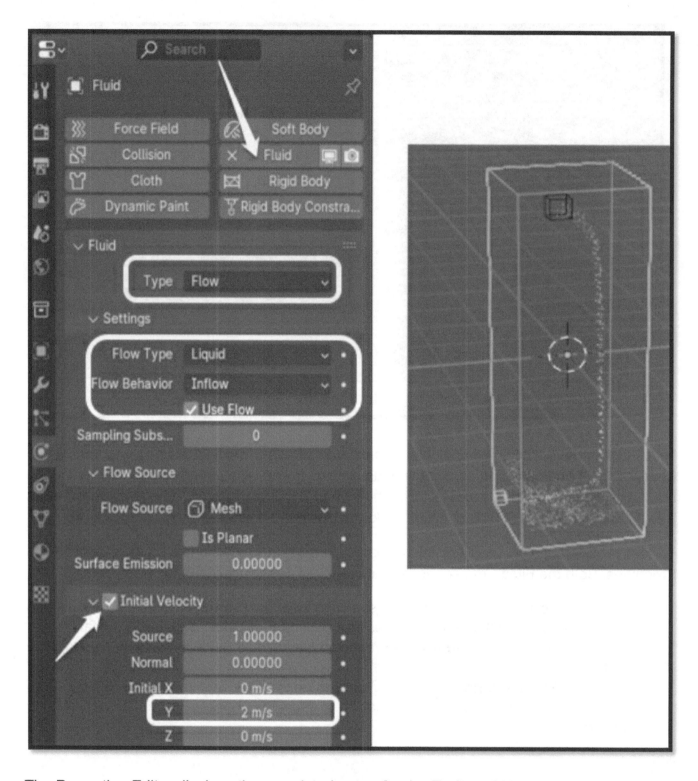

The Properties Editor displays the completed setup for the **Emitter** Object, as illustrated in the screen shot below. To control the Domain object, follow a process similar to setting up the Emitter Control.

7) To get started select the **Domain Cube**. Then, in the 3D Viewport Editor, navigate to the **Physics** Properties within the **Properties** Editor and click on "**Fluid**". This time, change the **Fluid Type** from "**None**" to "**Domain.**" Within the **Settings** Tab, adjust the **Do-main Type** from the default "**Gas**" to" **Liquid**" as illustrated below.

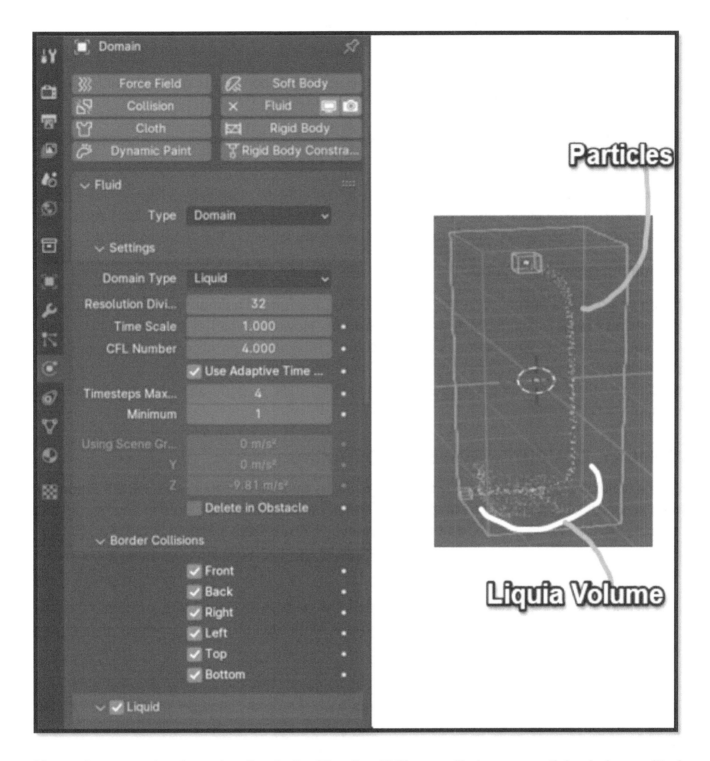

Now, when you play the animation in the Timeline Editor, you'll observe particles being emitted from the Fluid Cube. Initially, these parti-cles move along the Y-axis until Gravity takes effect, causing them to fall and splash at the bottom of the Domain, mimicking the behavior of a container. As the animation progresses, particles continue to be emitted from the Fluid Cube.

Within the **Domain,** the splashing particles appear to rise and accumulate, creating the impression of an upper surface of liquid.

At this point, the particles serve as a visual representation of the fluid flow, rather than an actual portrayal of the fluid itself. They offer an indication of how the fluid moves within the simulation. You should understand that these particles are generated by a particle system, as explained in

Chapter 10, and they interact with objects in the scene, responding to gravitational forces and interacting with obstacles or containers.

Remember that these particles do not render as the final fluid representation. Instead, they contribute to the overall visual feedback dur-ing the simulation process.

At this juncture, you have the flexibility to adjust control settings, modify the shape of the Domain, and resize or reposition the Fluid Flow Object to refine the particle display. After each adjustment, you can replay the animation to observe the impact of the changes made.

Examining Animation Length:

When you play the animation in the Timeline Editor, the default animation length is determined by the **End Frame** value, typically set to **250 frames**. However, you have the flexibility to adjust this value based on your needs. Decreasing the End Frame can accelerate the simu-lation, particularly when tweaking flow controls while increasing it allows for a longer and more detailed simulation. Hint: each time you play the animation, data is generated and stored on your computer's hard drive.

MEMORY, COMPUTER POWER, AND BAKING:

As the simulation progresses and you make revisions and adjustments, a significant amount of data is generated. During each playback of the animation, this data is stored in your computer's memory (RAM). While this might not be noticeable with relatively simple anima-tions, complex simulations can quickly consume memory, potentially slowing down your computer's processing capabilities.

To ease this issue, particularly in fluid simulation, the particle display data is written to the hard drive in a cache folder. This frees up mem-ory for future processing, ensuring smoother operation even with demanding simulations.

Initially, Blender automatically creates a Cache folder in the directory where the simulation Blender file is saved. This cache folder serves as a temporary storage location for the data generated during the simulation's development phase. However, for the final simulation, this data needs to be written to a permanent file for future reference.

The process of writing data to a permanent folder is referred to as **"baking"** When you bake, you specify the location on your hard drive where the data will be saved.

To access the **Caching** settings, select the **Domain** object in the 3D Viewport Editor, and navigate to the **Cache** tab located at the bottom of the **Physics** Properties in the **Properties** Editor. Blender automatically creates a folder named for saving the cache data with a **File Path** similar to the screenshot below.

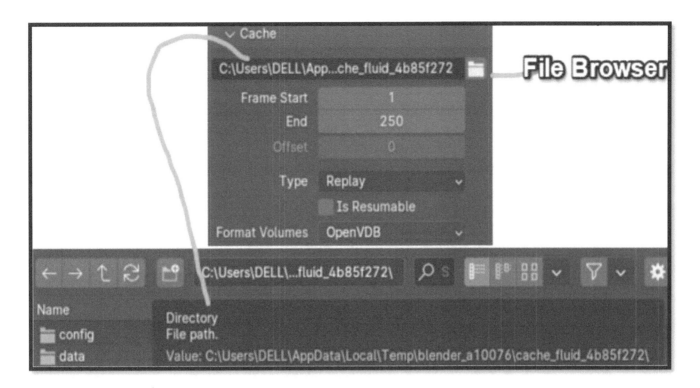

The Cache File is not readily accessible when searching for it on the computer. To make it more convenient to locate, it's advisable to create a new folder in a more accessible location.

The cache folder was created in the **C: Drive** as shown here. You can click to open the **File Browser** and designate a location for the new folder to ensure easy access to the **Cache** data.

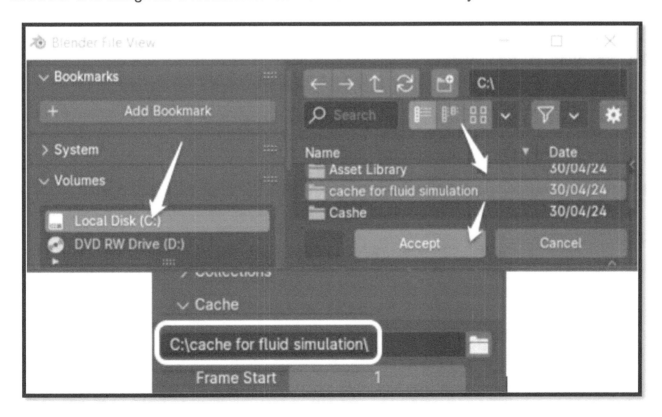

BAKING CONTROLS:

In the **Domain** Properties under the **Cache** Tab, you 'll find the **"Type"** option, which includes **"Replay** "among its three modes.

- ✓ In **"Replay"** mode, there are no **Bake** buttons available, and baking is not possible.
- ✓ **"Modular"** mode allows for individual bakes of **Baking Settings Data, Particle Data, and Mesh Data.**
- ✓ **"All"** mode, on the other hand, bakes everything simultaneously.

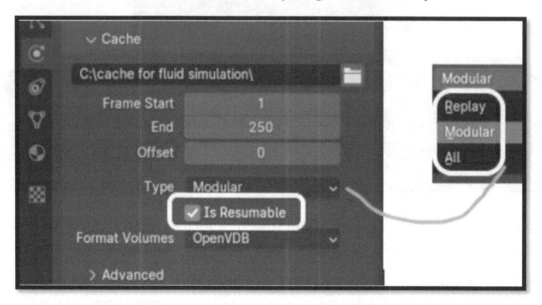

While in **"Replay"** mode, you can adjust controls, reconfigure arrangements, and replay the animation as mentioned previously, but you cannot bake. To initiate baking, you need to select either "**Modular"** or "**All"** mode.

FLUID SIMULATION CONFIGURATION

Blender integrates the Mantaflow Fluid Simulation Framework, a physically-based system designed for gas (smoke & fire) and liquid simulations.

- ✓ Hint: **Mantaflow** allows for pausing and restarting a bake, but this feature requires the "**Is Resumable"** option to be checked. With- out this option enabled, a warning will be displayed.
- ✓ With **"Is Resumable"** checked, you can pause the **Bake** by pressing **Esc**, which then reveals the **"Resume"** and **"Free"** buttons. **"Re-sume** "continues the bake, while" **Free"** clears the cache.

BAKING IN PRACTICE

To illustrate data storage and baking, consider the following exercise in the context of the previously set-up fluid simulation. The simula-tion duration is set to the default **250fram**es in the **Timeline** Editor.

- ✓ When the Domain is selected, navigating to the **Cache** Tab in the **Properties Editor, Physics** Properties reveals an automatically created folder named"/ /**cache_Fluid_4b8Sf2 72". Click the File Brower** to change to any directory of your choice.
- ✓ In the **Cache** Tab for the Domain, the **Cache Type** is set to "**Replay**", and the option **"Is Resumable"** is unchecked and inactive. In "Replay" mode, pausing and replaying the animation timeline while particles are being generated is supported, rendering the "Is Resumable" option unnecessary.
- ✓ However, having the **Cache** folder located in the "**C:\Users**" directory may not be the most convenient location for access. To address this, you can create a new folder and update the file path in the Cache Tab.

When you change the **File Path** to the new folder, subfolders named **"config"** and "**data"** are automatically generated, each containing a single **uni"** and ".**vdb"** file, respectively.

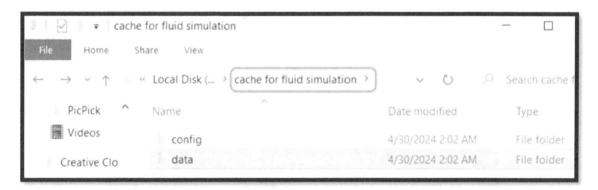

During playback of the animation in the Timeline Editor, multiple config and data files are generated, contributing to the caching process.

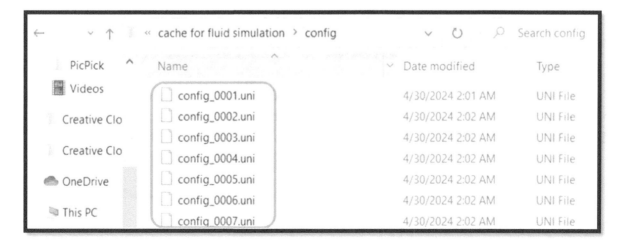

At this stage, there isn't an option available to bake the simulation. The".uni "and ".vdb" files serve as temporary files, enabling you to re- play the simulation and make adjustments as needed.

However, if you change the "Type" value to "All" In the **Properties** Editor, **Physics** Properties, under the **Cache** Tab, a "**Bake All**" button appears.

Hint: switching to "**Type: All**" deletes the config and data folders along with the ".**uni** "and ".**vdb** "**files.** As a result, replaying the animation at this point will have no effect. To regenerate the simulation, you must initiate the baking process. Additionally, changing to "**Type: All**" removes the display of particles (fluid flow) from the 3D Viewport Editor.

Hint: **Mantaflow** allows a bake to be paused and restarted, but this feature only works when "**Is Resumable**" is checked. If "**Is Resumable**" is unchecked, a warning will be displayed, indicating that the feature is note enabled.

USING BAKE ALL

When you choose to "**Bake All**", you're essentially regenerating all the necessary information for the fluid flow simulation. This informa-tion, organized into categories, includes **Bake Data** (found in the Settings Tab), **Bake Particles** (in the Particles Tab), and **Bake Mesh** (in the Mesh Tab).

To access the Bake buttons for each category, you need to select "**Modular**" in the **Cache** Type.

When you select "**All** on the Type menu, clicking the "**Bake All**" button starts the baking process. A progress bar appears in the **Timeline** Editor, indicating the progress of the bake. Meanwhile, the "**Bake All**" button transforms into an instruction to "Pause Bake" as shown below.

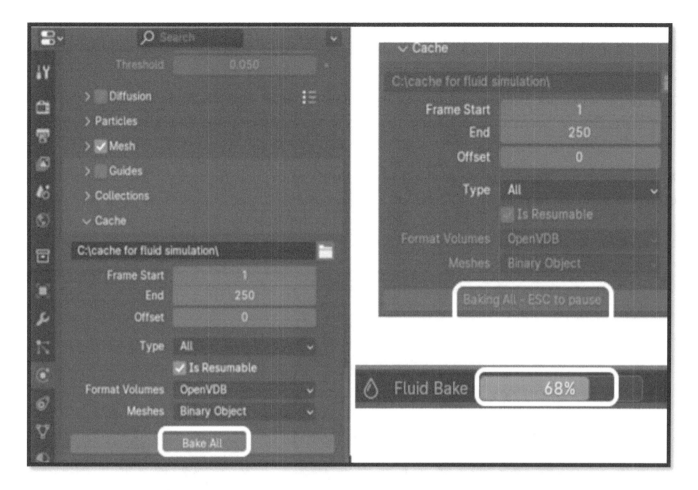

When you complete the bake, the **"Bake"** button changes to **"Free Bake,"** which allows you to delete all the data generated during the process.

In the 3D Viewport, the fluid is displayed as a mesh, ready for rendering. This signifies the successful completion of the baking process.

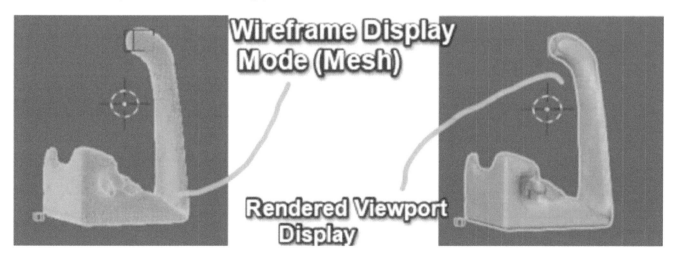

USING BAKE MODULAR

✓ When you choose **"Modular"** as t h e **Cache** Type, the **Bake** button in the **Cache** Tab disappears. Instead, separate **Bake** buttons are provided for each category, as previously explained.

✓ Hint: you need to **Bake Data** before you can **Bake Mesh** or **Particles,** and the **"Is Resumable"** checkbox must be checked in the **Cache**

Tab for t h is to work properly. Additionally, to bake Particles, you need to select (check) at least one of the **Spray Foam,** or **Bub-bles** categories in the **Particles** Tab. **Selecting Spray, Foam,** and/or **Bubbles** generates particles within the mesh, creating these specific effects.

At this stage, the **Rendered View** displays the **fluid mesh** in a gray color. This is because the demonstration started with the default **Cube Object** as the Domain, and the default gray material is applied. However, by making some adjustments in the **Material Properties**, you can achieve a nice, cool purple color or any color of your choice.

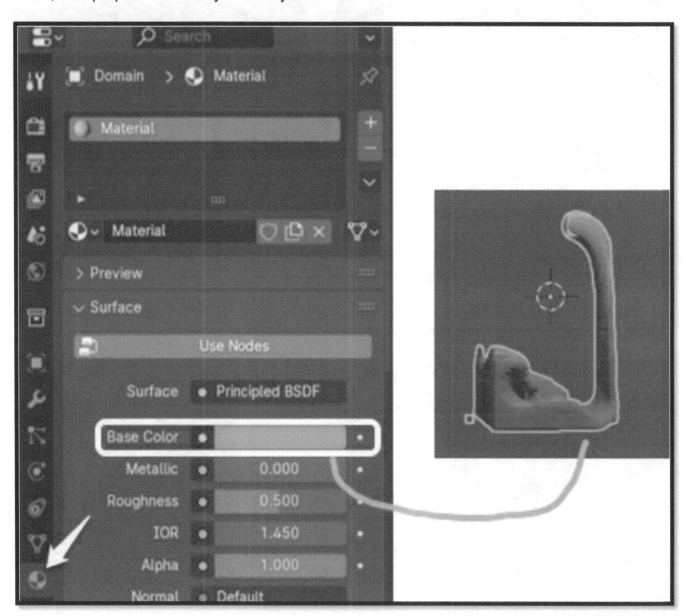

Hint: If your **Domain** is not created from the default **Cube** Object, you'll need to apply a new material to it to customize its appearance.

REBAKING WITH CACHE TYPE: BAKE ALL

During a bake with the **Cache Type** set to "**Bake All,**" you have the option to **pause** the process at any time by pressing the **Esc** key. Pausing allows you to preview the fluid being generated in the 3D Viewport Editor. If everything looks satisfactory, you can resume the bake, pro- vided that **"Is Resumable"** is checked.

In the **Properties** Editor, the bake but tons will display a **"Resume** "option, allowing you to restart the bake from where you left off. Hint: once the bake is initiated, the Physics button controls become grayed out, preventing you from changing settings. If you forgot to check "**Is Resumable**", you 'll need to free the bake and start over.

To make changes to settings during a bake, press Esc to stop the bake, adjust the settings, and then resume the bake.

REBAKING WITH CACHE TYPE: MODULAR

After baking with the **Cache** Type set to "**Modular,**" the "**Bake Data**" and "Bake Mesh " buttons change to "**Free Data**" and "**Free Mesh**", respectively. Clicking either of these buttons cancels the data saved to memory in the cache and reactivates the controls. This allows you to adjust settings and re bake if necessary. Hint: you can re bake the mesh without re baking the data.

As mentioned earlier, when you bake a simulation, data is written to the cache folder on your hard drive, freeing up RAM. Hint: when you save the Blender file, the data written to the cache folder is not saved along with it. Even when you close the Blender file, the data remains stored in the cache on the hard drive. However, if you create a new simulation using the same cache folder, the existing data will be over- written. Consequently, when you reopen the original Blender file, the simulation will not play as expected. To avoid this issue, it's advis-able to create a new cache folder for each new simulation you create.

INTRODUCING SPRAY, FOAM, AND BUBBLES

Up to this point, particles have been generated to mimic the flow of fluid. These particles were created during the baking process. In the **Particle** Properties section of the **Properties** Editor, having **Domain** selected, you'll notice that a **Particle** System named "**Liquid**" has auto-matically been applied to the **Domain**.

Hint: you cannot directly edit the **Particle** System applied to the Domain in the **Particle** Properties section. You can do this in the **Physics** Properties

To modify the **Particle** system, select(check) either **Spray, Foam, or Bubbles in the Fluid Physics** but ton s section of the Properties Editor under the **Particles** Tab.

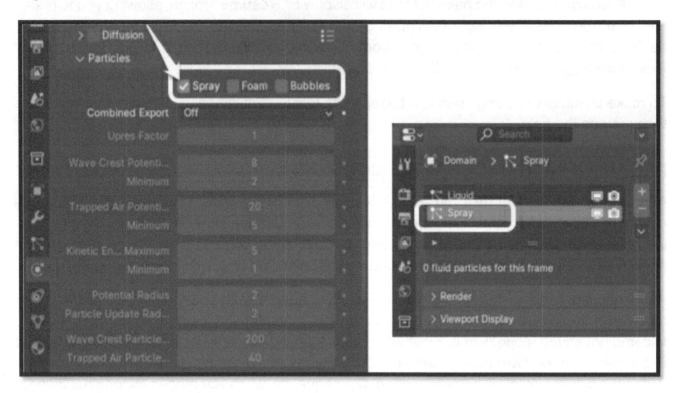

Additional particles can be created to represent **spray, foam, or bubbles** by toggling the corresponding buttons in the Fluid Physics but- tons section. These controls allow for adjustments to the particle system as a whole.

Recall: Particle systems themselves do not render.

To show the spray particles within the fluid in the 3D Viewport Editor, you need to add an **Object** to the scene and set the Particle System to render the particles as instances of that object. This allows for the particles to be displayed using the selected object as a reference.

INSTANCE OBJECT

To incorporate an **Icosphere** into the scene.

1) first, add it to the scene and scale it down appropriately, positioning it to one side. It's recommended to assign a vibrant material to the **Icosphere** to enhance its visibility.
2) Maintain the default subdivision level **(1)** for the **Icosphere** when in **Edit** Mode. This ensures that the object has a minimal number of vertices, reducing the computational load during the baking process.

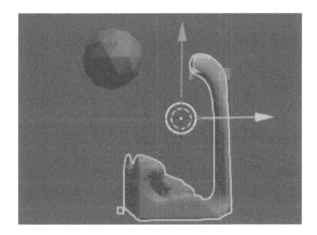

3) After selecting **Spray** Particles in the **Domain Physics** Properties, a **Spray Particle** System is introduced, as shown in the screenshot below. To render the particles as instances of the **Icosphere,** navigate to the Render Tab and set **"Render As"** to **"Object."** Then, in the Object Tab, designate the **Icosphere** as the Instance Object. Finally, in the **Viewport Display** Tab, set **"Display As"** to **"Rendered."**

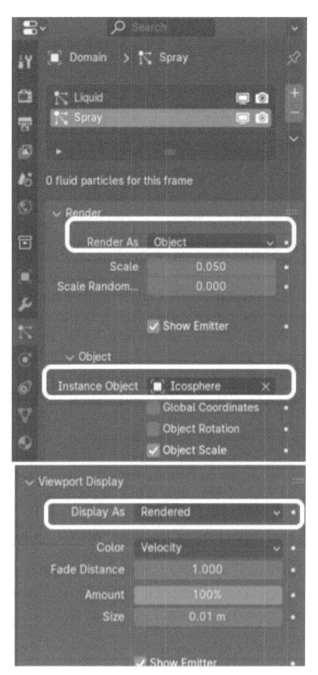

Rebake the simulation to observe the spray particles, represented by tiny Icospheres, dispersed around the fluid mesh.

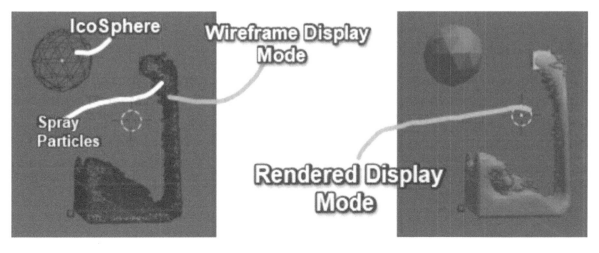

INCONCLUSION

As you progress through this exercise, it's easy to get lost, so let's recap.

- ✓ The default **Cube Object** serves as the **Domain** for the simulation.
- ✓ A second Cube, scaled down in size relative to the **Domain**, is positioned inside as the **Inflow** Object.
- ✓ Using the Properties Editor in the Physics Properties and selecting the Domain, **Fluid Data** and **Mesh Data** were baked.
- ✓ Keep in mind that the default animation length is **250frame**s, resulting in relatively short baking times. Longer animations can sig-nificantly extend baking durations. Therefore, it's not recommended to **have "Is Resumable"** checked in the **Domain's Physics** Properties, Cache Tab, as it may gene rate additional data during replaying.
- ✓ Within the Cache Folder, you'll find subfolders containing various file formats, which are data files for the simulation.
- ✓ Remember, this is supposed to be fun, and as you become more familiar with the settings, you'll achieve incredible results. You can set up and bake **Bubble Particle s and Foam Particles** simultaneously.
- ✓ This exercise has focused on minimal settings. However, there are numerous settings to explore. Nonetheless, the above informa-tion should provide a foundational understanding of the basic fluid simulation process.

ANOTHER INSTANCE OF FLUID SIMULATION

Continuing from the fluid simulation setup detailed in the previous section, we explored a basic configuration utilizing **a Fluid Flow Type with "Liquid" set as "Flow Type" and a Flow Behavior to "Inflow".**

When you set Flow Behavior to Inflow, fluid is continuously delivered throughout the animation. To explore further into this.

Let's examine how the Fluid Behavior differs when using **Type Geometry**. Instead of a continuous flow, Type Geometry delivers the fluid in a mass.

SCENARIO: FILLING A CUP

In this scenario, we aim to generate a volume of fluid to pour into a cup. The setup illustrated below displays the 3D Viewport Editor in Wireframe Viewport Shading Mode. The scene below comprises a fluid emitter **(a UV Sphere)**, a domain cube (a scaled-up default Cube), and an obstacle object (a cup).

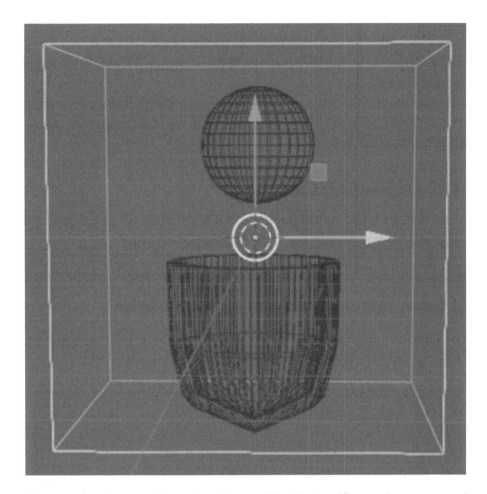

For details on the cup, refer to **Chapter Four (4).** Note: If you have saved a Blender file containing the cup, you can append it into a new Blender scene. It's crucial to apply the modifiers anytime you are developing the cup as discussed in **Chapter Four (4).**

DOMAIN OBJECT CONFIGURATION

The domain, represented by a scaled cube enclosing the sphere and the cup, serves as the setting for our simulation. For this demonstra-tion, default physics settings will be utilized.

1) With the **cube** selected, navigate to the **Properties** Editor within the 3DViewport Editor, access the **Physics** Properties, and click on Fluid to reveal the Fluid Ta b.
2) Set the **Fluid Type** to **Domain** and set the **Domain Type** as Liquid in the Settings ta b. Ensure to check **"Mesh"** at the bot to m of the panel.
3) In the **Cache** Ta b, adjust the default End Fra me to **50.** Set the End Frame to **50** in the **Timeline** Editor as well.

SETTING UPTHE GENERATOR OBJECT

The   fluid emission will originate from the sphere positioned within the d**omain** directly above the **cup**. This type of object is commonly referred to as the "**Generator"**. While it might be tempting to simply call the sphere the **"Fluid Object"** because it controls fluid generation, it's important to Hint: all objects included in the simulation with **Fluid Physics** applied are considered **Fluid Objects.**

To configure the setup,

1) select the **UV Sphere**, in the **Properties Editor** under **Physics Properties**, and adjust the values as follows:

a. Set **Flow Behavior** to "**Geometry**," which defines the fluid inflow to match the shape of the Generator Object. This means that the fluid will be generated as a spherical mass rather than a continuous flow.

SETTING UP THE OBSTACLE OBJECT

Objects that interact with the fluid in the simulation are referred to as Effectors. In this case, the obstacle impeding the fluid flow within the domain will be the cup.

1) Select the **Cup** and set the following **values** in the **Properties** Editor as shown below:

a. Fluid type to "**Effector**" and Settings Effector Type to "**Collision**".

Hint: The **Effector Object is** named "**Cylinder** "in the **Outliner Editor**, as the cup model may have originated from a default cylinder object and hasn't been renamed.

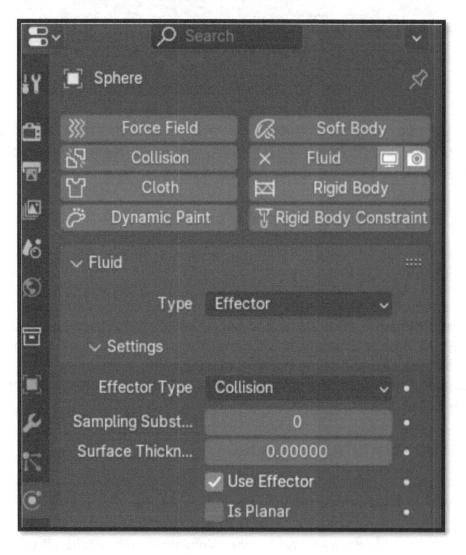

Also, take note of the **Effector** Type: **Collision**.

CONSIDERING SCALE ANDPROPORTION

When crafting a fluid animation, it's crucial to consider the proportion, otherwise known as the size relationship of objects. In this simula-tion, the size of the Sphere Flow object has been sized relative to the effector cup. The volume of the sphere determines the volume of fluid generated; thus, it's scaled accordingly to fit reasonably into the cup.

Currently, the cup is quite large, with a diameter of 1.97 meters, making it a sizable cup. If placed within a scene alongside other objects, the scale of everything would need to be relative.

Another aspect to consider is time. Assess the setup and determine how long you want the substantial drop of fluid to take to descend into the cup. To observe the outcome, perhaps around two seconds would be suitable.

The animation length has been set to **50** frames, with the output framerate defaulting to **24** frames per second (fps) in the **Properties** Editor under **Output** Proper ties. If you desire precisely two seconds, adjust the frame rate to 25 fps.

UNDERSTANDING VISCOSITY

Viscosity is another crucial factor to take in to account. It refers to the "**thickness** "of the fluid and essentially represents the force required to move an object of a certain surface area through it at a particular speed. In Blender, the viscosity used is kinematic viscosity, which is a type of dynamic viscosity.

The table provided below displays various fluids alongside their dynamic and kinematic viscosities.

Fluid Type	Dynamic Viscosity (cp)	Kinematic viscosity (Blender, in $m^2 s^{-1}$
Water (20 °C)	1.002×10^0 (1.002)	1.002×10^{-6} (0.0000001002)
Honey (20 °C)	1.0×10^4 (10.000)	2.0×10^{-3} (0.002)
Oli SAE 50	5.0×10^2 (500)	5.0×10^{-5} (0.0005)
Ketchup	1.0×10^5 (100,000)	1.0×10^{-1} (0.1)
Melting Glass	1.0×10^{15}	1.0×10^0 (1.0)
Chocolate Syrup	3.0×10^4 (30,000)	3.0×10^{-3} (0.003)

To adjust **viscosity** in Blender, navigate to the **P**roperties Editor under **Physics** Properties with the **domain** selected. You'll find the **viscos-ity** settings in the **Diffusion** Tab.

By default, the viscosity setting is for water as shown below.

✓ Base: 1.000
✓ Exponent: 6

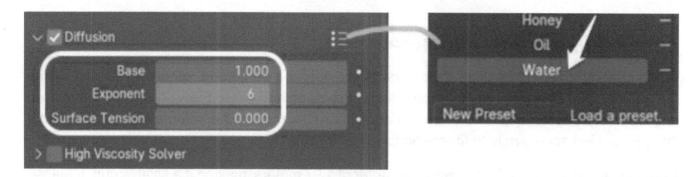

Note: The **Diffusion** Tab will only appear when the **Domain Type** is set to **Liquid,** and in the **Viscosity Presets**, the default display is **Fluid Presets.** Clicking the Fluid Presets button reveals a **selection** menu containing options like **Honey, Oil, and Water.** When you select an op-tion, **Fluid Presets** updates the chosen option.

With these fundamental settings specified, proceed to **Bake Data** and then **Bake Mesh**. The performance of the baking process will vary depending on the computing power of your system. Hint: many impressive video demonstrations found online tend to gloss over this process, so be prepared for potential wait times during baking. For this demonstration, on my PC, both Data Bake and Mesh Bake took some seconds.

Recall: In the **Cache** Tab, the default **Type** is set to **Replay.** Ensure to select **"Is Resumable"** and change the Type to **"Modular". Addition - ally, adjust the Cache Folder** to an empty folder (that means clear all the files in the Cache folder).

Bake the Data, and proceed to bake the Mesh by expanding the Mesh Tab. Upon completion of baking the data, the sphere will be displayed with a blue mesh overlay. When the mesh baking process finishes, the domain will consolidate and adopt the shape of the sphere.

Navigate to the **Timeline** Editor and play the **animation.**

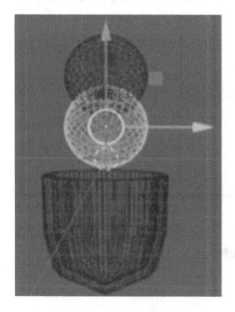 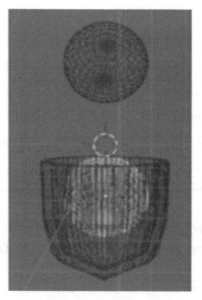 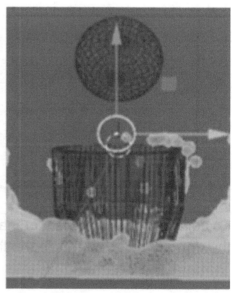

Now, the consolidated domain represents the fluid that descends into the cup. However, you may notice that it breaks through the cup mesh and ends up resting in what was the profile of the domain. This is not the desired outcome. It requires modification followed by a re- bake.

254

In the **3D Viewport Editor**, select the **cup**. In the **Properties** Editor under **Physics** Properties, navigate to the **Fluid** Tab. Here, you'll find the **Surface Thickness** parameter, currently set to **0.00000**. This value determines the distance around the effector object used when calculat-ing collisions. The default value is **0.00000.**

A suggested correct value for **Surface Thickness is 1.0000.**

Next, select the **Domain Cube** in the Outliner, which is now consolidated as a sphere on the Flow Sphere. Free the data and mesh bakes. Adjust the **Surface Thickness** value, clear the cache folder, and then **re-bake both data and mesh**.

Finally, play the animation to observe the fluid descending and filling the cup (depending on the sphere size).

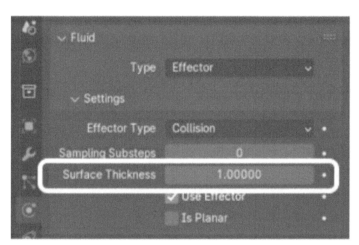
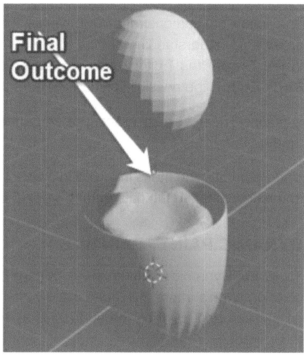

Note: If the baking process is not proceeding as anticipated, you can stop it by pressing the Esc key or clicking the **Cancel** button in the **Header**. Adjustments to the settings may be necessary to rectify the issue. To restart the simulation, select the **Domain** by clicking on the **Cube** in the **Outliner** Editor (which is now the blob attached to the sphere) and press **Resume** to continue the bake. Alternatively, free the bake and start the baking process again.

Additional Notes: if the demonstration does not unfold as expected, there may have been an error in the setup. Double-check your settings and adjust values accordingly. However, please note that after changing a setting, you'll need to free the data and re bake the simu-lation. Simply altering settings will not resolve the issue.

Before starting anew fluid simulation, ensure to clear the data from the cache file or designate a new location for saving the bake. If data remains in the cache when a new domain is created, Blender will attempt to utilize the existing data, which may lead to unexpected results.

CHAPTER 14: DYNAMIC PAINT TECHNIQUES

Dynamic Paint involves using one object to either color (paint) or deform the surface of another object. When coloring, the process resem-bles a painting on a canvas, with one object acting as a brush and the object being painted referred to as the canvas.

Despite its name, Dynamic Paint can also deform the surface of an object by either permanently displacing vertices or simulating wave formations as one object moves through the surface of another, creating a dynamic effect.

The following demonstration will reveal the basic setup for using Dynamic Paint, aiming to provide an understanding of how to set up the physics for basic operation. By altering settings in the **Properties** Editor under **Physics Properties** and creating node arrangements in the **Node Editor**, the possibilities for final outputs are limitless.

Caution: The following procedure is derived from experimentation and represents just one method.

Understanding the steps involved in creating a Dynamic Paint effect will enable you to research and follow detailed tutorials for further exploration.

DYNAMIC PAINT - PAINTING

To reveal Dynamic Painting, a UV Sphere object will be utilized as a brush to apply a material color onto the surface of a Plane object, referred to as the canvas. Although any object can serve as a brush and paint on the surface of any object, a Plane provides a suitable flat surface for this purpose.

The term **"Dynamic"** in the title indicates that painting occurs during the play back of an animation sequence in the **Timeline** Editor. As the brush moves across the canvas surface during the animation sequence, painting occurs. This introductory illustration will utilize the Format Type: Vertex, meaning that color will be applied to the vertices of the canvas where they intersect with the brush object.

1) Set up the scene with a **UV Sphere** object positioned to the side of a scaled-up and subdivided plane object as shown below. The plane should be subdivided **eighty** times in **Edit** Mode to ensure an adequate number of vertices. Additionally, the plane should have a material color applied, such as blue.

For ease of testing the procedure, animate the **UV Sphere** to move across the Plane along the **Y-axis** across **100** frames.

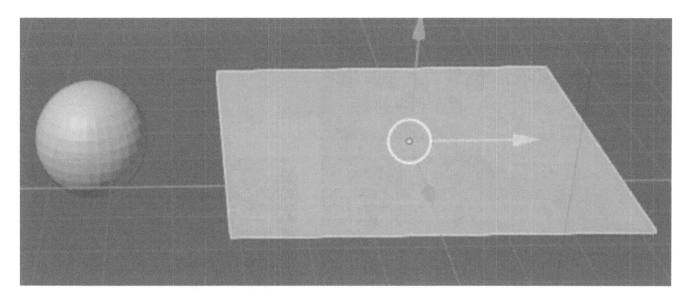

2) With the plane selected, subdivide it in Edit Mode **eighty** times to generate an ample number of vertices.

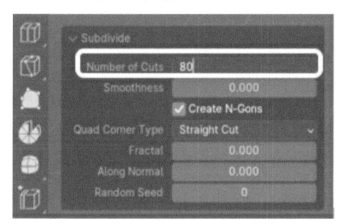

Note: Ensure that the **3D Viewport** Editor is set to **Solid Viewport Shading** Mode. As mentioned in the introduction, the UV Sphere object will serve as a brush to apply color on the **Plane** object, acting as a Canvas. These terms, **"brush"** and **"canvas,"** are utilized in the **Proper- ties** Editor under **Physics** Properties.

BRUSH SETUP

Begin by selecting the UV Sphere in Frame 1 in the animation. Note that the Sphere doesn't have a material applied, but it is displayed in the viewport with the default Blender gray color.

Go to the **Properties** Editor and access the **Physics** Properties. Click on **Dynamic** Paint, then in the **Dynamic Paint Tab**, Select **Brush** on the **Type** menu and click **Add Brush** to reveal the **settings** (which will subsequently change **Add Brush to Remove Brush**).

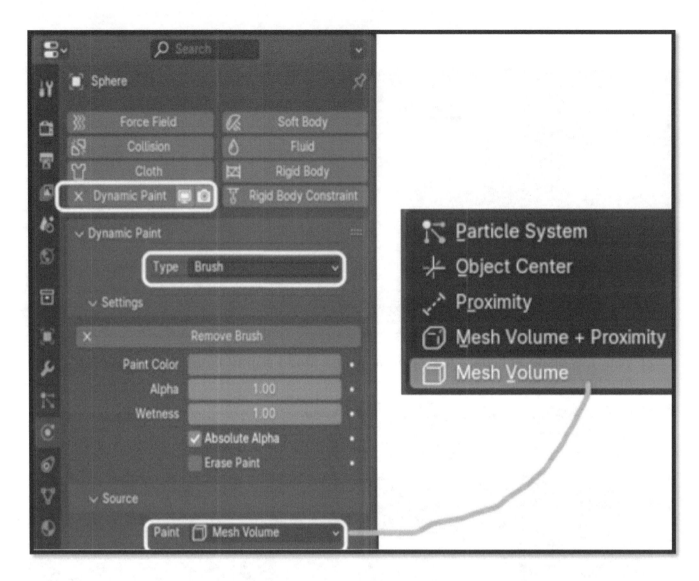

Hint: the paint color is set to dark blue, and in the **Source** Tab, Paint is selected as type **Mesh Volume**. These settings will be reconsidered later.

VIEWPORT SHADING SETTINGS

By default, the 3D Viewport is set to **Solid Viewport Shading** Mode. To prove Dynamic Painting, switch to **Rendered Viewport Shading**

Mode by selecting it from the options in the **Viewport Header.**

CANVAS CONFIGURATION

1) Select the Plane, switch to **Edit** Mode, and confirm that the mesh is adequately subdivided with 80subdivisions.
   Important Notice: Apply a material to the canvas with **"Use Nodes"** active. The default gray color is also okay.

2) Return to **Object** Mode and activate **Dynamic Paint Physics** in the **Properties** Editor. Set the **Dynamic Paint Type** to **Canvas** (the default). Click **"Add Canvas"** to reveal the **Dynamic Paint Properties**.

3) In the **Surface** Tab, the **Surface Type** is set to **Pain**t. Expand the **Output** Tab located at the bottom. You'll notice that both **Paintmap** and **Wetmap** Layers are highlighted in red.

4) Click the plus sign (+) next to the **P**aintmap Layer to create a paint layer named" **dp_paintmap".** Once created, the red highlight will change to black, indicating the presence of the paint layer.

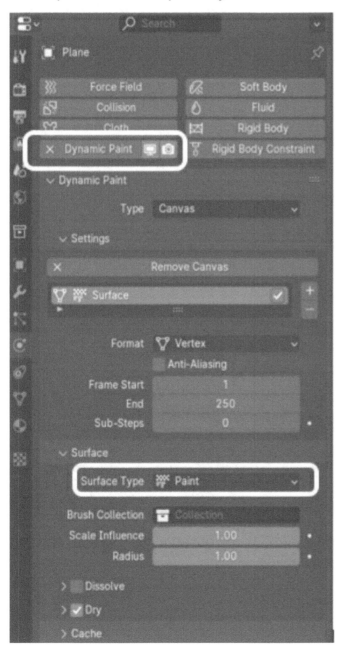

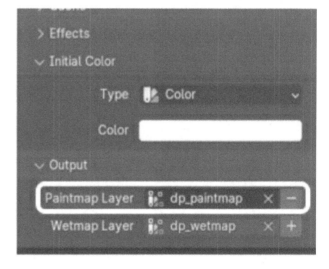

5) With the **Canvas (Plane)** selected, open the **Shader** Editor displaying a **Principled BSDF** Node connected to a Material Output Node. Add an **Attribute** Node.

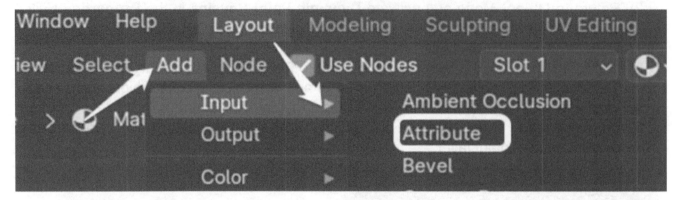

6) Connect the Attribute Node and Enter "**dp _paintmap**" in the **Attribute Node Name** field.

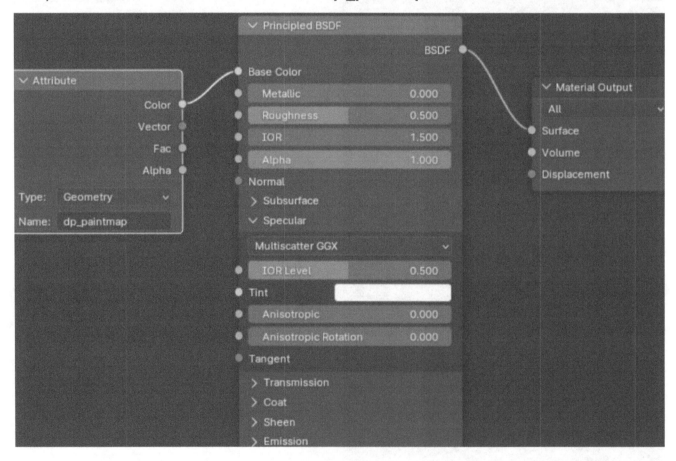

7) By playing the animation in the **Timeline** Editor, you'll observe the Sphere passing through the Plane, painting a blue stripe as it moves.

BRUSH PAINTSOURCE OPTIONS

The paint settings in the Dynamic Paint Source Tab for the brush (sphere) dictate the characteristics of the brush stroke. Refer to the screenshot below for visual guidance.

- ✓ **Mesh Volume**
- ✓ **Mesh Volume + Proximity**
- ✓ **Object Center - Distance: 0.500**

Note: When using Particle System, a Particle System must be created for the UV sphere in the **Properties** Editor under **Particle** Properties and then entered in the **Brush Settings Source** Tab. During playback of the animation, particles emitted from the **Brush (UV sphere)** make contact with the Plane, resulting in the application of color.

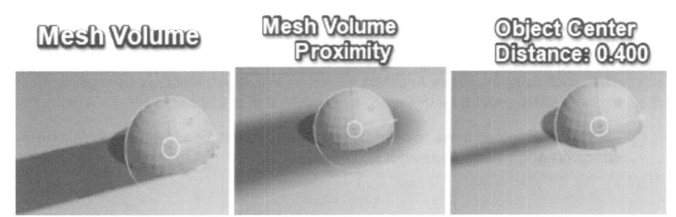

CHAPTER 15: RIGGING WITH RIGIFY AND ANIMBOX

The title Rigging- (Rigify- Animbox) signifies the step-by-step process of rigging a humanoid character and animating it to walk using

Blender's add-on s, Rigify and Rigify Animbox.

Rigify, when activated, offers a range of pre constructed armature assemblies with bones organized in parent-child relationships similar to a skeletal structure. It automatically generates control handles for these assemblies, forming what's known as the Armature Control Rig.

Rigify Animbox complements Rigify by generating an automated walk-cycle animation for the character. This animation, when played, depicts the character walking.

However, to utilize Rigify Animbox with a custom armature assembly, the custom assembly must align with the structure provided by Rigify.

Hint: Rigify Animbox is specifically designed to work together with the armature assemblies provided by Rigify Add-on.

REQUIREMENT

Before you can utilize the Add-ons, ensure you have a humanoid figure model and have installed and activated the Rigify and Rigify -Anim- box Add-ons on your computer. If you're unfamiliar with installing and activating Add-ons in Blender, refer to the instructions below:

INSTALLING AN ADD-ON IN BLENDER

Let's walk through using the **Rigify Animbox** add-on by **VALANGDANCE** as an example. First off, kudos to **VALANGDANCE f**or this excel- lent contribution to Blender.

1) Use the link provided below to download the **Rigify Animbox add-on: https://blender-ddons.or>grigif y -animbox-addon**

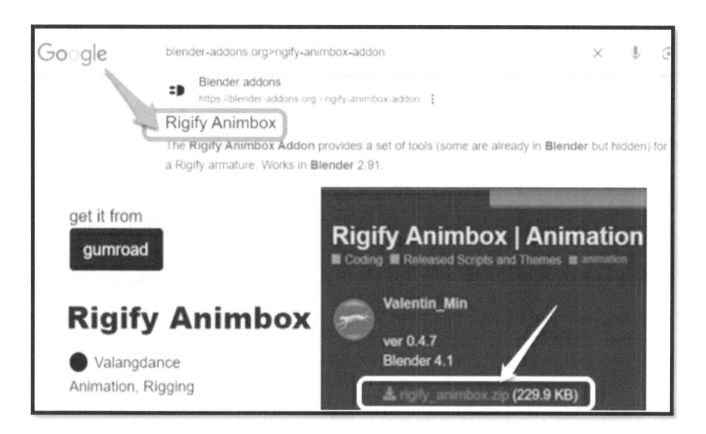

2) Downloading the add-on might seem a bit complex at first, but you'll end up with a ZIP file named Rigify animbox.

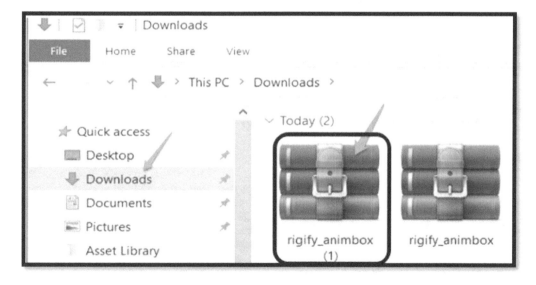

3) Open Blender and Go to **Edit > Preferences** in the Blender Screen Header. In the **Preferences** Editor, select Add-ons and click the Install button located in the Header to install it.

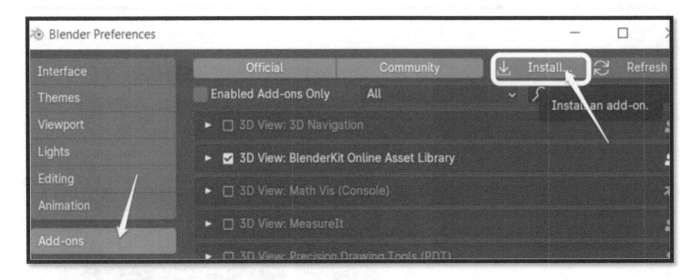

4) This opens the **Blender File View.** Navigate to find and select **the rigify_anirnbox.zip file**.

5) Click to choose the file, then click **Install Add-ons**.

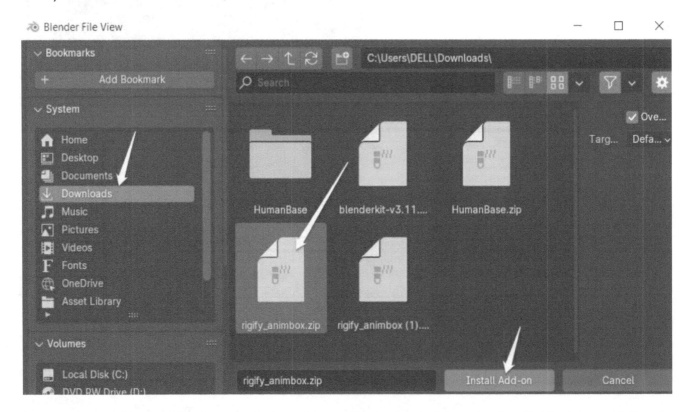

Remember: After installation, don't forget to activate **the add-on** in the Preferences Editor to start using it.

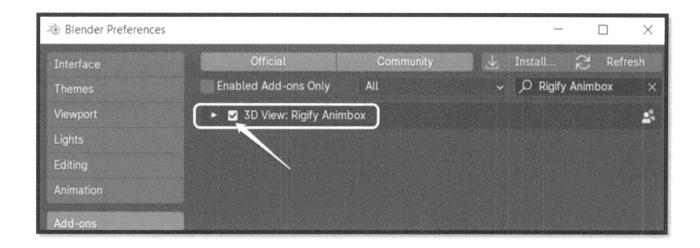

RIGIFY

Rigify offers a selection of pre-built Armature assemblies where the Bones are interconnected in Child-Parent Relationships. In our demonstrations, **Rigify and Rigify Animbox** will be displayed using the **Human Armature**, which is labeled as **Human (Meta-Rig).**

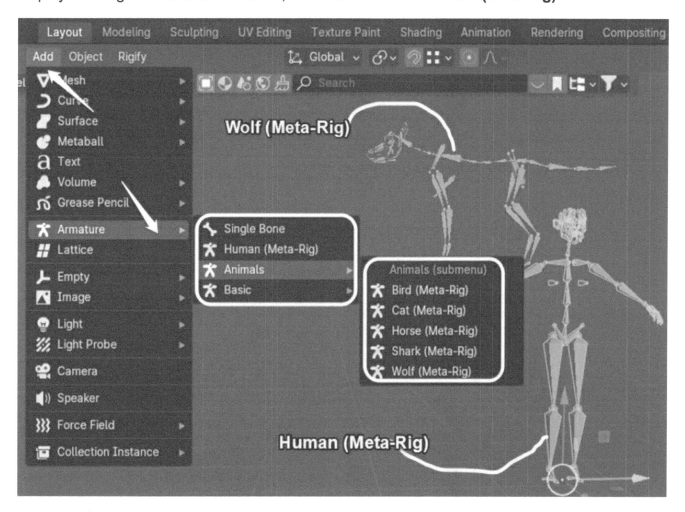

Let's go over how to rig a humanoid character and animate it walking using **Blender Add-ons Rigify and RigifyAnimbox.**

MODELS FOR ANIMATING

When it comes to choosing an animation model, you have a few options. You can create your own human figure model, making sure it's made of mesh and has enough vertices for smooth animation. Alternatively, you can download models from websites like Turbo Squid or Free3D. Just remember, whichever model you choose, it needs to be a mesh model with sufficient vertices for the best results.

You can find models on Free3Dhere: **https://free3d.com/ 3d-models/ blender-human**

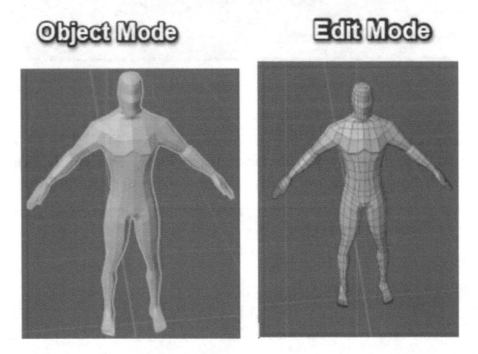

You can find models on Turbo Squid here: **https://www.turbosguid.com/Search/ 3D-Modelsf free/human/blend**

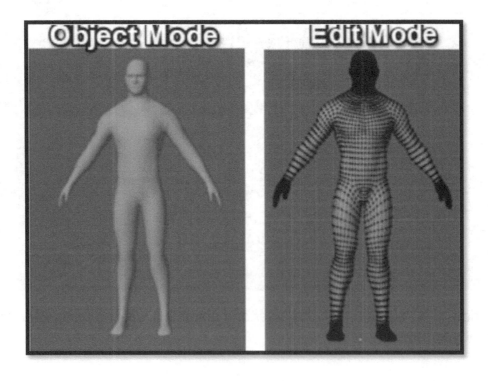

When considering downloading a model, it's important to recognize that not all models are created equal. For instance, let's take a look at the two models above. This model with insufficient vertices might present challenges when it comes to rigging it for animation due to its limited number of vertices in the mesh.

Another option for obtaining a human model is through the open-source program Make Human. By exporting the default human model from Make Human as a Wave front .obj file, you can then import it into Blender.

Instructions for this process are itemized below or on the Make Human website:

EXPORT YOUR MODEL FROM MAKE HUMAN

To export your model from the Make Human Website, start by:

1) clicking on the **"Export"** button located in the Make Human interface. This button defaults to exporting the current model.
2) Before finalizing the export, you can tweak the model's settings by adjusting the sliders found in the Macro panel. Once you're satis-fied with the adjustments, click on the **"Export"** button again to reveal the available mesh format options.
3) For Blender compatibility, choose the **Wavefront .obj** format. After selecting the format, input a suitable File Name in the header and designate a destination folder for the export.
4) Finally, click on the **"Export"** button to save the model. Upon clicking **"Export,"** your PC's file browser will prompt you to confirm the save action. Simply click **"Save"** to complete the export process.

A model with several vertices is more suitable for rigging and animating purposes. For this demonstration, we will stick to the Model downloaded from the Turbo Squid because it has sufficient vertices.

WHAT IS ARMATURE ASSEMBLY

The Armature Assembly is a collection of bones that form the skeleton of a character. It can consist of a single bone or multiple bones depending on the complexity of the model.

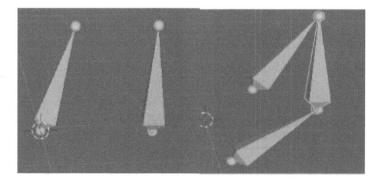

Rigify offers a pre-configured multi-bone armature specifically designed for humanoid models. Hint: An Armature can be several bones or a single bone.

To add a Rigify Armature Assembly to your scene:

1) Go to the **3D Viewport** Header, and click on **Add-Armature - Human Metarig**. This creates **an Armature Assembly named Metarig.**

2) The **Human Metarig,** also known as the **Armature Bone Skeleton**, is positioned between the legs of the model. In **Object** Mode, select the **Armature** and scale it up to fit the proportions of the model.

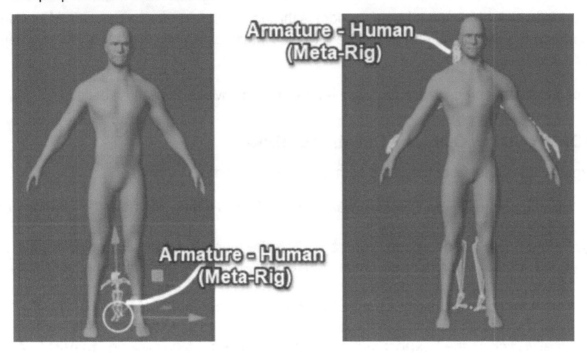

3) It's common for the Armature to be partially obscured by the model. To fully visualize the Armature, access the Properties Editor, go to Object Data Properties for the Metarig, and go to the Viewport Display Tab. Ensure the **"In Front"** option is checked to bring the Armature to the forefront of the scene.

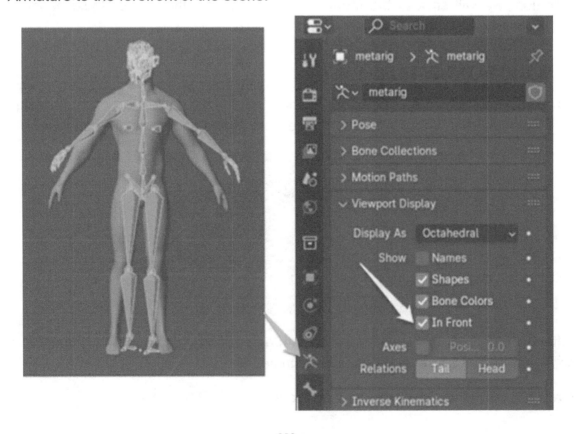

ENSURING PROPER ALIGNMENT OF ARMATURE SCALE

It's crucial to maintain consistency in scale alignment when importing a model into the scene. After import, the model's scale value is set to 1.000, which can be confirmed by pressing the **N** key to reveal the Object Properties Panel

Similarly, when the **Metarig** is introduced into the scene, it also possesses a scale value of 1.000, despite appearing much smaller. As the **Metarig** is scaled up to match the model, its scale value will increase accordingly, possibly reaching around **8.4.**

To ensure uniformity in scale between the model and the Metarig, it's imperative to reset the **Metarig's** scale value to 1.000. With the **Metarig** selected, press **Ctrl + A** and choose **"Apply-All Transforms".** This resets all transformations, including translation, rotation, and scale.

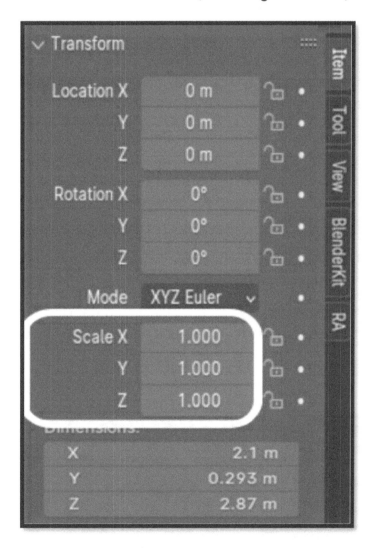

Alternatively, you can manually adjust the **X, Y, and Z** scale values in the **Object Properties** Panel.

Hint: The Armature Assembly obtained from **Rigify** is named **Metarig** and constitutes a multi-one armature. Armatures in Blender can be viewed in the 3D Viewport Editor in Object Mode, Edit Mode, and **Pose** Mode.

ACCURATELY ALIGN ARMATURE ASSEMBLY WITH THE MODEL

Make sure the armature assembly is properly aligned with the model, ensuring that the bones fit comfortably inside the mesh. Select the **Armature** and switch to **Edit** Mode by pressing **Tab**. To aid in alignment, activate **the X-Axis** Mirror located in the upper right corner of the **3DViewport** **by clicking on X.**

With the **X-Axis** Mirror active (highlighted in blue), positioning a right-hand bone in the armature will automatically adjust the position of the left-hand bone. The bones in the armature are interconnected through parent-child relationships, meaning when parent bones move, child bones follow suit. This relationship only applies when the armature is in Pose Mode.

Adjusting bone positions to fit the **Model** is done in **Edit Mode.** Select the bones and move them accordingly to fit within the Mesh of the **Model.** Moving bones in **Edit Mode** maintain their connection to the **Armature** and preserve the parent-child relationships, which are ac-tive in **Pose Mode**.

Armature bones can be linked to Vertex Groups in the Mesh. However, when using the armature assembly from Rigify, a control rig is cre-ated and linked to the mesh using the positions of the armature bones for association.

The Rigify- provided armature assembly **(Metarig)** includes detailed bones for the face, ears, and hands. For simplicity, these can be re- moved as demonstrated below.

zoom in and rotate the viewport. Use **Circle Select** to choose **bone**s and **press X** to delete them.

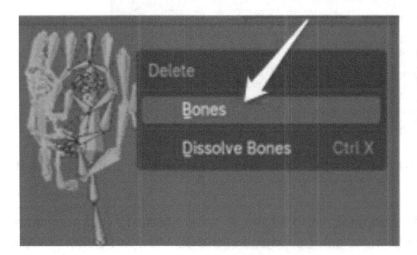

Repeat this process to delete the hand bones (both hands).

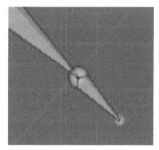

While in **Edit** Mode, select the **Bones** and place them within the Mesh Model. To view different angles, **press Num Pad 1** for the front view, **Num Pad** 3 for the side view, and **Num Pad 7** for the top view.

To properly align the **Upper Left** Arm Bone, **in Edit** Mode, select the **Tip and Base** of the Bone separately. Then, use the G key to drag them into position relative to the Model. You can also manipulate **Bone Bodies** by **translating, rotating, and scaling them**.

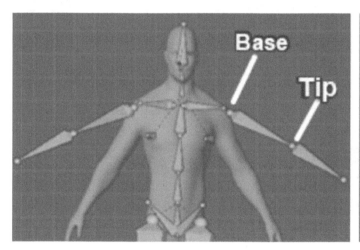
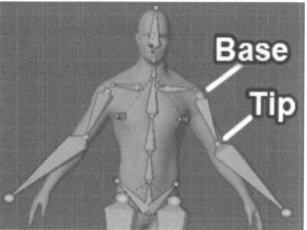

Take the time to go through the entire Model, aligning the Armature Bones. You don't need to create a detailed anatomical skeleton. The goal is to position Bones inside the Mesh Model so that the Mesh can be Parented to the Control Rig (as explained later) based on the Bone alignment.

To simplify the alignment, you can delete the **Face** and **Hand Bones** since the focus is on generating a Walk Cycle. However, adding hand and facial animations can enhance character and realism but requires more detailed alignment.

Once the Bones are aligned, switch to **Object Mode** by pressing **Tab, then press Ctrl + A** and select **All Transforms** again.

TIDY UP

When setting up a Control Rig, you might encounter a problem caused by an unusual **Bone** named **"face"** t h at remains inside the **"Head Bone",** under "spine.**006**", even after deleting other **Face Bones.**

You'll notice this Bone listed in **the Outliner Editor** when expanding the **Metarig** entries. To remove it, simply select **"face"** in **the Outliner Editor**, press the **X** key, and then choose **Delete.**

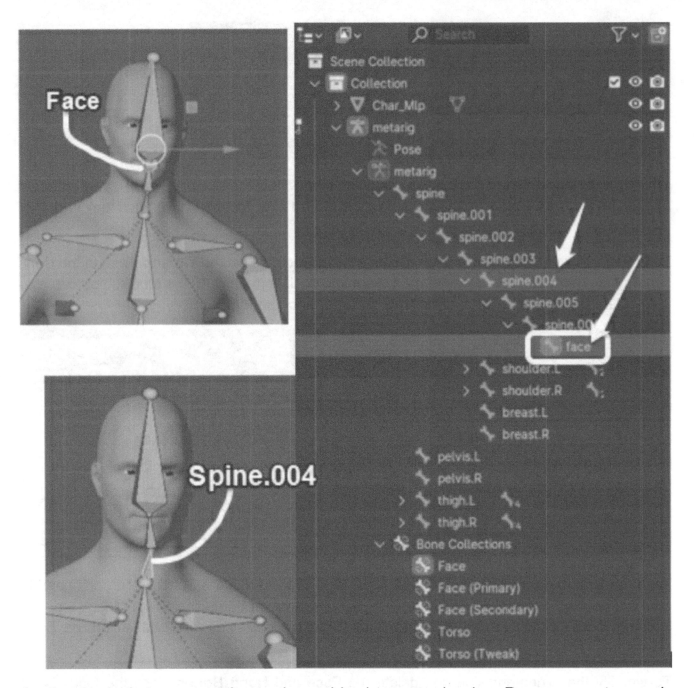

Another issue that can sometimes arise and lead to errors is when **Bones** are not properly aligned. For instance, the base of "spine.004" may not align with the tip of "spine.003."

To fix this, switch to **Edit** Mode by pressing Tab, **select "spine.004"**, delete it, then select the tip of "**spine.003",** and extrude a new **Bone up** to the base of "**spin e.005 ".** T h e new Bone will automatically be named "**spine .004**."

Once the Bones are aligned correctly, switch back to **Object** Mode by pressing **Tab**, then press **Ctrl + A** and choose **"All Transforms"** to apply the changes.

GENERATE THE ARMATURE CONTROL RIG

Let's breakdown the steps for generating the **Armature Control Rig.**

First, ensure that you've imported a model into the Scene and aligned an Armature called

"Human Metarig" with the model.

Hint: At this stage, the Mesh Mode I hasn't been parented to the Armature. Thus, moving a Bone in **Pose** Mode won't affect the Mesh. Rather than parenting the **Armature** Bones to the Mesh Model, we'll create a **Control Rig** for the **Armature Metarig** and then parent it to the Mesh using Bone positions. When you pose(move) the **Control Handles** in the Rig will make the components of the Mesh follow accordingly.

Ensure the **Metarig Armature** is selected in Object Mode, then go to **the Properties** Editor, Object Data Properties, and click on the Rigify **Buttons Tab**. Look for **the "Generate Rig"** option and click it.

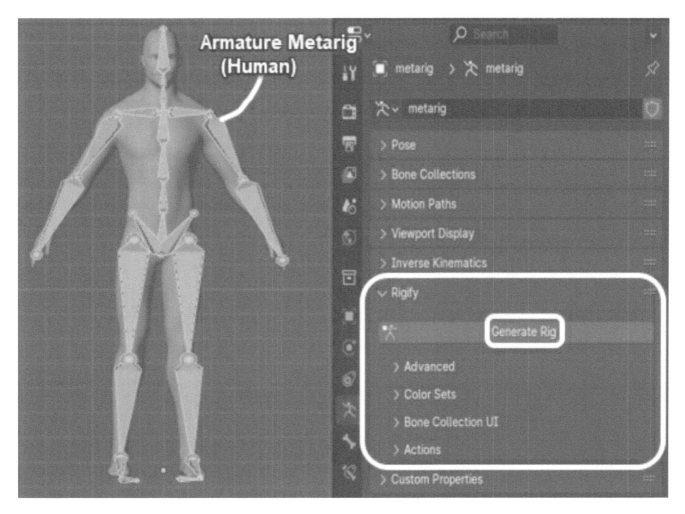

Blender will take some time to compute the Rig, based on your PC's performance. If everything goes smoothly, you'll see the Control Rig displayed as illustrated below.

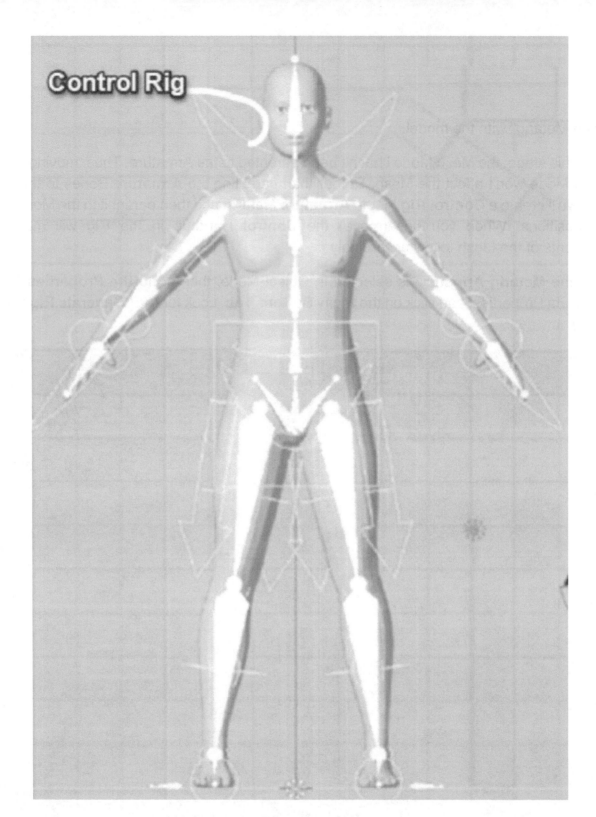

If you encounter an error message of any kind, it indicates a misalignment of bones, as explained earlier.

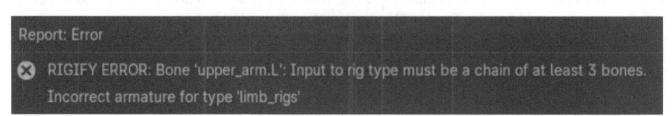

Report: Error

❌ RIGIFY ERROR: Bone 'upper_arm.L': Input to rig type must be a chain of at least 3 bones. Incorrect armature for type 'limb_rigs'

The control rig is generated and visible in **Object** Mode, it includes control handles positioned according to the armature m**etarig's** bones. Both the armature metarig and the control rig are independent of the mesh model; they are not parented to it.

In Pose Mode, within the **3D Viewport** Editor, you can select individual control handles. However, moving them at this stage won't affect the mesh. To deselect the **control rig**, click on it in the viewport.

To parent the control rig to the mesh model, stay in **Object** Mode, select the **Mesh Model** first, then Shift-Select the **control rig.**

Finally, press **Ctrl** + P and choose **"Set Parent To: With Automatic Weights"**.

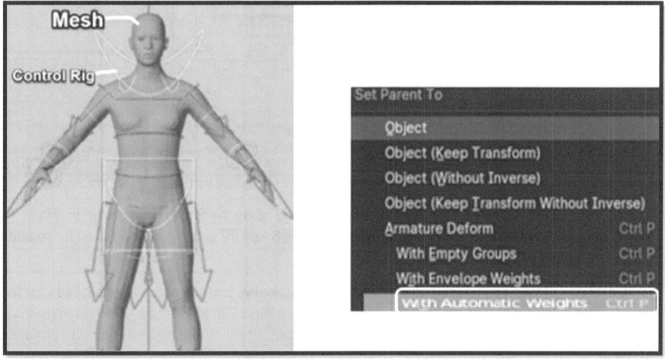

In Pose Mode, the Control Rig Handles appear in the 3D Viewport Editor with distinct colors. Switching to **Object** Mode, go to **the Outliner** Editor and hide the **Armature Metarig.** You have the option to hide the Camera and the Light (Lamp) as well (refer to the illustration below for guidance).

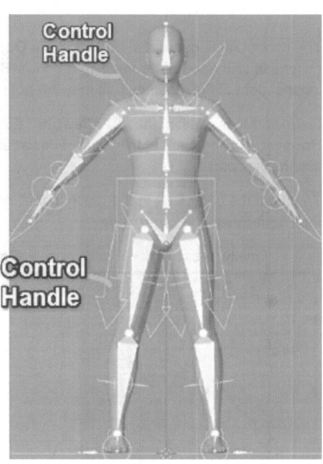

When you select **Control Handles** (by left-clicking), they become highlighted in blue. To manipulate the model, use the **G** key for grabbing, the **S** key for scaling, or the **R** key for rotating while interacting with the handles.

This process allows you to pose the mesh model. Typically, you'd create various poses for the figure (**Mesh Model** at different frames within the Animation Timeline to generate an animation. However with the assistance of Animbox, the figure can be automatically ani-mated to simulate walking.

It seems that when the **Make Human Model** was imported into **Blender,** the eyes weren't properly connected to the rest of the model. Additionally, when viewing the **Model** in Object Mode with **X-Ray** activated in the **3DViewport** Editor, it's evident that there's a Palette integrated into the Mesh. These discrepancies with the eyes and palette serve as a reminder that similar issues might arise when import-ing models from other programs.

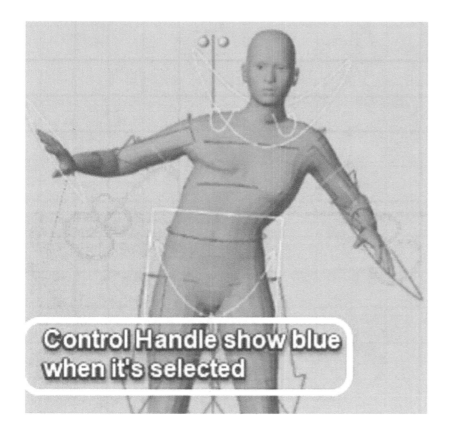

Control Handle show blue when it's selected

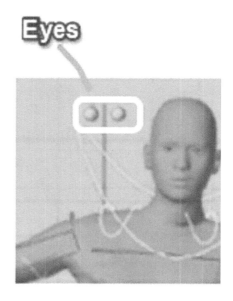

Eyes

DISCOVER THE WONDERS OF ANIMBOX!

This Blender Add-on is tailor-made to complement Metarigs provided by **the Rigify Add**-on. A **Metarig** from **Rigify** consists of a complex assembly of bones connected in parent-child relationships.

Now, here's where Animbox shines: it not only generates a **Control Rig** similar to what was just described but als offers the ability to create **Rigs for Animal Metarigs**. Plus, it goes a step further by automatically generating a walk cycle animation sequence. Packed with features, Animbox includes options like **Rig Box Eye Controls and Motion Paths**.

In our upcoming exercise, we'll animate a human figure using a walk cycle as a starting point. But remember, this is just the tip of the ice- berg. Once you get the hang of it, feel free to explore the endless possibilities of Animbox.

1) To get started, make sure **Rigify and Animbox** are activated in the **Preferences** Editor. In particular, Animbox needs to be activated in the **Add-ons** section of the Preferences Editor to reveal its C**ontrols** in the **3DViewpor**t Editor.

Check out the **RA** tab in the **Object Properties** Pan el, located on the upper right side of the 3D Viewport Editor. You can toggle the Object Properties Panel on and off by pressing the **N** key. The **RA (Rigify Animbox)** tab will only appear when **Rigify Animbox** is activated in the Preferences Editor.

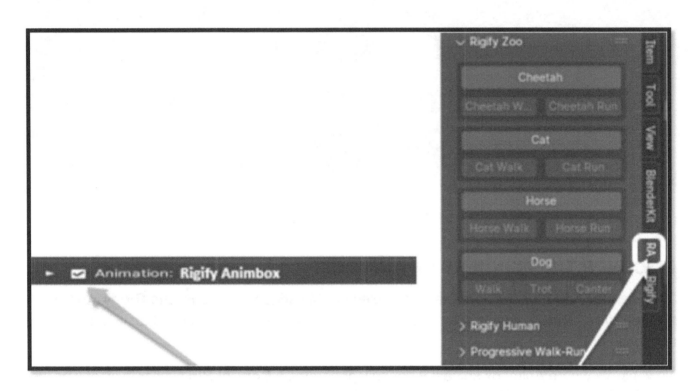

2) Ensure you have a Mesh Model in the **3DViewport** Editor with a **Metarig** added from **Rigify.** Scale and position the Metarig to match the Mesh. Remember to apply **Transforms after scaling the Metarig.**

3) For simplicity, remove **the Face** and **Hand Bones**, along with the hidden face bone inside the **Head Bone**. To avoid errors, delete the spine.**004** Bone and extrude a new **Bone** as instructed previously.

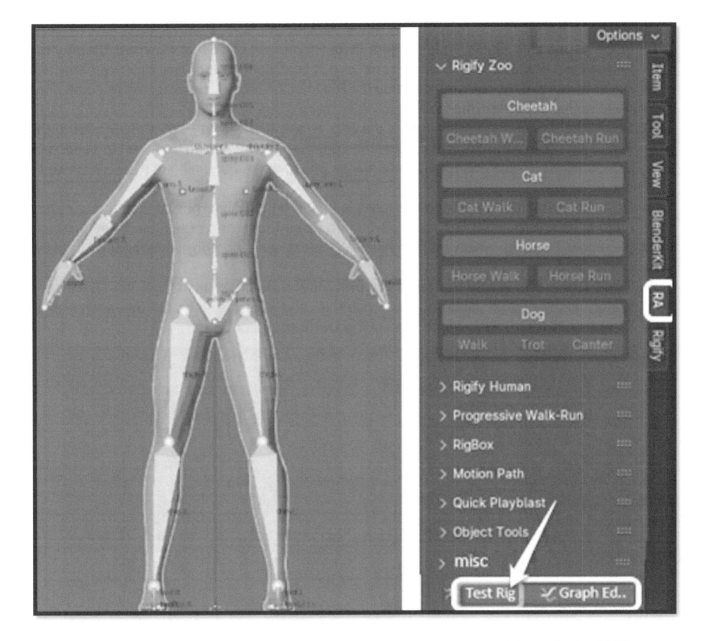

4) Next, in Object Mode, deselect both the **Metarig** and the **Model** Then, in the **3DViewport** Editor, still in **Object** Mode, press **the N** key to reveal the **Object** Properties **Panel**. Within the panel, navigate to the **R.A.** tab, then click the **misc** tab, and select **Test Rig.**

Hint: The Armature disappears from view.

The **Test Rig** now appears between the **feet** in **Pose** Mode. Although small compared to the **Model**, both have a scale value of **1.000,** as ob-served in the **3DViewport** Editor in **Object** Mode.

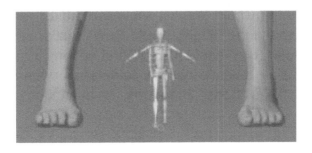

5) In the **Properties** Editor, under **Object Data** Properties, go to the **Viewport Display** tab for the **Rest Rig** and Tick the **"In Front"** check box. Zoom out on the view. With the Test Rig selected in **Object** Mode, scale up the Rig to fit the **Model**. deselect the Rig. You don't need to apply **Transforms** now.

6) Select the model, then, Shift-Select the **Rig**. Press **Ctrl + P** to Parent the **Model** to the **Rig** using **"With Auto Weights"**. Give the com-puter some time to perform the necessary computations. Once done, the model will be posed at the beginning of the walk cycle, as shown below.

7) Do not forget that the parenting process is based on the bone positions in the armature metarig, which may not be visible. Switch to **Pose** Mode and press the **A** key to select the whole **Test Rig**, which will turn blue. Adjust the scale and position if needed to fit the Model properly.

8) Press **Ctrl + A** to **Apply Visual Transforms** to the Pose. At this stage, the 3DViewport Editor might appear cluttered with controls and rigs. To tidy up the scene, hide **"metarig.001"**and **"Rig _Mesb"** inside the **Outliner** Editor.

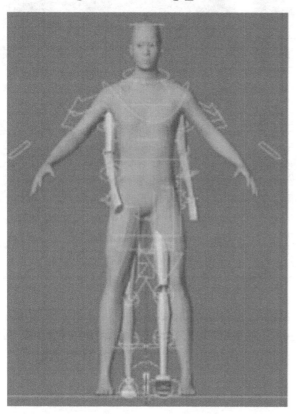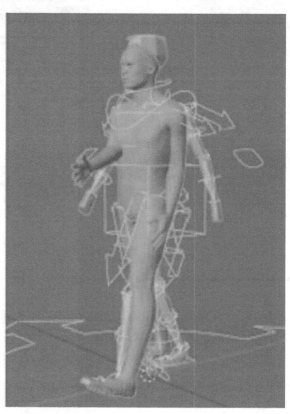

9) Now, you can animate the model to walk. In the **Outliner** Editor, right-click on **"Test_rig"** and select it. Ensure that the 3D Viewport Editor is in **Pose** Mode.

10) To select the entire **"Test_rig"** and have it highlighted in blue, press the **A** key. In the **Object** Properties Panel within the 3D **Viewport** Editor, ensure that the **"RA"** tab is selected, and then expand the **"Rigify Walk/ Run"** section, as illustrated below.

11) Within the **"Rigify Walk/ Run"** section, you'll find options to make the Model either **Walk** or **Run**. For either choice, select a number to determine the duration of the animation in frames. For example, if you choose 24 frames, the animation will play for **24** frames before repeating.

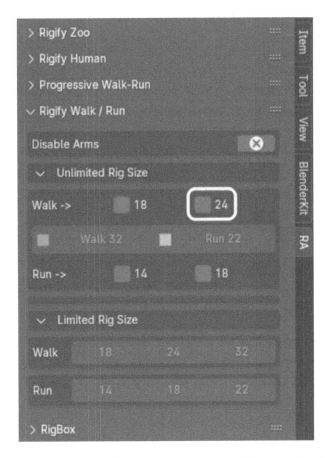

> Rigify Zoo
> Rigify Human
> Progressive Walk-Run
∨ Rigify Walk / Run

Disable Arms ⊗

∨ Unlimited Rig Size

Walk ->   ■ 18   ■ 24

■ Walk 32   ■ Run 22

Run ->   ■ 14   ■ 18

∨ Limited Rig Size

Walk   18   24   32

Run   14   18   22

> RigBox

12) In the Timeline Editor, the animation's end frame will be set to **24**. You can now hide the "**Test_rig**" in the **Outliner** Editor to observe the model walking by pressing the Play button in the **Timeline Editor.**

If you want to switch the animation from a **Walk** to a **Run** or adjust its **Length**, unhide the "**Test_rig**" in the Outliner Editor to reveal the rig in the 3D Viewport Editor. While in **Pose** Mode with the mouse cursor in the 3D bEditor, press the **A** key to select the "**Test_rig**" and reactivate the options in the **Object Properties** Panel.

13)Make your desired changes, then hide the "**Test_rig**" again. Finally, replay the animation to see the updated changes.

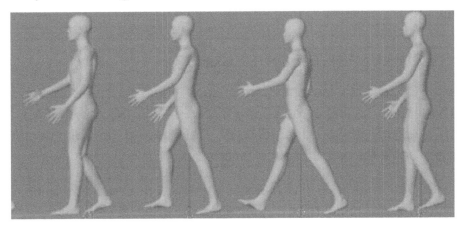

CHAPTER 16: EXPLORING BLENDER RENDER ENGINES

The render engine serves as the crucial software within Blender, transforming a scene crafted within the platform into a tangible image or movie file. Within Blender, three primary render engines exist **Eevee, Cycles, and Workbench.** While external render engines can be inte-grated with Blender, this guide will focus on utilizing its internal systems for simplicity.

Eevee stands as the default engine, offering a preview of the final render within the 3D viewport when the 3D Viewport is set to **Rendered viewport** display mode. On the other hand, Cycles, an integral part of Blender, specializes in generating photorealistic images and provid-ing an interactive workspace where scenes evolve in real time.

However, achieving photorealism and high definition through Cycles entails significant computational resources and render time. While Eevee yields impressive results, Cycles shines in scenarios demanding enhanced fidelity.

Both render processes leverage Blender's suite of tools and controls for scene generation, even though with variations in their respective Node Systems. Meanwhile, Workbench Render streamlines the previewing of scenes during the construction phase before committing to a final render.

This chapter focuses on guiding users through the utilization of the Cycles render engine.

CYCLES RENDER

Cycle rendering offers a comprehensive simulation of various effects typically needing manual inclusion in other rendering methods. These effects encompass depth of field, soft shadows, caustics, motion blur, indirect lighting, and ambient occlusion.

Described as a raytracing-based engine, the Cycles Render Engine supports interactive rendering. This interactive aspect allows users to witness a real-time rendered view of their work directly within the 3D Viewport Editor, particularly when in Rendered Viewport Shading Mode. Cycles also employs a Shading Node system, a distinct material and texture workflow, and uses GPU acceleration.

COMPUTER REQUIREMENTS FOR CYCLES

Before diving into Cycles, it's essential to ensure your computer meets the necessary specifications. This entails having a robust processor, ample memory (RAM), and a graphics card capable of handling advanced processes. Referencing the Blender Wiki's hardware require-ments is advisable for precise specifications.

To fully leverage Cycles, a speedy processor, substantial memory allocation, and a graphics card equipped with **OpenG**L and **CUDA** capabil-ities are imperative.

Hint: While Cycles Rendering is activated directly from the main Blender interface, enabling CUDA and GPU acceleration requires an addi-tional activation similar to installing an add-on.

If you're new to Blender, some of the terminologies and specifications might seem a bit technical, but it's important to ensure your com-puter meets the requirements to fully utilize Cycles' capabilities. The following steps will guide you through activating Cycles and check-ing if your system is compatible.

GET STARTED WITH CYCLES

1) Activate Cycles by s wit chi ng from **Eevee** to **Cycles** in the **Properties** Editor, under Render Properties.
2) To witness **Cycles Rendering** in action, set up a scene in the **3D Viewport** Editor as illustrated below.

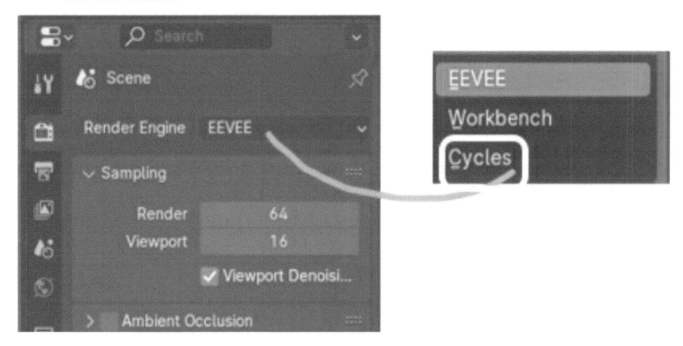

You'll see a **UV Sphere** positioned slightly above a **Plane** (ground plane). Another Plane (Plane.001) is situated above and behind the UV Sphere, opposite the Camera's perspective. The ground plane is adjusted to fill the Camera's aperture, as illustrated in the inset Camera View, while Plane.001 is positioned outside the Camera View. The UV Sphere is enlarged and smoothed, with a single Point Lamp illumi-nating the scene.

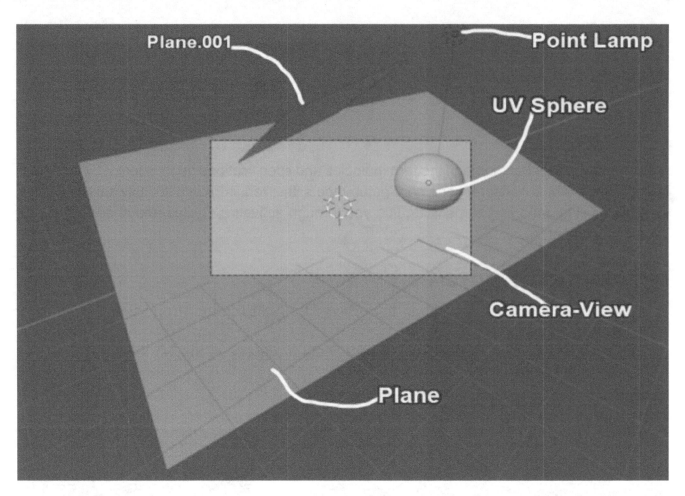

3) To witness **Cycles** in action, switch the **3D Viewport** Editor to **Rendered Viewport Shading** Mode. You'll notice the Objects dis- played against a dark gray background. As you rotate the scene, observe how the Objects are dynamically re-rendered to reflect changes in perspective.

Solid Viewport Shading   **Rendered Viewport Shading**

If your processor isn't sufficiently fast, the render may appear blocky and grainy and could take a significant amount of time to complete. With **Rendered Viewport Shading** enabled, the 3DViewport Editor continuously re-renders with each modification made to the scene. As time passes, the render progressively becomes clearer, though there's a limit to this improvement.

To prevent your computer from getting stuck in an endless rendering loop, Blender includes timeout settings to cap the rendering process. Whenever the scene is adjusted, such as being rotated, the rendering process starts.

In the upper left side of the **3D Viewport** Editor, you'll find a progress display indicating the number of render samples. Once rendering is finished, it'll show **"Rendering Done"**.

Within the **Properties** Editor, in the **Render** Properties under the **Sampling** Tab, you can adjust the render quality. This quality is mea-sured in terms of the amount of noise visible in the view. Noise refers to the speckled or clear appearance of the render. Adjusting these set- tings allows for finer control over the final out put's clarity and detail.

4) In the **Sampling** Tab, you can adjust the render quality for both the Viewport display and the final **Render**. Note that rendering can be time-consuming, so when constructing a scene, it's wise to minimize render time where possible.

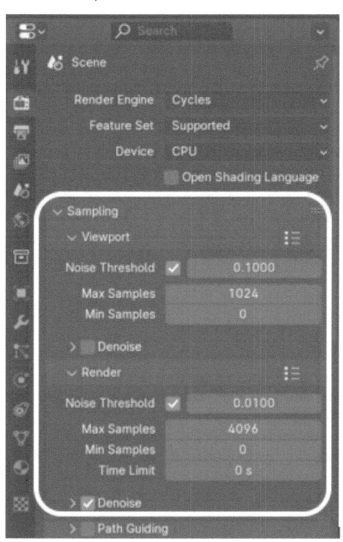
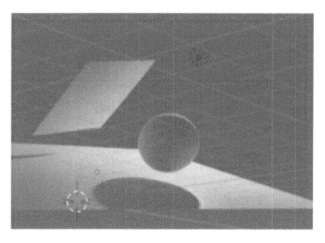

There are several methods available for setting render limits:

✓ **Noise Threshold:** This option sets a limit for the amount of noise present in the render.
✓ **Max Samples**: Determines the maximum number of samples used in the render.
✓ **Min Samples:** Sets the minimum number of samples required for the render.

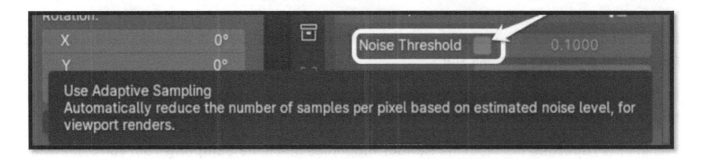

By default, the Noise Threshold controls the sample settings. If you prefer to set maximum and minimum sample values manually, simply uncheck the **Noise Threshold** option.

Your choice of Render Settings will ultimately hang on the desired quality for both the Viewport Display and the Fin al Render. Keep in mind that higher quality settings in both cases will result in longer render times, which are based on your computer's capabilities.

SCENE CONTENT AND CYCLES

The composition of your scene significantly impacts render time. For instance, on a standard machine running the default Blender scene with just a single cube object, the elapsed time for viewport rendering in **Rendered Viewport Shading Mode** is around 00:10:10seconds. When rendering the full image by pressing F12, it takes approximately O1 :20:10 seconds. Doubling the size of the cube increases the pre- view time to about 01:13:21seconds, with a full render taking around 01:38:42 seconds.

Hint: These render times are approximate and may vary depending on your PC.

Numerous factors influence render times, including your computer's specifications, operating system, graphics card (display adapter), and installed drivers. Understanding some key terminology is helpful before proceeding:

- ✓ **NVIDIA Graphics:** NVIDIA provides graphics chipsets for graphics cards. Blender is currently configured to utilize NVIDIA with Open CL and CUDA or OptiX enabled for GPU rendering.
- ✓ **OpenCL**: A global set of graphics standards designed to maximize GPU performance.
- ✓ GPU (Graphics Processing Unit): The processing device within the graphics card that performs computations in parallel with the CPU.
- ✓ **CUDAT" (Computer Unified Device Architecture):** A parallel computing platform and programming model that enhances comput-ing performance by leveraging the GPU's power.
- ✓ **OptiX**: A specialized API for accelerating ray tracing, utilizing RT Cores on NVIDIA RTX GPUs to boost performance.

In summary, the GPU collaborates with the CPU to accelerate graphics processing, crucial for on-the-fly rendering. However, whether the **GPU** outperforms the **CPU** depends on your computer setup. If you have an NVIDIA GPU, you can choose between CUDA and OptiX. OptiX, optimized for ray tracing, is likely faster than CUDA, designed for general computation. Blend e r's OptiX option utilizes NVIDIA RT technol-ogy, available on newer NVIDIA cards like GeForce, Quadro, and Tesla products with Maxwell and newer GPUs.

Another technical consideration is the **Compute Capability** rating of your graphics card, typically ranging from 1.1 to **3.5**. Currently, Blender only supports graphics cards rated at 1.3 and above for GPU processing. Therefore, unless your system meets these requirements, you may not fully explore Cycles' capabilities.

Now, Cycles has been activated and you'll see a display on the screen, but additional functionalities like CUDA, OptiX, and OpenCL aren't active yet. You'll need to activate them separately.

Keep in mind that what you see in the Blender controls can vary based on your system setup.

To activate CUDA, **OptiX, or OpenCL**:

1) Go to the Blender Screen Header, click on **Edit,** and open the **Preferences** Editor. Then, select **System** in the left-hand column to access the **Cycles Render Device** settings as illustrated below.

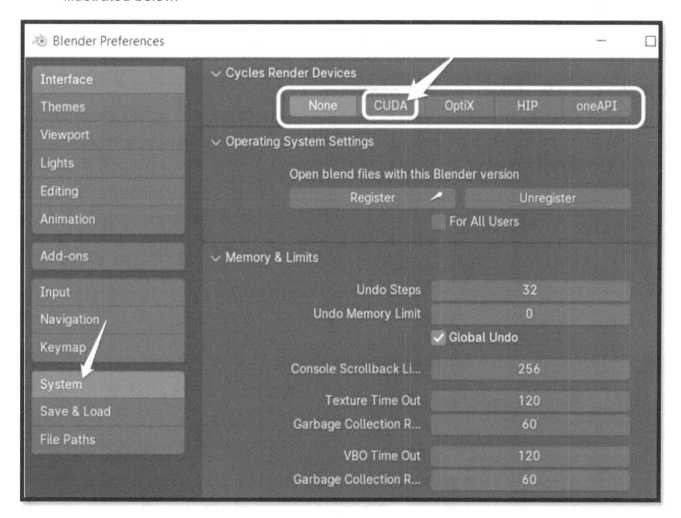

If you don't have an NVIDIA graphics chipset, or if your drivers for the card are out-of-date, you'll receive a message saying "No compatible GPUs found." As a result, the Cycles rendering process will rely wholly on the CPU.

2) Assuming you have the appropriate graphics chipset, you can simply click on CUDA, and the Cycles Render Devices Tab will reveal the name of your graphics card as shown below. Note that this display is unique to your PC setup.

3) In the **Properties** Editor under Render Properties, you'll find the option to choose **GPU Rendering**. Click the **GPU** to select it.

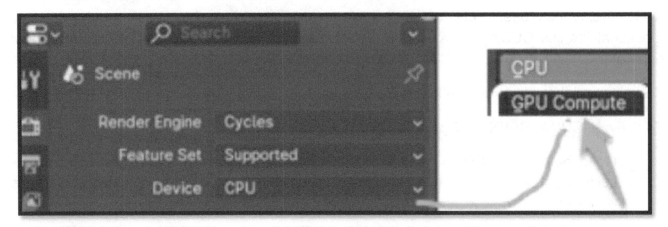

Now that Cycles is activated, it's time to explore its capabilities.

CREATING AN OBJECT LIGHT SOURCE

When Cycles Render is activated, objects can serve as light sources. In the previously created scene, none of the objects have materials applied, appearing in Blender's default gray color in the **3D Viewport** Editor when the Point Light in the scene is set to default white (RGB: all l) as shown below.

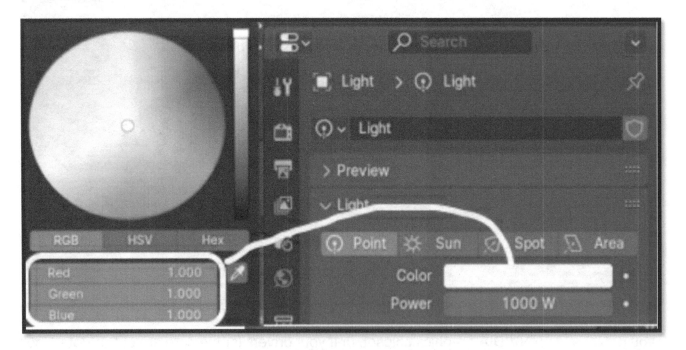

By changing the color of the **Point** Light, the objects in the scene will reflect that light color. To begin:

1) Select the **inclined Plane (Plane.001)** in the scene. In the Properties Editor under Material Properties, click the "New "button to add a material. Note that the Base Color defaults to gray.

2) Scroll down to the **Surface** and select the **Emission tab**. The **Emission** color bar initially displays black. Click on the black color bar to bring up the color picker. Adjust the **Brightness** Slider and choose a **vibrant color**. Increase the Emission Strength value also.

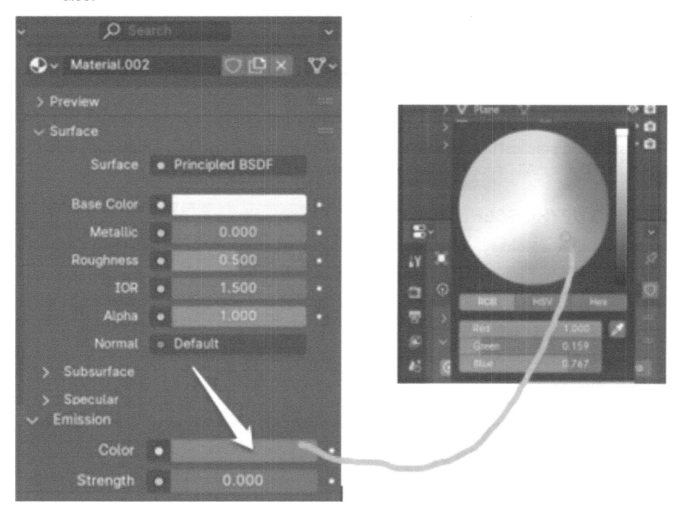

3) With the 3D Viewport set to **Rendered Viewport Shading Mode**, you'll observe Plane.001 emitting light, which illuminates the objects in the scene.

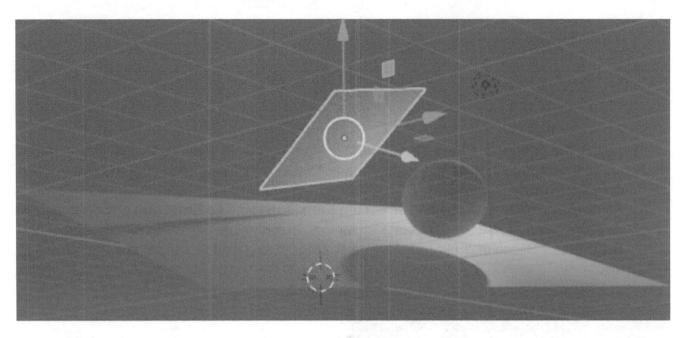

4) By altering the default color of the Point Light, you can blend the scene color accordingly

APPLYING CYCLES RENDER IN PRACTICE

To illustrate the practical utilization of Cycles Render, the following demonstration will compare Eevee and Cycles. All Render Properties will remain at default values.

SETTING UPTHE SCENE

Arrange a **Cube**, a **Monkey**, and a **UV Sphere** Object just above a **Plane** so that they are visible within the **Camera** View (Camera View short- cut is Num Pad **0**)

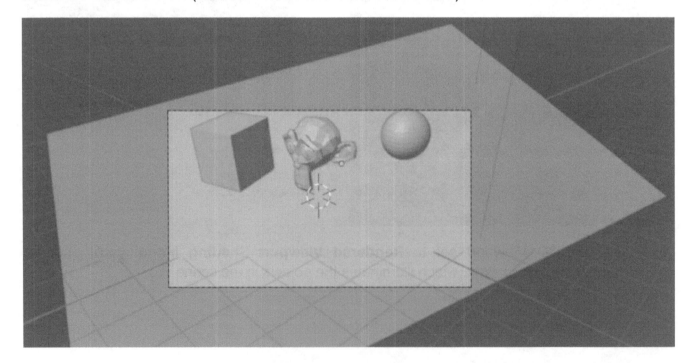

For each Object, adjust the Material Properties to different colors as shown below. Consider the Specular and Metallic values for each Object

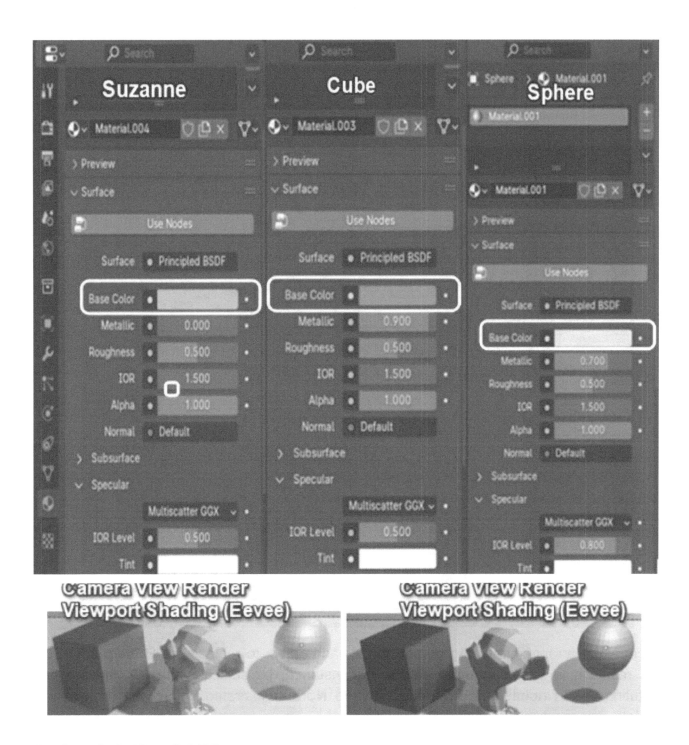

CYCLES AND NODES

In the example provided in the last section, the materials assigned to each object in the scene have been configured in the **Propertie**s Edi-tor under **Material** Properties.

By accessing the **Shader** Editor and selecting each object individually, you'll notice that the **Material Properties** of each object are repre-sented by a **Principled BSDF** Node connected to a **Material Output Node.**

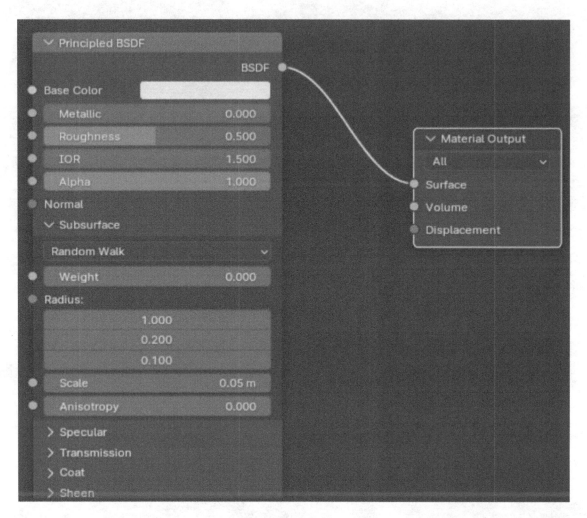

Different Node arrangements can be set up for each object to replace the **Principled BSDF Node,** resulting in varied material effects. For instance, by selecting the **UV Sphere** and substituting the **Principled BSDF** Node with the **Nodes** illustrated below and then mixing mate-rials, you can achieve diverse color effects.

Hint: The colors of the materials being mixed are those indicated in the Glassy BSDF and Diffuse BSDF Nodes.

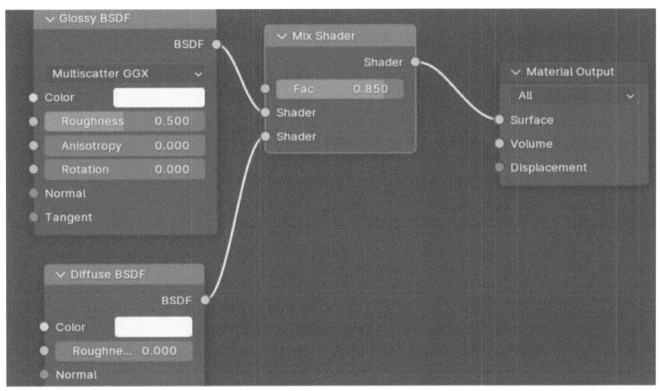

Mix Shader-Factor 0.850   Mix Shader-Factor 0.600

CONCLUSION

As we bring this journey to a close, it's important to reflect on the immense strides that have been made. The transformation from a complete beginner to someone who can confidently navigate, model, and render within 3D space is nothing short of remarkable. The realm of 3D design, particularly with such a versatile and powerful tool, offers a nearly limitless creative frontier. Along this path, there have been challenges, moments of uncertainty, and a learning curve that at times may have felt overwhelming, but that's precisely where the growth happens. Embracing the complexity, experimenting with new techniques, and gradually mastering the intricacies has led to a more profound understanding of not only the software but also the creative process itself.

The beauty of 3D design is that it's never about perfection on the first attempt. It's a discipline that encourages trial and error, where mistakes often lead to unexpected discoveries and breakthroughs. Each project undertaken in this space adds to your skill set, slowly building up a toolbox of knowledge that enables you to take on increasingly complex challenges. The journey, therefore, is never truly finished. It's a continuous process of learning, refining, and experimenting.

One of the key takeaways is that efficiency plays a huge role in creative workflows. Keyboard shortcuts, tool customizations, and a deep familiarity with the user interface are all essential in turning a dauntingly intricate software environment into an intuitive creative space. The importance of these efficiency tools cannot be overstated. They allow you to spend less time navigating through menus and more time focusing on the creative aspects of your work. Efficiency isn't just about speed, though; it's about creating a workflow that minimizes friction and lets your ideas flow seamlessly from your mind to the screen.

Throughout the process, understanding the basics of 3D objects and their interactions has laid a solid foundation. Grasping the fundamental concepts, such as how objects are manipulated in the viewport, has opened the door to a myriad of creative possibilities. With this foundational knowledge, even the most complex designs become manageable, and new techniques can be absorbed with confidence. Every project builds upon the last, and with time, tasks that once seemed impossible become routine.

The power of editing tools, modifiers, and curves cannot be underestimated. These features allow for a level of control and flexibility that transforms even the simplest objects into highly detailed, complex models. The versatility offered here ensures that creators can approach a project from a variety of angles, using different tools to achieve the same end goal. Whether it's generating a new object from a base shape, manipulating that object using modifiers, or applying detailed edits through curves, the editing process is an art form in itself.

Another critical aspect of the learning process has been mastering materials and textures. This is where models come to life, where they transition from abstract geometric forms into tangible, realistic objects. Materials are what give a 3D model its identity, and learning to apply, edit, and manipulate them has brought a deeper understanding of how light, texture, and surface detail interact to create stunning visual effects. The principles learned here can be applied not only to simple objects but also to complex, highly detailed scenes, allowing for a level of realism that is crucial for everything from architectural renders to game assets.

The journey into constraints, shape keys, and action editors has opened up new dimensions in design. These tools are essential for creating animations, adding movement and life to static objects. They offer a nuanced understanding of how objects behave within a scene, whether through complex rigging systems or simple constraints that dictate how objects interact with one another. This deeper dive into animation and object interaction has added layers to your creative abilities, allowing for the production of dynamic scenes that can be used in everything from short films to interactive environments.

Exploring particle systems and physics simulations has been an exciting adventure. These features allow for the simulation of real-world phenomena—things like smoke, fire, water, and other natural effects—that add a new level of realism and excitement to any project. The ability to manipulate these elements within a controlled environment has pushed the boundaries of what is possible, allowing for the creation of environments and scenes that feel grounded in reality, yet are entirely a product of the digital space.

Dynamic paint techniques and rigging tools like Rigify have further extended the range of creative possibilities. Dynamic paint adds an interactive layer to models, allowing objects to influence each other in real-time, much like they would in the physical world. Meanwhile, rigging has introduced the capacity to animate characters, mechanical objects, and anything else that requires movement. These tools are vital for animators and anyone working in fields that require motion, making complex animation projects not only possible but manageable for even beginner users.

Another cornerstone of this journey has been the exploration of different render engines. Choosing the right render engine is essential for getting the most out of your projects, as different engines offer different strengths. Whether aiming for real-time previews with lightning speed or high-fidelity, photorealistic renders, understanding how to leverage the strengths of each engine has become a crucial skill. The ability to balance speed with quality ensures that projects can be completed on time without sacrificing visual excellence. This knowledge is essential for optimizing workflows, especially in professional environments where deadlines and quality are both critical.

Perhaps one of the most valuable insights gained is the understanding that the journey of learning and mastering 3D design is never static. It's a field that is constantly evolving, with new tools, features, and techniques being introduced regularly. This constant state of evolution means that the learning never stops, and the opportunity for growth is always present. What is key, however, is the strong foundation that has been built throughout this process. With this, you can confidently continue to explore new features, integrate new techniques, and apply your knowledge to an ever-expanding array of projects.

Creativity in 3D design is a muscle that grows stronger with use. The more time spent experimenting with the various tools and features, the more confident and skilled you become. Each new project represents an opportunity to flex that creative muscle, to try something new, and to push your limits a little further. In this way, every success builds upon the last, and every challenge overcome opens the door to new possibilities.

As you move forward, it's essential to remember that mastery comes with time and experience. What was once unfamiliar and challenging is now second nature, and that sense of progress is something to celebrate. At the same time, there is always more to learn, more techniques to master, and more creative ideas to explore. This balance between progress and potential is what makes working in 3D design so rewarding. It is a field where growth is continuous, and the possibilities are truly endless.

Looking back, it's clear that the path from beginner to a more advanced level was filled with learning moments, each one contributing to a broader understanding of the software and the 3D design process. There were moments of frustration, where things didn't seem to work as expected, but those were balanced by moments of triumph when everything clicked into place. Those moments of success—whether it was a perfect render, a flawless animation, or a beautifully textured model—are the fuel that keeps the creative fire burning.

As you continue your journey in 3D design, it's important to stay curious, stay creative, and most importantly, stay patient with the process. There will always be new challenges, but there will also be new solutions. The path forward is filled with exciting opportunities to learn, grow, and create.

With the skills and knowledge gained so far, there is no limit to what can be achieved. From creating professional-grade animations and models to crafting unique visual experiences, the tools are now at your disposal. The key is to keep pushing the boundaries of what's possible, to stay engaged with the software, and to never stop exploring new ways to bring your creative visions to life.

The world of 3D design is vast and ever-changing, but with a strong foundation, the right mindset, and a passion for creativity, there's no limit to what you can accomplish. The future is bright, and the potential is boundless—so go forward with confidence, knowing that you have the skills to turn even the most ambitious ideas into reality.

Made in United States
Cleveland, OH
01 May 2025

16582686R00171